BEHIND THE LINES
Case Studies in Investigative Reporting

BEHIND THE LINES

Case Studies in Investigative Reporting

**Margaret Jones Patterson
and Robert H. Russell**

**COLUMBIA UNIVERSITY PRESS
NEW YORK**

Columbia University Press
New York   Guildford, Surrey

Copyright ©1986 Columbia University Press
All rights reserved

Printed in the United States of America

Library of Congress Cataloging-in-Publication Data

Patterson, Margaret Jones.
   Behind the lines.

   1. Reporters and reporting—United States.
I. Russell, Robert H.   II. Title.
PN4781.P37   1986   070.4′3′0973   85-22422
ISBN 0-231-06058-0 (alk. paper)

c 10 9 8 7 6 5 4 3 2

Book design by Ken Venezio

CONTENTS

ACKNOWLEDGMENTS

We thank everyone who helped us produce this book. The reporters and editors named in these pages, and many newspaper employees who are not, gave their time wholeheartedly. The journalists we interviewed seemed to enjoy having the tables turned. Experts at the process themselves, they helped to structure the interviews, making their own notes to return to points raised out of turn. Some helped to trace wayward facts and then double-checked our accuracy. The enthusiastic cooperation of these journalists and the high standards of their work encouraged and inspired us.

Our travels, tapes, transcription and typing costs were funded by a Faculty Research Award from Indiana University of Pennsylvania and by special grants from Oliver Ford, dean of the College of Arts and Sciences; Lee Bowker, dean of the Graduate School; and Norman Norton, provost. Dr. Ford interceded several times on our behalf to find the ways and means to move the project along, and we especially appreciate his ongoing faith and support.

William Bernhardt, associate executive editor at Columbia University Press, gave the manuscript a skilled edit and helped us pare it down to a reasonable size. Tom Gordon, Nan Walkowiak, Bob Nelson, and Peggy Renner put us up and put up with us during our travels. Richard Issacson generously gave legal advice. Maggie Patterson's husband, Rob Ruck, read and edited these pages and guided the work from its inception. Author Patterson would like to dedicate her part of the book to him and to their son, Alexander Morgan Ruck, who was hoped for, conceived, and born during its production.

Bob Russell dedicates his portion to the special people in his life: Mary Ellen Lieb and Robin Stahl Jennings, his friends; and Mildred and Edward Adolph, his parents.

BEHIND THE LINES
Case Studies in Investigative Reporting

INTRODUCTION

Investigative reporting has been the fastest-growing segment of American journalism since the Watergate exposures made national icons of Bob Woodward and Carl Bernstein. Movies such as *All the President's Men* have bestowed on the nation's ink-stained newspapermen and women some of the glory and popular acclaim they had not known since *The Front Page* immortalized the "jazz journalism" of the 1920s.

The average reporter on the average newspaper in the average city was more likely to be covering a sewer board meeting than arranging a clandestine encounter with a faceless source in a dark garage at midnight, there to learn the secrets that would bring down a president, but no matter. The drama was irresistible, and the public seemed caught up in it. Newspapers faced with declining circulation, soaring costs, and aggressive competition from television were quick to oblige.

Some of what has passed for investigative reporting since then has been pretty shoddy. Hyped headlines and glittery graphics have too often substituted for careful research and meticulous documentation. The bombshell revelations promised by the promotion blurbs often evaporate on close inspection. And all of this has damaged the credibility of the profession that the Watergate triumph had helped to restore.

Still, a great deal of useful work was being done around the country by newspapers that were willing to devote the time and resources to painstaking, long-term inquiries. The subjects were often less glamorous than ferreting out corruption in high places; the reporters spent more time poring over records than having dramatic encounters; the results might be measured more in terms of modest reforms and heightened public sensitivity than in indictments returned or officials resigned in disgrace. This book profiles six such investigations.

These are not the breathless accounts of journalistic derring-do so common to the how-I-got-my-big-story genre. Instead, they try to show the student of investigative reporting just what happens when an in-depth project is undertaken. How did the idea come about? How was the decision made to pursue it? How did the reporters and editors decide the overall strategy? What sort of working relationship evolved—between the reporters themselves and between the reporters and the editors—as the investigation developed? What problems did the project pose for the editors as they sought to balance the needs of the project staff and the relentless demands of publishing a daily newspaper? When the research was completed, how were the daunting tasks of writing and editing handled? And when the work was published, what were the results?

Each chapter cannot answer every one of these questions, of course, for each involved an individual set of circumstances: for example, the *Charlotte Observer*'s decision to commit a significant portion of its staff to the brown lung series forced it to make compromises and adjustments in its daily routine that did not have a precise counterpart in the atomic-testing story because that was handled largely by a Utah paper's one-man Washington bureau. But each does go beyond the necessarily limited perspective of the reporters to consider the roles of the editors and of the newspaper itself, for we believe that they play a pivotal but often overlooked part in the process of investigative reporting. The reporters do the legwork but it is the newspaper that must make the commitment of personnel and resources without which no serious in-depth project could be carried through. It must also create by its receptivity to suggestions for projects and its willingness to persevere over weeks, months, or even years the atmosphere in which reporters and editors develop fruitful ideas for investigations and then stick with them. This is not glamorous work, despite its image; only those journalists and news organizations willing to settle in for the long haul need bother. We hope that these chapters make clear the institution-wide nature of the commitment.

How did we select the six examples? We make no pretense that they represent every kind of investigative project being undertaken by American newspapers today. But we do think they are an intriguing mix:

The *Charlotte Observer*'s comprehensive examination of brown-lung disease among textile-mill workers in the Carolinas is our only example of a private industry target; beyond that, the newpaper had selected the region's largest employer.

The *Salt Lake City Deseret News*'s revelation of the link between atomic testing in Nevada during the 1950s and the incidence of leukemia in later years also struck us as significant on several grounds. The target was the federal government, in particular the super-secret defense establishment. The issue, furthermore, was one of extreme sensitivity with national security implications. And in sharp contrast to the group effort at Charlotte, the *News*'s one-man Washington bureau handled most of the reporting (with intermittent help from the paper's local reporters).

At opposite ends of the country, we found newspapers skillfully penetrating two close-knit professional fraternities. The *Long Beach (Calif.) Independent, Press-Telegram* had to break through the speak-no-evil public facade of the medical profession to tell its story of indigent patients being improperly transferred from private to public emergency rooms. And the *Philadelphia Inquirer* found itself tackling the entire municipal government of the nation's fourth largest city when it sought to document systematic brutality toward suspects by the police department's homicide detectives.

When Tucson's *Arizona Daily Star* began documenting illegal practices in the University of Arizona's popular football program, the feisty little paper found itself the target of public hostility and advertiser retaliation. As if that drama were not reason enough to include it here, the investigation provides a classic example of the investigative technique known as "the paper trail," in which the reporters rely on public records (aided, in this case, by computer analysis) for most of their information rather than interviews.

Finally, we offer the *Nashville Tennessean's* inside look at the Ku Klux Klan as a modern example of that most venerable reportorial tool, the undercover infiltration. In the tradition of nineteenth-century reporters who posed as mentally retarded patients to expose conditions in insane asylums, *Tennessean* reporter Jerry Thompson assumed a false identity and joined the KKK.

In each case, we visited the reporters and their editors to talk with them about their work. We had to talk to a few of them by telephone some time after the initial interviews because they were not available when we visited their newspapers. We found all of them remarkably generous with their time and informative and articulate as interview subjects. We suspect that journalists, who spend so much of their professional lives interviewing others, enjoy the rare opportunity to talk about themselves and their work while someone else handles the tape recorder and takes notes. We enjoyed meeting and talking with them.

Owing to space limitations, some of the newspaper articles have been omitted and others condensed.

1

THE *PHILADELPHIA INQUIRER*

Jonathan Neumann and William K. Marimow, 27 and 29, respectively, in April 1977 when "The Homicide Files" was published, were reporters at the City Hall bureau of the *Philadelphia Inquirer.* City Hall in Philadelphia houses not only the mayor's office and city council but all the county's civil and criminal courts. We interviewed the pair around a small conference table in the *Inquirer's* photography department. Neumann had moved to the *Washington Post* in July 1979, but he traveled to Philadelphia because he and Marimow felt it was important for us to see and to interview them as a team in order to understand how they worked together.

Marimow was born in Philadelphia, grew up in Havertown, a Philadelphia suburb, and graduated from Trinity College in Connecticut before joining the *Inquirer* in 1972. Neumann, from New York City, was graduated from City College of New York. He joined the *Inquirer* in 1976 after four years at the *Daily Hampshire Gazette* in Northampton, Massachusetts.

"The Homicide Files," published April 24-27, 1977, won the Pulitzer Prize for Public Service, the Sigma Delta Chi National Public Service Award, the Roy A. Howard Public Service Award from the Scripps-Howard Foundation, the Silver Gavel Award from the American Bar Association, the Robert F. Kennedy Journalism Award from the Robert F. Kennedy Foundation, along with numerous state and local awards.

Jonathan Neumann was puzzled. The new man on the city-courts beat for the *Philadelphia Inquirer* heard defendants in one trial after another complain that policemen had beaten them during interrogation. But the revelations seemed to startle no one except the reporter.

"I was really stunned, but no one else in the courtroom seemed to be really surprised," Neumann recalls. "The judge, the prosecutor, the defense lawyer were all just staring at the ceiling like nothing was being said. The guy was describing torture techniques that no one expects to hear about in America, but it was routine to hear that kind of testimony. I thought either that everyone knew this wasn't true, that the defendants were routinely lying, or there was some kind of a grand-scale investigation going on into it." None of these, it turned out, was the case.

He told his city editor, John Carroll, what he was hearing. "Welcome to Philadelphia," Carroll replied.

Carroll, now editor of the *Lexington Herald* in Kentucky, remembers Philadelphia of the mid-1970s as "an incredible cesspool. I'd never seen corruption and brutality so wide open and accepted. I hadn't seen any more corruption in wartime Saigon. . . .

"Neumann told me that in the trials he covered, the police didn't even bother to collect fingerprints. They never investigated crimes; they just beat the shit out of everyone in sight." Some of the problem was the news media's fault, Carroll concedes. "The newspapers had been letting Philadelphia down for years," he said, noting that for years the *Inquirer* had assigned only one reporter to the court beat, where he or she had been nominally responsible for 90 courtrooms.

Neumann's predecessor on the beat, Bill Marimow, shared his colleague's concern. In the spring of 1976 Marimow had been covering the trial of Robert "Reds" Wilkinson, charged with murder in the firebombing of Radames Santiago's home. Mrs. Santiago and her four children had been killed in the blaze in a racially tense neighborhood. Wilkinson was convicted in May 1976. Despite the verdict, Marimow was skeptical. "There's more to this story than has come out coherently," Marimow recalls telling Neumann.

A defense witness, a woman who lived across the street from the Santiagos, testified at Wilkinson's trial that she had seen another neighbor, not Wilkinson, throw the firebomb. Furthermore, evidence had been admitted that the same man the neighbor said she saw, David McGinnis, had volunteered a confession but the district attorney had allegedly disbelieved him and destroyed the tape of his statement. Finally, Wilkinson—who said he had nothing to do with the crime—had passed a polygraph test.

Over the summer, Neumann went to work on the Santiago case, publishing a series of articles in partnership with the *Inquirer*'s federal court reporter, Jan Schaffer. The reporters and a concurrent federal investigation affirmed Wilkinson's own testimony that he had gone out late on the night of the fire to buy his wife a pack of cigarettes. Seeing the blaze at the Santiago home, he ran to the corner to pull the fire alarm and returned. It was then that the prosecution's main witness, a 13-year-old boy who had been sleeping on the porch, saw Wilkinson. Later the boy was prodded by police into implicating him.

Although Wilkinson, a retarded automobile mechanic, could neither read nor write, police said he wrote a confession. Ronald Hanley, who actually masterminded the incident, had also confessed, but charges against him had been dropped after the courts found the police had severely beaten him to get his statement. In fact, at least seven people from the neighborhood had been beaten or threatened by police in an effort to extract the witnesses' statements against Wilkinson.

(Eventually, the federal investigation led to a conviction of Hanley, and Wilkinson was freed after spending 15 months in jail. Six police officers involved in the interrogations were sentenced by the federal court to the same term, 15 months, that Wilkinson had unjustly served.)

As the federal investigation proceeded, Marimow and Neumann sat around some afternoons in City Hall talking about the implications of the Wilkinson case. Perhaps, they conjectured, this case was not an exception to the homicide squad's behavior during investigations, but the rule.

"We talked about it so much that we got to the point where we said maybe we could do something about it," Neumann said.

"The crucial question was: if this was a pattern, how could we prove it?" Marimow recalled.

The two reporters talked to John Carroll, who told them to give it a try.

Almost immediately, they got a big break. They asked an administrator in the Court of Common Pleas, Dennis Moran, if he could get a list of every homicide case over the previous three years in which a judge had ruled on the legality of a police interrogation. Moran, a former police officer, might have surmised what they were up to, the reporters thought. Nevertheless, he was back in two days with a computer printout listing 433 cases in which a homicide defendant had confessed, then later challenged the legality of his statement in a pretrial motion. The printout gave the reporters the name of the judge in each case and whether he had found the confession legal, illegal, or moot.

In 80 cases, nearly one in five, the police interrogation had been declared illegal. To Neumann, "it was almost like watching 'Columbo,'" the television show in which the viewer sees the crime committed at the beginning and watches to see how the supersleuth solves it. The reporters were fairly sure of the outcome at this early point in the investigation. The pattern they had suspected was on the printout; now they had to find the proof and flesh out the details. That, they knew, would be difficult.

The printout did not prove that the police were knowingly and routinely breaking the law, Marimow points out. "But it was the strongest piece of documentary evidence that there was a pattern of illegal interrogation," he says. As it turned out, in all the months of work that lay ahead no one raised a serious doubt about this basic conclusion, Neumann said.

"Had someone come up at any point and said, 'That conclusion isn't true,' we would have very seriously examined that," he said.

Poring through the city's legal directory, they selected the names of 40 to 50 current and former assistant district attorneys and defense lawyers who would have tried homicide cases in the preceding three years. Then they called all of them, telling them what the computer printout showed and asking if they had been involved with any cases in which they believed the police had beaten the defendant to get a statement.

Most knew of such a case, usually one in which they had been involved, in which there had been evidence of a beating beyond their client's testimony, usually medical records or the testimony of someone who had heard the police beating the suspect or had seen his condition afterward.

But few of the attorneys agreed there was a pattern of police brutality; most argued there had been only few isolated incidents. Many prosecutors blamed the "Holmesburg Bar Association" for all the accusations against the police. Holmesburg is the city prison in Philadelphia. According to some prosecutors, prisoners who had become well-versed in the law were advising defendants to claim they had been coerced or beaten as a ploy to get a confession thrown out by the courts.

Judges, too, told reporters that although they had ruled against the police and knew of other such findings, there was no pattern, only isolated cases.

"The psychology was really interesting," Neumann recalls. Their story would require another dimension, the reporters realized. In addition to the hard news, they would have to examine the politics, sociology, and psychology of the criminal justice system, which they did in "The Homicide Files," Part IV.

Mayor Frank Rizzo was the city's most powerful politician. He had risen through the police department from rookie in 1943 to police commissioner until he became mayor in 1972. He also controlled the local Democratic Party, the only party to have a mayor in office since

1952. The party endorsed most of the successful candidates for judges so the judges "were aware that the mayor and the former police commissioner are not going to be happy to find a ruling in which they criticize the police for anything, let alone for beating the smithereens out of somebody," Marimow said.

Later, when the reporters began looking at the transcripts, they found that even when the judges made a ruling against the police, they appeared to take great care in their remarks for the court record. For example, in the case of William Hoskins (see Part III), Judge Sam Smith listened to homicide detective Michael Chitwood's testimony for a few minutes, then cut it off and called the attorneys into his chambers. Only there did he say he did not believe Chitwood and that he was dismissing the case.

Except for the Santiago firebombing case, which Neumann had investigated, few cases of beatings by the homicide squad had been exposed to the public. "People were testifying routinely in the court about how cops were beating them, and nobody would notice this," Neumann said incredulously.

After talking to the lawyers and a few judges, the reporters began to feel anxious.

"We were two individuals, and here we were challenging the police department and the city's perception of what was happening. We were challenging, in effect, what hundreds of thousands, or millions of people accepted every day," Neumann said. "That was a pretty tough burden for us."

At this early stage, they knew only what a good number of other people knew or could have known with the same check of the public record. "Maybe," Neumann wondered, "we were just seeing things funny. I know I felt that way for a long time, because it's not easy to sit in City Hall and have everybody see something one way and you see it differently. . . . That's where a partnership helps a lot, because we could talk to each other and support each other on that."

The pair shared their facts and feelings with city editor Carroll at almost every step of the way. "When we found something that made us gasp, he would gasp with us," Marimow recalled. "And when we needed time or freedom, he was always supportive."

The interviews with the legal community helped the pair shape the story and gave them some specific leads on cases to look for. Next was step two.

"I guess it was the step that dispels anyone's romantic illusions about investigative reporting," Marimow said, laughing. The City Hall elevator made its last stop on the seventh floor. After that, they had to thread their way through a maze of bureaucrats' desks up a steep spiral staircase to room 951, a dark and dusty room of row upon row of old files. Here, in the records of all homicide cases tried in Philadelphia, the reporters read testimony and examined evidence in suppression hearings dating back to 1974. Although they found testimony of physical violence by the police in many of the cases, the reporters honed in on those 80 cases in which the judges had found that police methods were illegal. Along with the transcripts were medical records, photographs, or references to photographs that could be obtained, and the names and addresses of defendants and attorneys involved in the cases.

"When we were going into that file room, the only thing we had behind us was a theory and the list of cases that proved that there was a pattern, but we didn't have human beings yet," Neumann explained.

Then they began to read. "Each time we saw a new case," Neumann remembers, "we looked at each other and we said, 'Holy shit! Look at what's happening here!" The files included a case in which a 13-year-old boy, picked up because there had been a murder in his neighborhood, was handcuffed and beaten by six cops. Or a case in which two young men had been arrested together. One was strapped into a metal chair where a policeman grabbed and twisted his testicles, while the other boy was forced to watch and listen to his screaming friend. He was warned that if he, too, did not sign a confession, he was in for the same treatment.

"I'd be reading one case and Bill would be reading another," Neumann recalled. "He'd say something like, 'You're not gonna believe this!'"

"Emotionally it builds up, you know," Neumann said. "We saw what was really happening, the kind of torture that people were suffering. ... It became, to us, a real story now, and it became that much more frightening and that much more important for us to get it out right away." He began to feel the police were not just beating prisoners to get confessions; they seemed to enjoy the violence.

Marimow, soft-spoken and even-tempered, feels he was slow and deliberate in reacting and in drawing conclusions. For him, reading the cases was still impersonal, "like reading an awful book." Neumann, by contrast, has quick and usually accurate instincts, Marimow says.

"I know I got emotionally involved. I always get emotionally involved in things in my life," Neumann explained. "I don't think there's any such thing as objectivity. I think that's absolutely ridiculous. ...

"To me, the only thing that's important for a newspaper reporter is to be thorough, accurate, fair, and make sure that you report all sides."

He was, he says, determined to write his story rationally, not emotionally.

"I wanted to make sure something happened as a result of the story. I think the skill of this kind of reporting is knowing how to write a story so that it can't be challenged rationally."

They knew they could not allow emotional reactions to impede the story. "Basically, we knew that we were taking on the Philadelphia Police Department and lurking behind there, not very far, the mayor, the Democratic Party, the power structure of the Philadelphia government," Marimow said. As horrifying as he might have found the police tactics, he was not out for revenge, he said. "I wanted to make sure that this story was documented in an ironclad way. . . . I wanted to make 100 percent sure that we were totally thorough, fair, and accurate. . . . It was the subject of many of our conversations: 'Are we right?'"

The two men spent much of January and March 1977 in room 951 of City Hall, reading transcripts and examining evidence. (There was a strike at the *Inquirer* during February.) After concentrating on the 80 cases in which the defendants' statements had been ruled illegal, the two reporters narrowed their focus to 15 or 16 in which there was evidence beyond the defendant's testimony that police had beaten or coerced him into making a statement. They wanted medical records or supporting testimony.

Neumann concedes that the reporters had prejudged the guilt of the police and had then gone out to find the strongest cases to support that contention. "But we didn't predetermine it out of emotional prejudice. We predetermined it out of facts. . . . We saw how many cases were illegal, and from that we did start the story with the conclusion."

The next step was to spend several weeks tracking down defendants, witnesses, and other participants in those 15 or 16 chosen cases and interview them. The reporters also searched for and examined evidence introduced or mentioned in the hearings, such as medical records, police logs, and photographs in which wounds or discolorations could be discerned.

Neumann and Marimow did 90 percent of the work together, although dividing it might have saved legwork. Why? "Because of the sensitivity of the work," Marimow says. "We knew what we were up against, and we wanted to make 100 percent sure that when we saw someone we had two gauges of the person's veracity. When we looked at evidence, we had two people to say, 'Well, it looks to me like those are pretty serious injuries.' We just wanted to be careful as opposed to efficient."

While most of the defendants and witnesses were cooperative, Neumann and Marimow had more difficulty with the last step of their research, talking with the police. During the Rizzo administration, there was a standing order that only the police commissioner was authorized to speak for the police to the press. No officer or patrolman could talk to reporters without risking his job. This rule blocked the reporters' access to the homicide detectives, but they began early to try to make contact through unofficial channels. The reporters asked assistant district attorneys, who worked with the 84 members of the homicide squad every day, to help them set up interviews.

"We specifically asked [the assistant district attorneys] if they would talk to their friends on the homicide squad—and we didn't limit it to anyone, as many as they could—and tell them what we were working on, everything," Neumann recounted. The reporters were willing to meet the police under any circumstances they named. Although much of the police side of the story was contained in the court transcripts, the reporters wanted to talk to the police to find out if some argument or explanation of theirs might confound the reporters' conclusions or debunk their evidence.

Only a handful of police responded. All refused to allow their names to be used. Yet, the interviews with the police yielded such "incredible material," as Neumann described it, that the writers developed the sidebar, "Interviews with 3 Detectives on Interrogations by Police," to incorporate it.

"More than anyone else we interviewed, the cops confirmed that police beat people routinely in interrogations, because they didn't deny it," Neumann said. "They explained it. Most of them didn't justify it. Most of them said, 'This happens. I don't like it. I don't do it, but it happens.' Some of them said, 'This happens, and I do it, and this is why.' And, they presented really forceful reasons why it happened."

One Saturday afternoon just before the February strike, Marimow and Neumann drove to the outskirts of the city to the basement gameroom of one of the homicide detectives who was in a position to know firsthand what had happened in many of the most violent cases. The officer gave them each a beer and began telling stories.

Identified in the sidebar as the "young detective," he admitted he had beaten defendants. As he talked he grew more and more angry, standing up, shouting, and waving a finger over the reporters. He was outraged by crime, he shouted, and by the inadequacies of the criminal justice system. He had, in essence, taken matters into his own hands.

"His means of telling the stories was so frightening that when we left I knew that everything we had reported was absolutely true," Marimow said. The officer was aware, Neumann added, that the guilty were going free, but he blamed that on the courts. He believed, Neumann felt, that the innocent never went to jail, because the police would never arrest the wrong man.

"I remember the feeling leaving that house," Neumann said, "which is a very common feeling, if you're a reporter—that you have just interviewed the person, who, in effect, is the target of your story . . . and you're sympathetic with the guy. One of the first human reactions that you have as a reporter—and I know that I had it then and I always do—is to go easy on the guy." Neumann contends that many news-paper stories never see print because the reporter becomes paralyzed at this point by his own conflicting sympathies.

The solution, Neumann advises, is not for reporters to deny their emotions but to keep a clear and rational mind. "Always keep your eye on the facts" and on the story, he suggests.

Just before the series was printed, the reporters made another, more formal, attempt to contact police. As the articles were written, and it was clear what was going to be said about whom, Neumann and Marimow sent registered letters requesting interviews to all 31 police officers mentioned in the series. A few more responded. All asked for anonymity. None had much that was new to say.

So many police mentioned the lucrative overtime pay earned by the homicide detectives as a result of the marathon interrogation sessions that the reporters obtained the salary figures from the city controller's office. Neumann and Marimow came to regret the prominent play given this aspect of the story, with its implication that overtime pay was a main motivation behind the police beatings. The implication came, they say, from the police themselves.

Verification, usually the last and one of the most tedious steps in investigative reporting, was not a serious part of Neumann and Mari-mow's work. Because much of the series was based on testimony from cases in which a judge had made a finding of fact, the legal issue of what was a fact had already been determined, Neumann points out. "But if there was a dispute, we reported what the dispute was," he added.

The one exception to documenting their facts with sworn testimony or attributed quotations came in reporting the aftermath of the William Hoskins case in Part III. The reporters relied on anonymous sources, the only instance in which they did so in the series, to report a politi-cally sensitive situation.

Investigators from District Attorney Emmett Fitzpatrick's office had concluded that there was sufficient evidence to prosecute four homicide detectives for beating Hoskins. In a later meeting of high-level officials, according to the story, Fitzpatrick was persuaded not to prosecute. Instead, the four officers were merely transferred briefly out of the homicide division. The account of that meeting in which Fitzpatrick allegedly changed his mind is attributed only to "sources," a tactic disliked by some journalists.

Marimow, explaining why it was done in this case, noted that Fitzpatrick was up for renomination in the May primary, which in a one-party city is, in effect, the election. Any bad light shed on the police department by the district attorney's office could cost Fitzpatrick the party's endorsement. So no one who had been in that meeting was going to cross his boss, Fitzpatrick, on the record.

For the reporters, the reconstruction of events was a matter of building blocks, Marimow explained. The facts of the Hoskins beating had been determined in court. The fact that the four officers had been transferred because of their participation in the beatings was a matter of public record. Only the middle part was missing. Only the details of the meeting in which the decision had been made to transfer rather than prosecute had been locked in privacy. For that information, the reporters relied on sources inside the district attorney's office whom Marimow had known and trusted for years, he said.

Even though the bulk of the reporting relied on legally established fact, being fair, accurate, and thorough was seldom easy. "Here's one little anecdote about the kind of internal struggles we had on being fair and accurate," Marimow reported. "It's what we called the Chitwood argument."

William Hoskins met with the reporters and gave them his account of the beating that had included a stab in the groin. Officer Chitwood refused to talk but the reporters had his brief testimony before Judge Sam Smith which the judge had rejected when he had made his ruling. Neumann thought a major portion of Chitwood's testimony should be included in order to tell his side of the story. Marimow disagreed. If the judge had dismissed it as unbelievable, Marimow argued, including much of it in the story would disrupt the account of what probably happened. The two compromised on the account that appears in Part III.

City editor Carroll had continued meeting with the reporters almost daily, listening to stories about what they were finding and feeling. He knew what he was going to get. When Neumann and Marimow began writing in April, there were no surprises. The only question remaining was whether the reporters, Carroll, and executive editor Eugene Roberts could all agree on an appropriate presentation.

The editing process was painstaking. It went on for three weeks, often 16 hours a day, as the reporters recall. The opening sections of the lead-off article were rewritten 40 times, the reporters estimate. "Would it be too colorful, hyperbolic for us? Would it be too dry for them?" Marimow said. Neumann added: "We all wanted it to be as low-key and matter-of-fact as possible, and yet we did not want the drama to be lost."

As new drafts made changes in style, Neumann and Marimow checked each carefully to make sure the factual content remained the same. They rode herd on the headlines, the commas, and capital letters as each installment was assigned to a copy editor who went through it with a diamond-cutter's precision.

What makes this process excruciating for all sides is that the reporters are eager to get the story into print but the editors want to slow things down. "Because we'd invested so much time on it, we wanted everyone to view it as urgently as we viewed it," Marimow said.

But for editor Gene Roberts, this was one of those six or seven projects a year that get intensive scrutiny before being published.

"One of the things that I feel very strongly about and the paper institutionally feels very strongly about," Roberts said, "is that if you're going to inflict 10,000 or 50,000 words on the reader, you owe it to the reader, to the paper, and to yourself to make sure that it is well-organized, that it reads well, that it flows properly, and that it's accurate, accurate, accurate. That takes some time.

"I've seen lots and lots of stories in American journalism that when you really look at them or really dig into them, you know that a great deal of reporting effort has gone into them, but the stories are not well presented," Roberts said. The reporter understood his subject, but failed to explain it clearly. Roberts likes to use what he calls "nut graphs," paragraphs at the beginning of the story that sum up the heart of the matter for the readers, so that they start off knowing the real magnitude of the project.

Roberts also believes that because investigative reporters may spend several months on a project, they may get too close to it to see things clearly. To "build in distance," he says a tough editor must approach the story with a fresh eye and demand to be convinced.

Another reason for caution, former city editor Carroll notes, is that "you're launching something that's attacking the honesty and careers of many people. You've got to be nervous. I always wondered, 'Is there some horrendous mistake somewhere?' "

As he worked on the material, Carroll worried that the phone would ring with information that would destroy the story. He bombarded

Neumann and Marimow with questions and remained unsatisfied until they answered all of them and he could think of no more.

Although they saw the careful editing as helpful, the reporters were determined to fight, if necessary, to protect their work from any changes that might erode its substance. Reporters who have grown weary after months of work on a story often fail to stick with it through the editing process, Neumann contends, forgetting that all of their effort is meaningless until the reader sees the printed result.

In this case, nothing of substance was changed. Nor was the editing period complicated by any fears that the *Inquirer* might back down on its commitment to print the highly controversial series. "I always trusted the *Inquirer* from a moral point of view entirely, that they wouldn't do something cowardly," Neumann said. "If they knew the story was true, they would publish it."

"Roberts never flinched when Rizzo tried to stare us down on anything," Carroll added. "I never thought for a minute that the rug would be pulled out from under us; that never happened under Roberts," Carroll said. Such an atmosphere is essential for investigative work, he believes. "No staff," he said, "can do investigative work in spite of its editors."

As it turned out, Rizzo never seriously tried to block the investigation. From January 1977 when the research began, Neumann and Marimow made no secret of their project. Early on, they were straightforward with the assistant district attorney, police, and others in City Hall about what they were finding.

Roberts thinks the politicians knew any pressure on the paper would have been futile. "There had been several years of other efforts and other attempts to get stories killed that never came to fruition," he notes. "I don't think by '77 anyone in a political position around here would think that they could succeed in getting a story killed."

In April, as the series was being written, Marimow called the mayor for an interview and read a few key paragraphs of the series to his press secretary. Two minutes later, as Marimow recalls, Rizzo called back and in "loud threatening tones" told him that he would sue him and Neumann and the *Inquirer* for libel as soon as the series hit the streets. He never did. Even at the time, the reporters dismissed the threat as bombast.

Stories such as "The Homicide Files" seldom crop up and get done properly on a paper without an on-going commitment to in-depth reporting, associate editor Michael Pakenham claims. According to both reporters and editors at the paper, the *Inquirer* has gradually made and deepened that commitment since 1969 when Knight Newspapers, Inc. (now Knight-Ridder Newspapers, Inc.) bought the paper and changed the management.

Why then, we wondered, are reporters involved in such long-term projects not freed from their daily beats? During their investigation, Neumann and Marimow stayed with their beats, although, they admit, their daily coverage grew progressively weaker. Toward the end of the project, Carroll sent another reporter to City Hall to replace Neumann in the courts and buttress Marimow at City Council.

"A lot of what you do on a beat is self-initiated. . . . And during the time that we were working on 'The Homicide Files,' I personally was not initiating anything," Marimow recalled. "It was only when there was a major story that was unavoidable that I was working on it." Other City Hall reporters helped out.

"One of the great things about the *Inquirer* is that it's such a team effort," Neumann said. "Everyone wants to see a good story in the paper even if it's not theirs."

Some reporters perform better and some projects evolve better when the writers maintain day-to-day contact on a beat, Pakenham says. Few reporters, he adds, can be full-time investigators without "burning out." Sensitive editors should foresee that and take action before it happens, Pakenham contends.

"I would much rather have 20 good reporters, each of whom spends six months every four years on one of these kinds of projects," he says. Frankly, he adds, "This kind of stuff done well takes an almost patho-logical personality. . . . What always happens is that at certain points in the process it becomes a totally obsessive thing."

Carroll agrees that investigative reporters must be handled carefully. Some people may think an editor simply turns an investigative reporter loose for 90 days, Carroll said. "But the reporter needs someone to talk to every day; he needs an editor even more than a reporter doing daily stories does," Carroll contends. Daily contact keeps the investigative reporter from feeling isolated. "An investigative reporter can get men-tally shaky, even paranoid, wondering what the paper really thinks of him. He can get off-track, thinking someone's following him or that the editor has made a deal with the mayor. He must know the paper's interested in what he's doing and that no one will do anything but support him," Carroll believes.

Executive editor Roberts can afford to have his staff pursuing two or three investigative projects at any given time. Beyond that, the risk of dislocation must be weighed against the potential value of the story.

"We never turn down an idea that seemed strong enough, but basi-cally, the rule is that any editor can, on his own without higher approval, detach a reporter for two weeks on a hunch," Roberts explains. "At that point I would assess whether the information and evidence warrant a further investigation."

"The Homicide Files" dispells a popular notion that investigative reporters reveal scandals to the public eye from where criminal conspiracies have hidden them. Many of the facts Marimow and Neumann "exposed" were already known.

"I imagine that 90 percent of all major investigative stories that are done are stories that are already known, except for federal secret conspiracy stuff, which doesn't happen often," Neumann said. "If they weren't known, they couldn't be very good stories. They wouldn't affect anyone."

The best examples are in Washington, where 50 to 100 potential exposés wait openly to be done, Neumann believes.

Why isn't more such work done?

"I would speculate that most individuals do not feel it's their responsibility to decide, 'I'm going to challenge something, which the entire society looks at and doesn't challenge,' " Neumann said. If everyone else reports what happens at press conferences or follows the president around, most reporters don't feel compelled to go beyond that, he said.

Marimow pointed out that reporters covering beats often see only a fragment of a larger problem. One may "suspect that there's a larger problem, but unless you actually have the time and the inspiration and the courage to investigate it, you're only going to see two pieces of a thousand-part jigsaw puzzle."

Roberts says his commitment to in-depth reporting, a term he prefers to investigative reporting, "comes from what I hope is a deep-seated conviction in our newsroom that society has grown ever more complex, and that if all a paper is doing is a conventional what-happened-yesterday type of reporting, the chances are it's not really adequately reporting on its community to its community."

One cannot read "The Homicide Files" without wondering what happened after it was printed. What follows is a brief summary of those events:

—In March 1977, just before "The Homicide Files" appeared, the Pennsylvania Supreme Court handed down the Davenport ruling. Aimed at ending protracted, 24-hour interrogations in order to obtain a statement, the new ruling, in effect, limited police interrogations between the time of arrest and the time of arraignment to six hours.

—When the series was published the *Inquirer's* phone lines in City

Hall began ringing almost constantly with reaction. Many callers told the reporters they had only scratched the surface. Many readers, who came from all sections and strata of Philadelphia, said they had witnessed or been the victim of other police beatings, not by the homicide squad but by police on the beat. Although Marimow and Neumann say they were washed out physically and emotionally after their work on "The Homicide Files," they almost immediately began a new phase of their investigation. The result was a series of articles published in late spring and summer 1977, a set of case studies of street violence by police officers, entitled "On the Street: Police Violence in Philadelphia."

—In May 1977, two weeks after "The Homicide Files" appeared, U.S. Attorney David Marston began a civil rights investigation of the Philadelphia Police Department. A special federal grand jury was empaneled in July 1977 to gather evidence in police cases. It met through January 1978, when Marston, a Republican, was fired by the Carter administration. After Marston's dismissal, that federal investigation was moribund, but between July and January, 15 police were indicted. Six were convicted of conspiring to violate the civil rights of suspects and witnesses in the Santiago firebombing case. Three others were acquitted in another case.

—In the May 1977 primary election, District Attorney Fitzpatrick lost his bid for renomination by the Democrats. His opponent, Edward G. Rendell, campaigned on a promise to fight police brutality. He won the May primary and the November election.

—The State House Subcommittee on Crime and Correction and the NAACP held public hearings on police violence in Philadelphia during the summer of 1977.

—In August 1977, Common Pleas Court Judge Charles Durham threw out the confession of Carlton Coleman on the grounds that it had been obtained through illegal coercion. Coleman, whose case is discussed in Part I, had been charged with shooting an off-duty policeman. In October 1977, the district attorney's office dropped all charges against Coleman because there was no evidence except for his statement.

—One year after "The Homicide Files" was published, Neumann and Marimow did a brief follow-up. While they had been working on the original series, a city solicitor had warned the reporters not to publish it. Once it ran in the paper, he argued, every criminal defendant in Philadelphia would claim he had been beaten. The reporters went back to the records in a year to see if such was the case. What they found was that while there were 433 allegations of illegal interrogations by police in homicide cases during the period from January 1974 to April 1977—the three years preceding the publication of "The Homicide

Files" (well over 100 per year)—in the year that followed the publication of the series, only three defendants brought similar allegations. Once the spotlight was on the homicide officers and they knew they would be subject to prosecution, "they cleaned up their act," Marimow surmised.

—In April 1979, two years after "The Homicide Files," the U.S. Civil Rights Commission investigated police violence and held public hearings in Philadelphia.

—In August 1979, the U.S. Justice Department brought a police brutality suit against the city of Philadelphia. The core of the suit was dismissed that October by U.S. District. Judge J. William Ditter, who ruled the government had exceeded its authority to intercede in local affairs.

—In January 1980, Rizzo's term as mayor expired. He had lost a referendum in November 1978 which would have amended the city charter to allow him to run for a third consecutive term. William Green took over the office.

—In July 1981, the Justice Department allowed the police brutality suit against Philadelphia to die by allowing an appeals deadline to expire. Officials said the climate in Philadelphia had changed since the suit had been filed during the Rizzo administration.

THE HOMICIDE FILES, PART I

AT THE ROUNDHOUSE: HOW DETECTIVES COMPEL MURDER "CONFESSIONS"

By Jonathan Neumann
and William K. Marimow
Inquirer Staff Writers
© 1977 The *Philadelphia Inquirer*

It can be said with certainty that two things happened in the 22 hours between Carlton Coleman's arrest and his arraignment last October.

One is that he was interrogated by homicide detectives. The other is that his health went from good to poor. When it was all over, he spent the next 28 days hospitalized for injuries of the abdomen, arms, shoulders, chest, calf, spine, and back.

Medical problems are not rare among those interrogated by the Philadelphia Police Department's 84-member homicide division. In fact, a four-month investigation by the *Inquirer* has found a pattern of beatings, threats of violence, intimidation, coercion, and knowing disregard for constitutional rights in the interrogation of homicide suspects and witnesses.

The study shows that many homicide detectives, in beating or coercing suspects and later denying it under oath, have come to accept breaking the law as part of their job.

As a result of those practices, the *Inquirer* has found, there are cases in which murders have remained unsolved, killers have gone free, and innocent men have been imprisoned.

From 1974 through this month, judges of the Common Pleas Court have been asked to rule in pretrial hearings on the legality of police investigations in 433 homicide cases. Those rulings require the judge to decide who is telling the truth—the police or the suspect. In most cases, the judge believes the police.

In 80 of those cases, however, judges have ruled that the police acted illegally during homicide interrogations. The judges found in many cases that police had used either physical or psychological coercion. In some cases, the victims' injuries were documented by X-rays, medical records, and photographs.

Extensive interviews with homicide detectives and prosecutors who work with detectives every day confirm these findings. The interviews—

including some with detectives who frequently have been accused of beatings—make it clear that top officials in the Police Department know of and tolerate the coercive measures.

The illegal interrogations follow a pattern:

• They are conducted by teams of detectives in tiny rooms at police headquarters—known as the Roundhouse—at Eighth and Race Streets. The suspect or witness is often handcuffed to a metal chair, which is bolted to the floor. Some of these sessions have lasted 24 hours.

• Some of the techniques used in the beatings leave no severe marks. Those techniques include placing a telephone book on a suspect's head and hammering it with a heavy object; beating his feet and ankles; twisting or kicking his testicles; and pummeling his back, ribs, and kidneys.

• Other techniques do leave marks. Testimony about interrogations that judges have ruled illegal has shown that suspects have been beaten with lead pipes, blackjacks, brass knuckles, handcuffs, chairs, and table legs. One suspect was stabbed in the groin with a sword-like instrument.

• The detectives make use of one-way mirrors through which the interrogation rooms can be observed. Suspects and witnesses have testified that they were forced to watch beatings through such windows and were told that they would receive the same treatment unless they cooperated.

"What we're living in at the Roundhouse," a former homicide detective said, "is a return to the Middle Ages. All this nonsense about the 'thin blue line between society and the underworld,' it's bull—. Police are breaking the law every day, and they know it."

Why are detectives doing this?

The main reason, detectives say, is outrage—outrage at the heinousness of the crimes they investigate, and outrage at a court system that allows murderers to "walk," or go free.

"It's a fight every day," one detective said. "The homicide detective must fight the lawyers, the judges, the Supreme Court—and he must fight crime."

But there is also another reason: money.

To get a statement from a suspect, a detective often works round the clock—and that means overtime. Once he gets a statement, he becomes a court witness—and court time means more overtime.

City payroll records show that the average homicide detective got $7,575 in overtime pay last year. One, Michael Chitwood, more than doubled his base pay, earning a total of $36,293, which is higher than the salary of Police Commissioner Joseph F. O'Neill.

Do high police officials know about the crimes in the interrogation room?

They, like all citizens, have access to court records, including the 80 recent homicide cases in which interrogations have been ruled illegal. They also work extremely closely with the elite homicide division.

In one case, testimony by an assistant district attorney showed that a homicide investigation was under the direct supervision of Commissioner O'Neill and Chief Inspector Joseph Golden, who set up a temporary "command post" office at the Roundhouse.

In that case, a judge later concluded, a suspect named Larry Howard was beaten. Howard testified that he was hit with a lead pipe, punched with brass knuckles and handcuffs, and grabbed by the testicles. Another suspect, Richard Atkins, testified that he was forced to watch Howard's interrogation through a one-way mirror.

Within the Police Department, there is constant pressure to get suspects to talk. Detectives say that Chief Inspector Golden has a standing order to the homicide division: "Get a statement."

At times, the emphasis on getting statements can produce odd results.

On Jan. 19, when a North Philadelphia shopkeeper named George Lewis was murdered during a holdup, investigators determined that he had been killed by a single bullet.

Homicide detectives questioned two suspects, and by the time they emerged from their respective interrogation rooms, each had allegedly admitted firing the shot. Their cases are pending.

So far this year judges have heard 31 formal allegations of illegal interrogations and have ruled for the defendant 11 times.

One case that is expected to come up in 1977 is that of Carlton Coleman, the man who was hospitalized for 28 days after his interrogation. Coleman, 26, is charged with shooting an off-duty policeman. He allegedly signed a confession, but he is expected to argue that he was beaten and coerced.

Does the Police Department care that murder cases are lost because illegal "confessions" are thrown out?

As individuals, the police care very much. But their concern does not carry over into the department's official gauge of its effectiveness—the rate at which murder cases are "cleared." A "cleared" case is one in which someone is charged with the crime—but not necessarily convicted.

The department is proud that it has "cleared" nearly 87 percent of its cases in recent years. But 20 percent of the homicide defendants who went to court last year were acquitted or were freed because the district attorney's office dropped the charges for lack of evidence.

An example of a murder that was "cleared," but apparently not solved, is the well-known Santiago firebombing case. As the *Inquirer* reported in November, the police rounded up seven neighbors, beat the men, threatened the women, and forced them to sign false statements implicating Robert (Reds) Wilkinson in five murders. He was convicted, but the verdict was overturned when another man, David McGinnis, confessed.

Why are homicide detectives not forced to obey the law?

No homicide detective has been prosecuted in recent years—if ever—for a crime committed during an interrogation. This apparent immunity can be explained in part by the detectives' close working relationship with the district attorney's office.

Prosecutors depend on the police for testimony and cooperation in presenting evidence. If the district attorney's office were to press criminal charges against detectives, the cooperation could collapse.

In the 80 cases in which judges have ruled interrogations illegal, the record shows that the police do not discriminate: The victims have been white and black, guilty and innocent. Women, too, have been coerced and threatened, but the *Inquirer* has seen no testimony that women have been beaten in interrogations.

Judges, in hearing these cases, have taken extensive testimony and examined documentary evidence, including photographs, X-rays, and other medical records, before making formal findings of fact.

Based on these cases, here are several incidents from the Roundhouse interrogation rooms:

William Hoskins, 23, a black murder suspect, was handcuffed to a metal chair bolted to the floor. During an interrogation by homicide detectives Michael Chitwood, John Strohm, Daniel Rosenstein, and Rosborough McMillan, Hoskins was stabbed in the groin with a swordlike instrument and blackjacked on his feet, ankles, and legs until the blackjack broke in two.

Lawyers present on the scene that night—Nov. 5, 1975—said Hoskins was carried out of the Roundhouse and driven by police to Philadelphia General Hospital, where he was carried in on a stretcher.

Medical records show that Hoskins could not stand up when he was admitted to the hospital's emergency ward. Doctors wrote that Hoskins suffered severe injuries to his kidneys, that he was urinating blood, and that the left side of his body, from his shoulders to his buttocks, was swollen and bruised. The prisoner, handcuffed to his hospital bed, was placed on intravenous feeding and remained at the hospital for five days.

Common Pleas Court Judge Samuel Smith ruled that the Hoskins interrogation was illegal. "There is no question he was beaten," Judge Smith said in an interview. "This guy was hurt bad."

Hoskins was later convicted of murder. The verdict is being appealed. Richard Rozanski, 28, a white murder suspect, was kicked in the testicles and beaten on the back with a wooden chair by Detective Richard Strohm. He was punched on the head and face by Detective George Cassidy until he was "numb," Rozanski testified.

That same night—Dec. 22, 1975—Detective Strohm approached Rozanski's brother-in-law, Joey Kedra, 22, who was in another interrogation room. According to court testimony, Strohm pointed a gun at Kedra's head and said: "I'm going to blow your motherf—ing brains out, Punch."

Judge James R. Cavanaugh ruled that the 17-hour interrogation of Rozanski was illegal and that the defendant had been "subjected to physical and mental threats and coercion. . . ."

Judge Cavanaugh made his ruling after reviewing photographs and hearing the testimony of Rozanski, homicide detectives, and Dr. Daniel Jacobs, who examined Rozanski a day after his interrogation.

Last July, after spending six months in prison, Rozanski was acquitted by a jury in Common Pleas Court. The murder of Joseph Lucano Jr. remains unsolved.

[Ed. Note: Neumann and Marimow described in this article nine other cases of brutality.]

INTERVIEWS WITH 3 DETECTIVES ON INTERROGATIONS BY POLICE

By Jonathan Neumann
and William K. Marimow
Inquirer Staff Writers

The *Inquirer* conducted extensive interviews with a number of homicide detectives, all under an agreement that they would not be quoted by name.

Three interviews were selected for publication at length. The three were chosen in part because they bring different perspectives to the subject of illegal interrogations.

In the first interview, a younger, "tough" cop, who has frequently been accused of beating suspects and witnesses, explains why he believes that the homicide division is doing its job properly. He says the public does not understand the difficulty of detectives' work.

In the second interview, a veteran homicide detective, who has also been accused of beatings, talks about "the new breed" in the homicide division. He has mixed feelings about the methods used by most detectives.

The third man is a recently resigned detective who says that coercion and beatings are routine at the Roundhouse and that detectives knowingly break the law to obtain evidence.

The Young Detective

"After a brutal death, who the hell cares? Who cares about the victim? It's the most horrifying thing that anyone can experience. The district attorney doesn't care—it's publicity for him. The defense lawyer doesn't care—it's money for him. The judges? They're gutless, inhuman and all they give a damn about is collecting their salaries. The cops that handle it? Damn right. They care. But no one else cares.

"It's a fight every day. The homicide detective must fight the lawyers, the judges, the Supreme Court—and he must fight crime . . . not to mention newspapers. . . . A homicide detective must know the law as it is now, and he must know the law as it is going to be interpreted five years from today. . . .

"Well, the courts want to ask you [the homicide detective], 'Why did you do this wrong?' . . . 'You did this wrong'. . . . 'You're not a doctor.' The judge says to me, 'You're not an expert. . . . You're not educated. . . .' Nowhere do they ask you about the victim. As soon as it goes to court, no one asks about the victim. . . .

"The cops are asked, 'Did you beat the defendant? . . . Was he beaten?' Whose side is the D. A. on? It's one big game. . . .

"Did I ever hit anyone just because of the crime he committed? Knowing this system the way I do, knowing the killer is going to be out on the street in a short time, did I ever hit anyone just because I was so angry at the crime he committed? . . . Be your own judge on that. I'm a human being.

"So what—what would be the big deal if they [detectives] did beat a cold-blooded killer? Who cares? Only the liberal society. . . . For what reason do I have to sit in that interrogation room and look at this son of a bitch and talk to him like he's a human being? Why do I have to sit down and care about the feelings of a killer? . . .

"Homicide—anybody can get away with it. Just kill a person without anyone seeing you. No matter how much circumstantial evidence there is, if you [the detective] didn't get a statement from the defendant, 99 percent of your cases would be thrown out.

"In today's day and age, innocent until proven guilty. Bull——! If you're arrested, you're damn right you committed the crime. Today a policeman cannot afford to make a mistake. I have never seen the wrong person arrested in a murder in Philadelphia. . . . All my jobs [cases] are solved. Not the conviction—that's on the D. A. . . .

. . . .

"A right to remain silent? Bull——! Everyone has an obligation to talk about a crime if they know about it. That's the law. If you know something about a crime, you have an obligation to talk.

"Everybody in this country knows what their rights are. By watching TV, everybody knows. You watch 'Starsky and Hutch,' you know what your rights are when you're 7 years old. Who are we trying to kid? . . .

"I hate niggers. But it doesn't affect the way I handle a job. We're all prejudiced, every damn one of us. Yeah, I hate niggers. I wouldn't let my kids go to school with those lazy loafers who don't want to work. . . . We're all prejudiced, let's face it. The whites hate the blacks. The niggers hate the whites. The Chinese hate the Americans. The Poles hate the Russians. We're all prejudiced—let's be open about that. But it doesn't affect my work. A murder is a murder. It doesn't matter what color the body is. . . ."

. . . .

The Veteran Detective

"I'm not going to defend the Police Department now. No way. I work on my own. There're people there [in the homicide division] I'd refuse to work with.

"We've got a new breed of guy now. Years ago we'd sit there [in the interrogation room] and talk with the defendants. The detectives used to think with their heads, not their hands. They were good, damned good, and they got the evidence clean.

"Now, all they care about is statements [from suspects]. I think statements are bull——. Don't let Golden know I said that. Suppose a guy is locked up. It's hard factual evidence that makes or breaks a case. There are guys [in homicide] who believe the statement is Almighty God. . . .

"There's little cliques down there [in homicide] now. Certain guys hang together. I'll admit it: There are some real assholes down there. I'm not going to defend it. The place could use some cleaning up. But what am I supposed to do? Tell me, what am I supposed to do? I just do my job on my own.

"Are there beatings? I don't know. I haven't seen any, but I've seen people who were obviously beaten up. Don't ask me who did it. I can't speak for the guys because I don't know them that well. And I can't speak against them, because I don't know them that well, either. I can only tell you what I've seen personally.

"They have imported a lot of assholes down in homicide. I can tell you this—when the housecleaning comes, the good guys will be pushed out and the assholes will move up. That's the way it always is in this Police Department. . . .

"Here's how I run an interrogation. I go in and say, 'I know you did so and so because I have such and such.' I don't know what the psychologists say, but after years on the job you know how to feel people out.

"I say, 'I have a witness.' Sometimes I do, sometimes I don't. I'll bluff sometimes. You got to feel him out. Then he'll explain it to you. It works. When you got somebody caught, he'll talk to you. The suspect is guilty as sin, so after I read him his rights he says, 'I don't want a lawyer.' You see, he thinks that if he asks for a lawyer, that means he's guilty. So he won't ask for a lawyer.

"The guy gives you a story, and at first he denies everything. Then he'll say, 'I had a gun and it went off . . .' I'll ask him, 'What do you mean, "It went off?" ' He'll try to explain it, like it wasn't his fault. He'll try to ease the guilt. . . . But he won't come right out and admit it.

"After his story I ask him to take a lie-detector test. 'If you did nothing wrong, you have nothing to be afraid of,' I say. So he goes upstairs, and he flunks. He always flunks. Because he's lying. Then I talk to him more, and eventually his story comes around. . . .

"If I think a guy is innocent, I'll go out of my way to get him off. If I think he's guilty, I'll go out of my way to get him in. . . .

"First time I was accused of beating someone I got bloodcurdling mad. . . . After a while, you start to think: 'Why should I worry about this? The tough reputation isn't going to hurt me down at the Round-house during an interrogation.'

"Me, I never laid a hand on one of them fish [suspects]. For one thing, I know if I was being beaten, the only thing I'd think is, 'Someday I'm gonna get out of here and I'm gonna get back at him. . . .' "

The Recently Resigned Detective

"I'll tell you from the start that I'm prejudiced against the department, but it's for a good reason. And everything I'm telling you is true. I feel guilty for having taken part in some of what goes on down there. I never beat anyone, but I played along with their game—and I'll feel guilty for it for the rest of my life because I know I treated human beings unfairly.

"[Chief Inspector Joseph] Golden runs that place like a czar. He got rid of an accumulated, experienced background of 500 years and brought in all inexperienced men, and they all aim to please. Because it's a very lucrative job, bringing them a lot of overtime pay. Believe me, the money is something they think about.

"The rule down there: Convictions at any cost. A detective will say, 'Chief, we know it's him, but we haven't got it yet.' And then Golden will say, 'Get it.' And they know it doesn't matter how they get it. Beatings? Yes, I've seen them. Really. Why beatings? It's very simple. They do it because they're told to. It's very lucrative. The only thing Golden has to do to maintain discipline is threaten to transfer. . . . They listen because Golden has them lock, stock, and barrel.

"Convictions is the name of the game. Not truth . . .

. . . .

"Miranda—when the Supreme Court first came down with the ruling [in 1966], it was regiment to read the defendant his rights. . . . No longer. I've asked defendants down there if they were read their rights and they said no. The detectives didn't deny it. . . .

"They'll interview him [a suspect] and then they will feel they have one person lined up and the pressure is put on. Then they'll bring in a goon. He'll start slapping, take him [the suspect] out of the chair. He'll hit him, again and again, and then [the detective will] read him the statement and say, 'You did it, motherf——ker and you're gonna talk.' Bang, bang, bang—across the guy's face. . . . Sometimes they'll keep him handcuffed in the chair and slap him open-faced and kick him on the shins.

"They'll punch you hard in the chest and heart area—they know where it hurts and where there won't be any marks afterwards. They know what they're doing. . . . What I'm telling you I've seen. I know it's true.

"If a man passes a lie-detector test they'll tell him he flunked, and he's interrogated again.

"Do the detectives know they may be breaking the law? Of course. Certainly. They know exactly what they're doing, and they know there's a law against assault and a law against perjury, and a law against falsifying police records. They certainly know the law. . . . If they thought beating a defendant was legal, why would they go to court and lie about it? If they thought it was legal, they would march into the courtroom and say, 'Yes, I beat the s——out of this guy because he's a vicious killer and he deserves it.'

"Their attitudes are built for them by their superiors. Yes, I'm talking about Mayor Rizzo. Who do you think built this police department? . . .

. . . .

"The attitude is the same in all the Police Department—setting apart the policemen from society. The first day you're in the academy they drill it into you: 'Your friends won't like you anymore. The only friends you'll have are police' . . . and so on. . . .

"I don't mean to intimate that everyone's brutal. They're not. That's why they have the goon squad. You've got to have some brains working in there, or you'd come out with nothing but bruised bodies.

"Conviction, win—that's where it's at. It's not justice. You can see it in the Wilkinson case. They're filly-fallying around with that and still hoping to win. They'll never admit they were wrong, not even when an innocent man's life is at stake.

. . . .

"A policeman is flying high on his arrest record. He's one of the 'in' boys. He's tough, and they like it that way. If he's not tough, he's not 'in.' It's like the Army. If the boss is happy, everybody is happy. You do it to please the boss. . . . You'll play their game or you'll leave quietly, and you won't look back."

RIZZO DEFENSE: IT IS A TRADITIONAL VIEW

By Jonathan Neumann
and William K. Marimow
Inquirer Staff Writers

Mayor Frank L. Rizzo refused to be interviewed for the *Inquirer*'s series on homicide investigations.

However, on March 17, when the State Supreme Court handed down a new ruling requiring that all suspects be arraigned within six hours of their arrest, Rizzo, in a telephone interview with the *Inquirer*, made these comments that touch on some of the issues in the series:

"It seems to me we have to consider the entire community. What are we talking about here? Murder. It's not like 'Kojak,' when you just look out the window and solve a crime. It has to be done with detective work. A lot of painstaking hours, walking the streets, talking to witnesses, checking records.

"Take the case of a variety store owner being shot. It's bad enough there's an innocent victim, but then, tell me, in a city of 2 million people, how are you going to come up with the killer? You hope he leaves evidence behind—a gun, a bullet we can run down—but it's not that easy.

"Sometimes we come up with a guy. So we got to talk to him. He comes in without a lawyer. There has to be a dialogue between criminals and police. The man talks to us and he tells us he had nothing to do with it. So we let him go and track down his alibis.

"Do we ever use the rubber hose [to beat people]? I've never seen it. We would not permit it to ever happen in Philadelphia. . . .

"So we go out and investigate his alibi. Then the man comes back with a lawyer. . . . It used to be you could use any statement [police obtained from a defendant], before they had Miranda and Escobedo [two U. S. Supreme Court rulings requiring that police inform citizens of their rights to remain silent and to consult with a lawyer]. But now the courts are tying you down, more and more.

"The police aren't going to suffer. It's the people who are going to suffer. In the violence that's sweeping through the nation, this court ruling will only make it more difficult to protect a free society. . . .

"I'm as concerned with the rights of the criminal as I am about anything else. But the scales of justice have to consider the innocent victim. You have to weigh the difference between a lawful society and an unlawful society.

"The scales are shifting too much to the rights of the criminal. It's unfair to the law-abiding citizen. . . .

"You tell me they [police] bring in the wrong people and question them? Unfortunately, that happens. But unfortunately, these are the times we live in."

"THE ONLY RIGHTS YOU GET . . . ARE RIGHT FISTS"

By Jonathan Neumann
and William K. Marimow
Inquirer Staff Writers

Anthony Prado, a murder suspect who turned out to be innocent, remembers what a detective said when Prado asked about his constitutional rights.

"Rights?" a detective replied. "You've been watching too much 'Kojak.' This is murder we're talking about."

Many have shared Prado's experience. Again and again, suspects and witnesses who have been interrogated by homicide detectives have later reported that their rights—especially the constitutional rights to remain silent and to consult a lawyer—were treated as a joke.

Richard Rozanski, who a judge found was beaten and illegally interrogated, said a detective told him: "The only rights you get down here are right fists."

In another case, Judge Robert A. Latrone became incredulous upon hearing a homicide detective, Chester Koscinsky, testify that he had interrogated 600 suspects in three years and that not one had asked to see a lawyer.

The judge interrupted to ask the detective: "You never have the defendant answer in response to the Miranda warnings that he desired to have a lawyer . . .? You never had that happen?"

"Not that I can recall, no sir," the detective replied.

Even when suspects do have lawyers, and the lawyers advise them to remain silent, the interrogations sometimes go on.

In one instance, Frank Lowery, 22, a murder suspect, surrendered voluntarily to police with his attorney, Dennis E. Haggerty, present. Haggerty testified that he told Detective John Ellis that Lowery was not to be interrogated. Ellis said he would not interrogate Lowery, and he did not.

But Detective Richard Strohm did.

Ellis later testified that he had indeed said he would not question Lowery. He added, however, that he had never made any promises on behalf of other detectives.

Under cross-examination about the Lowery interrogation, Strohm testified that Haggerty "doesn't advise me to do anything. He may advise his client of his constitutional rights, but he doesn't advise me."

Longtime criminal lawyer Louis Lipschitz supplies some of his clients with a two-page letter to the police in case they are arrested. It says:

"I am specifically advising you that you do not interrogate him [the client] . . . expose him to threats of any kind or any form of psychological, mental, moral, or physical coercion.

"Please do not expose him to any rides in your elevator or any lie detectors which you may suggest will induce him to 'have a change of heart' or 'unburden himself' or 'make peace with his Maker' . . . or subject him to any other form of persuasion, inducement, wile, seduction, or suggestion. . . .

"I am aware of the possibility that I have not mentioned all of the things for your consideration which in the past have been asserted through the ingenuity of pseudo-legal minds. I do feel that the above thoughts may serve to remind you of those I have forgotten."

THE HOMICIDE FILES, PART II

HOW POLICE HARASSED A FAMILY

By Jonathan Neumann
and William K. Marimow
Inquirer Staff Writers

On Dec. 29, 1975, the family of Mrs. Dolores Kedra was awakening on a leisurely holiday morning when 15 policemen surrounded their Frankford rowhouse and then smashed through the front and back doors with shotgun butts.

Inside the house, the police—according to testimony, interviews, and medical evidence—ran up the narrow staircase, pistols and shotguns drawn. In a bedroom, they overturned the bed, ripped out dresser drawers, and threw furniture against a wall.

Charging downstairs again, they used nightsticks to crack the heads of four Kedra children. Patti, 17, fell to the floor and cried: "My head is split!"

Only then did police find what they were looking for: Richard Rozanski, Mrs. Kedra's son-in-law. He had been sitting the whole time at the kitchen table, telling his lawyer by telephone what was happening and asking for advice.

The police had come to arrest Rozanski for murder—a murder he did not commit.

When Rozanski was acquitted last July, even the prosecutors acknowledged his innocence. By the time he was acquitted, however, Rozanski had been arrested three times for the murder and had spent six months in jail. In addition, his relatives had been beaten, coerced, and harassed by Philadelphia police, according to court testimony.

In reconstructing the Rozanski case from court rulings, medical records, police documents, and extensive interviews with the family, police officers, prosecutors, defense lawyers, and judges, the *Inquirer* has found that:

• The raid on the Kedra home was conducted without a search warrant.

• There was no warrant for Rozanski's arrest. In fact, his lawyer had offered earlier to bring him to the police voluntarily.

• The police entered the house brandishing shotguns and pistols—notwithstanding the testimony of Officer James Brady, one of the first to enter, who said he "could not recall" seeing any weapons drawn. Even when shown a photograph taken by Joe Kedra that showed an officer pointing a revolver through the front door, Brady testified: "I didn't notice it, no sir."

• Rozanski was beaten, threatened, and coerced in a 17-hour interrogation session at police headquarters, according to a finding by Judge James R. Cavanaugh Jr. of Common Pleas Court. Judge Cavanaugh made his finding on the basis of testimony, police reports, and medical records.

• At least nine persons, including five of Rozanski's relatives, were held in all-night interrogation sessions at the Roundhouse (police headquarters). Court testimony and interviews show that they were coerced and intimidated.

• During the interrogations, relatives sitting outside the interrogation rooms heard the pleas and screams of those being beaten inside.

• Edward McKenna, a friend of Rozanski's, testified that he was beaten by the police and pressured to sign a false statement against Rozanski. Another friend, Joseph McCullough, testified that a detective told him that he would be "locked up" if he refused to sign a false statement against Rozanski.

. . . .

The Rozanski case began on Dec. 22, 1975, when the body of Joseph Lucano Jr., 21, washed ashore along the Delaware River. He had been shot twice in the chest and stuffed head-first into a sleeping bag.

The police immediately had two prime suspects: Joey Kedra, 22, Lucano's former roommate, and Richard Rozanski, Kedra's brother-in-law.

Rozanski was known to be angry at Lucano, who police suspected was a drug dealer, for urging Kedra to use heroin.

Rozanski's in-laws, the Kedras, are a large family. In December 1975 five brothers and three sisters were living with their mother, Dolores, who is separated from her husband. Rozanski was also living there at the time.

On the evening of Dec. 22, seven days before the break-in, police went to the Kedra home to bring the family to the Roundhouse.

The first to arrive at police headquarters was Rozanski's wife, Elizabeth, 21, a slender woman with short blonde hair. She was taken to a small interrogation room at 9:30 P.M.

Between that time and 4:30 P.M. the next day, twelve persons, six in Rozanski's family and six others, would be interrogated at various times. Nine of them later said they were coerced.

"We just found Lucano's body in the river," Detective Richard Strohm said, according to Mrs. Rozanski, "and youse are all gonna get locked up for it." She said she was told at first that her brother, Joey Kedra, was the murderer.

"I Got Hysterical"

"I got hysterical crying when I found out Joey Lucano was dead," she recalled. "The police were talking to me like a piece of trash. I said, 'I have an ulcer, and I'd like to call a lawyer and my mother.' They said, 'No, you ain't seein' nobody till you tell us Joey did it.' "

Detective Strohm, 34, a policeman for 10 years, headed the Rozanski investigation. Strohm is a lanky, intense, and serious man. Now a sergeant in the narcotics division, he has developed a reputation in the department as a tenacious investigator who never lets up until the crime is solved.

Strohm was also the first to question Dolores Kedra, a waitress.

. . . .

Mrs. Kedra recalled that "all they were saying at the Roundhouse was mother f——er; f—— this; f—— that; scum bag."

Later that night, in the continuing roundup of the family, police sought out Rozanski, a 6-foot, stocky truck driver who speaks of his past criminal record in witty, tough language. "Look," he said in a recent interview, "I'm no angel, but I'm no killer . . . . I've served time [for two aggravated robberies], but I've been clean since 1969. I did some dumb things as a kid, but I've straightened up for good. I'm never going back to jail—I've learned my lesson."

. . . .

The Interrogation

According to court testimony, Rozanski's interrogation began with his being handcuffed to a bolted-down metal chair. Detective Strohm asked him if he had killed Lucano. Rozanski said he had not. He did say that he had recently been in a fist-fight with Lucano because Lucano had been "trying to pump Joey [Kedra] with heroin." But he added that he had no idea who had shot Lucano.

Police asked Rozanski if he would take a lie-detector test. He said he would. Then, he testified, he asked Strohm: "Can I call a lawyer? I don't know if I am supposed to do this, because when it comes to the law, I know nothing about it."

"No," Strohm replied. "If you ain't hiding nothing, take it [the lie-detector test]."

Rozanski was taken to the polygraph room and took the test. He was told that he had lied, according to his testimony.

At that point, Rozanski said, Detective Strohm "burst into the room, and spread my legs apart and kicked me in the [groin]. He said, 'Richie, you ain't never gonna have another [woman] the rest of your life.'"

According to Rozanski's testimony, the following took place:

George Cassidy, a heavy man nicknamed "Kong" by fellow detectives, came into the polygraph room and yelled to Rozanski: "Who did it?"

Rozanski said: "How can I say who did it if I don't know?"

Cassidy, standing behind Rozanski, who was now handcuffed to a wooden chair, smacked Rozanski's head to the left.

. . . .

After eight hours of questioning and beating, Rozanski was weary, and his head, he said, "was spinning." He said his face was "numb" from the pummeling by Cassidy, and that his back hurt. His shirt was torn open; his right eye was black and puffy, and his head was bleeding.

When Rozanski refused to confess, he said, police told him: "Look, if you didn't kill him, your brother-in-law [Joey Kedra] killed him."

Rozanski repeated that he did not know who the killer was.

"Tell us you killed him or your brother-in-law killed him," Rozanski was told, according to his testimony. He did not answer.

As Rozanski was being beaten in the polygraph room, his relatives were under questioning in other nearby rooms.

"I Can't Take It"

"I heard Richie hollering," Mrs. Kedra testified. "He was screaming: 'Mother of God, I can't take it anymore.'"

Rozanski's wife was in another room. She testified that she heard her husband screaming: "Dear God, I didn't do nothing. Don't hit me."

Rozanski's brother-in-law, Joey, was in another room.

. . . .

Kedra, an ex-marine, was then taken back to an interrogation room. He later testified that Detective Strohm pulled out a gun and pointed it at his face, saying, "I'm going to blow your motherf——ing brains out, Punk."

Kedra testified that, although he was frightened, he told Strohm: "Go ahead. You'll be charged with murder."

At the same time, detectives were questioning Joseph Lucano Sr. as a suspect because of his relationship with Geraldine Fox. The Kedras recall hearing shouting and moaning coming from the interrogation room in which Lucano was being questioned.

"I was sitting in the hallway," Mrs. Kedra testified, "and I heard . . . a detective screaming at him. And then I heard—I heard like a smack, and then Detective Strohm came out of the room and told me to sit on the other side."

By about 8 A.M. Dec. 23, 10 hours after the interrogations began, Rozanski was led into a hallway. There was dried blood on his face, according to Mrs. Kedra's testimony.

She recalled: "He said to me, 'Dee, they beat the balls off me,'" Mrs. Kedra testified. "And I said, 'Yes, I know.'"

The Kedras and Rozanskis were released in late afternoon of Dec. 23. No one was charged with Lucano's murder.

Just before his release at 6 P.M., Rozanski said, he was approached by Detective Cassidy, who said: "Richie, I believe you. After the beating you took, you gotta be innocent."

But Detective Strohm apparently did not agree.

Police continued to try to gather evidence against Rozanski. On Dec. 23 and 24, they brought in two possible witnesses in the case—Joseph McCullough and Edward McKenna, friends of Rozanski's since his high school days in Tacony.

Both men have since testified that the police tried to coerce them into signing false statements, saying that they had overheard conversations in which Rozanski implicated himself in the killing.

In court testimony, McCullough said he was taken to the Roundhouse on Dec. 23 and held into the morning of Dec. 24. He said he was interrogated by Detective Brian Muldoon.

. . . .

Refused to Sign

But McCullough did not sign, and he was eventually released.

McKenna testified that he was handcuffed and threatened at the Roundhouse that night. He also testified that he was beaten by police before he was called to testify against Rozanski.

After Rozanski and the Kedras were released by police on Dec. 23, Rozanski called his lawyers—Raymond Takiff and Anthony Baratta—and told them about the interrogations. On Dec. 26, Baratta met at the Roundhouse with Capt. Donald Patterson, the chief of the homicide division, and Lieutenant Leslie Simmins.

Baratta testified that he asked Patterson if Rozanski should turn himself in voluntarily, and Patterson replied: "Absolutely not, we don't want him . . . . We have nothing whatever to do with him at this point."

But only three days later—on that Monday morning of Dec. 29—the police conducted their raid on the Kedra home for the purpose of seizing Rozanski.

The incident began when police cars and vans filled the narrow street on which the Kedras lived. Fifteen policemen—including patrolmen from the 15th District, uniformed stakeout officers with shotguns, and plainclothes homicide detectives—surrounded the house.

According to testimony and interviews, the following happened:

At 10:05 A.M. officers James Brady and Robert Pitney knocked on the door. Mrs. Rozanski opened it, and the policemen asked to see Rozanski to serve him with court papers.

Rozanski, who had been in bed, came down the stairs. When he reached the front door, the officers grabbed at his arm and tried unsuccessfully to pull him out of the house.

Both Rozanski and his wife pushed the door shut. Rozanski immediately went to the kitchen and called Baratta, one of his lawyers.

Rozanski was advised to stay on the telephone while Baratta called police headquarters on another line. Baratta reached Detective Strohm at 10:15 A.M. The lawyer said he asked, "Is there a warrant for Richard Rozanski?"

No Warrant

Baratta testified that this was Strohm's response: "There is no warrant for anyone, but if I see Rozanski on the street I'm going to pull him in for questioning."

(Strohm, in court hearings, at first denied having that telephone conversation with Baratta. Later, however, he admitted under oath that the conversation had, in fact, taken place.)

Baratta again offered to turn Rozanski in voluntarily if the police obtained a warrant. The attorney then spoke to Rozanski, and suggested that Joey Kedra take out his camera and take pictures of the police around the home.

As Rozanski stayed on the telephone, Baratta then called the 15th Police District to find out why policemen were at the Kedra home. No one could answer his question, he said.

At 10:45 A.M., with Rozanski still on the phone to his lawyer, policemen smashed the butt of a shotgun through the Kedras' glass front door and kicked the door open. Police officers marched into the house with pistols drawn, aimed directly toward members of the Kedra family who were in the living room.

The police went to the staircase and hurried to the second floor, according to the Kedras. They did not say anything. Minutes later, more policemen broke through the back entrance of the house. They, too, did not say why they had rushed in.

Rozanski said the policemen who entered through the back walked right past him while he was on the telephone with his lawyer. He did not know they had come to arrest him; they did not know who Rozanski was.

Policemen upstairs rifled through dresser drawers and bedroom furniture.

"What are you looking for?" asked one of the Kedra sisters who said she thought they were seeking Joey Kedra. "My brother couldn't be in the drawers."

Mrs. Rozanski said she asked the police to leave, "but they just ignored me."

"We Got Rozanski!"

Finally one detective yelled out: "We got Rozanski! He's in the kitchen!"

As policemen began running down the stairs to the kitchen, Joey Kedra was following Baratta's instructions and taking pictures. Lt. Augustus C. Miller and Sgt. John J. Tiers spotted the camera, but before they could reach it Kedra threw the camera to his sister, Patti.

As Patti clasped the camera to her chest, Lt. Miller struck her on the head with a nightstick, she and other Kedras said in an interview. Holding on to the camera, she fell to the floor clutched her head, screaming.

According to several family members, Michael, her 16-year-old brother, shouted to police: "You're not going to hit my sister."

Michael and Joey were clubbed on the head with nightsticks and Elizabeth was hit on the back. Kenny, 20, was struck on the head, splattering blood on the floor.

Robert Kedra, 10, remembers being dazed with fright: "There was fighting for five minutes. It was wild. I got hit in the arm . . . .I don't know who hit me."

(Police never seized the camera. The pictures taken by Joey Kedra, although out of focus, were clear enough to be used in court to disprove policemen's testimony that no guns were drawn.)

. . . .

After the scuffle, Joey, Kenny, Patti, and Michael were taken to hospitals to be treated. Kenny required seven stitches in the head; Joey needed four stitches in the head; Patti had head injuries and serious knee damage. She has been treated at Frankford Hospital, Nazareth

Hospital, and by a private physician for her injuries. She must wear a rubber brace on her knee as a result.

Letter of Complaint

The three Kedra boys were arrested on charges of aggravated assault, resisting arrest, and hindering the apprehension of a criminal. (They were later acquitted of all charges.)

Four days after the raid and Rozanski's arrest, Baratta wrote a letter to Police Commissioner Joseph F. O'Neill complaining about the break-in and the arrest.

"I am shocked and horrified beyond all measure of time and place to think that the Gestapo-like tactics could occur in the fourth largest city of the United States. . . . I do not consider myself a bleeding heart. I do consider Detective Strohm's actions to be intolerable," he wrote.

In response, Capt. Patterson of homicide agreed to instruct his men to avoid future incidents of the kind, according to Rozanski's lawyers.

However, Rozanski faced more difficulties with Strohm.

At a preliminary hearing on Jan. 16, 1976, Takiff, who represented Rozanski and the Kedras at the trials, successfully argued before Municipal Court Judge Joseph McCabe to have the charges against Rozanski dropped.

Minutes after the hearing, Strohm rearrested Rozanski—on the same charges. Rozanski was then held without bail until the next preliminary hearing.

At the second hearing, Joseph McCullough—Rozanski's friend who had earlier said he was coerced at the Roundhouse on Christmas Eve—testified that he had been threatened again, this time in a City Hall corridor.

"I was threatened by Strohm," McCullough testified, "that if I didn't testify I was under immediate arrest and that he would never let up on me."

At that hearing, on Jan. 22—although the district attorney presented substantially the same evidence and Takiff made the same arguments for the defense—Judge Bernard Goodheart upheld the murder charge for trial.

Last July 13, Rozanski was acquitted.

The Lucano murder remains unsolved.

Epilogue

The unsolved murder of Joesph Lucano Jr. was followed by another death that some think may have been related.

In March 1976, the body of Geraldine Fox, Lucano's girl friend, was found in the back seat of a car at Philadelphia International Airport. The death was ruled a suicide by drug overdose.

But lawyers involved in the case are dubious.

Miss Fox knew four men who, at one time or another, were suspects in the Lucano murder. According to testimony, she was intimate with at least one—Joseph Lucano Sr.

Was it possible, the lawyers wondered, that she was murdered by one of the suspects to prevent Lucano's killer from being revealed?

If she was murdered, one thing is certain: Richard Rozanski, the police department's prime suspect in the Lucano murder, was not directly responsible.

At the time of Miss Fox's death, Rozanski was in prison awaiting trial.

Although Rozanski was acquitted in Lucano's death, police are no longer actively investigating the death of Joey Lucano Jr.—or Geraldine Fox.

THE HOMICIDE FILES, PART III

A POLICE BEATING . . . AND A DECISION
NOT TO CHARGE DETECTIVES

By Jonathan Neumann
and William K. Marimow
Inquirer Staff Writers

Shortly after 10 P.M. on Nov. 5, 1975, Judge Paul A. Dandridge of Common Pleas Court received an urgent call from Barry H. Denker, a well-known criminal lawyer.

"There's a man here who's hurt bad, judge," Denker said, according to the accounts of both men. "He's got to get to a hospital."

Denker was calling from Philadelphia police headquarters—known as the Roundhouse—and he was talking about William Roy Hoskins, a murder suspect who had been in a tiny interrogation room for the previous six hours. Hoskins lay crumpled on a metal bench, his face swollen, his right eye oozing blood, his kidneys severely damaged, his groin punctured by a stab wound, and his feet so swollen that they would no longer fit into his brown-and-tan loafers.

Judge Dandridge agreed to intervene and ordered that Hoskins be given medical care. Hoskins was admitted on a stretcher to Philadelphia General Hospital.

Within days, a team from the district attorney's office began an investigation into Hoskins' injuries. They found that Hoskins had been beaten by the police and that there was sufficient evidence to prosecute four detectives.

However, District Attorney Emmett Fitzpatrick, Police Commissioner Joseph F. O'Neill, and City Managing Director Hillel S. Levinson decided not to prosecute.

The decision was in keeping with long-standing practice in Philadelphia.

....

The unusual aspect of the Hoskins case was that prosecution was actually considered.

A team of investigators and lawyers from the district attorney's office concluded in a written report that there was a prima facie case of assault against four detectives—Michael Chitwood, John Strohm, Daniel Rosenstein, and Rosborough McMillan.

Just the fact that the district attorney's office was considering prosecution created a serious rift between homicide detectives and the assistant district attorneys, who try murder cases.

The high-level decision against prosecution was made after two secret meetings. At the first, Fitzpatrick and his staff discussed what should be done about the findings of the investigators. At the second session, O'Neill and Levinson met with representatives of Fitzpatrick's office and agreed to a compromise: The detectives would not be charged with crimes, but they would be transferred out of the homicide division. (Fitzpatrick, O'Neill, and Levinson have refused to discuss the case.)

But even that decision was reversed. Within several months, the detectives were transferred back to their old jobs of interrogating suspects in homicide.

When the Hoskins case came to court, Judge Samuel Smith, after hearing police testimony and examining medical evidence, ruled that the interrogation was illegal.

"There's no question he was beaten," the judge said later. "This guy was hurt and hurt bad. The injuries were there. And the police rationale was not convincing."

The Hoskins case began in the afternoon of Nov. 5, 1975, when police arrested three men in a dark-green Cadillac on the Schuylkill Expressway. In addition to Hoskins, those arrested were Lonnie Dawson and Joseph (Jo-Jo) Rhone. All three were suspects in the murder of Hershell Williams, a Black Mafia figure who, because of his size and style of dress, was known as the "Jolly Green Giant."

(Hoskins and Dawson were both convicted; they are appealing to the State Supreme Court. Rhone fled while free on bail and is a fugitive.)

According to court testimony, police records, hospital files, interviews with persons who were at police headquarters that night, and the ruling by Judge Smith, this is apparently what happened in the Hoskins case:

At 4:10 P.M., Hoskins arrived at the Roundhouse and was placed in interrogation room 121—a 10-by-10-foot cubicle containing three metal chairs and a table.

As detectives led him into the interrogation room, Hoskins, 23, a slender, 135-pound black man with a record of four arrests in five years, asked to see a lawyer.

"Do you think you're on television or something?" was the sneering reply from one of the detectives.

According to court records, the first man to question Hoskins was Detective Bernard C. Carr, 48, a policeman for 23 years.

"I'm going to whip your ass," Carr said to Hoskins, according to sources who were in the Roundhouse that night. Hoskins was seated in a widebacked metal chair that was bolted to the floor. Then, after reflecting a moment, Carr said, "I'm too old for this. I'm going to get some . . . [others] . . . to do it."

Carr left. According to sources who were in the Roundhouse that night, Hoskins was then handcuffed to the chair, one hand secured to an arm of the chair, the other hand locked to the chair leg on the opposite side.

For the next three hours, the sources said, Chitwood, Strohm, Rosenstein, and McMillan shuttled in and out of the interrogation room. Hoskins later identified the four from photos he was shown by the investigators from the district attorney's office.

Chitwood, 33, is the highest-paid homicide detective on the force, who last year earned $36,293.17, more than half of it in overtime pay. A tall, curly-haired man with a mustache, Chitwood, the most decorated man on the police force, was recently named one of the police department's two top investigators by the Fraternal Order of Police.

The other man so honored was John Strohm, a stocky broad-shouldered man who also participated in the Hoskins interrogation. Strohm, 34, was the third highest-paid homicide detective in 1976; he earned $30,288.83, including overtime pay.

Chitwood was carrying a small blackjack when he entered interrogation room 121, according to sources who were in the Roundhouse that night. Another detective removed Hoskins' shoes. Chitwood then bludgeoned Hoskins on his feet, ankles, and legs until the blackjack broke in two.

When the blackjack broke, Chitwood returned with a table leg. Shouting "black motherf——" and "black faggot," Chitwood repeatedly struck the shackled Hoskins on the feet, legs, stomach, arms, and face, the sources at the Roundhouse said.

Medical evidence has confirmed that Hoskins' injuries corresponded to such a beating.

Threw a Chair

At one point, after several hours of beating, a detective entered the room, picked up a metal chair, and threw it at Hoskins, the *Inquirer*'s reconstruction of the case shows.

The detectives continually taunted Hoskins, sources said. One detective reportedly said, "We're going to kill you. Maybe we should take his pants down and f—— him."

It was Chitwood, Hoskins told investigators from the district attorney's office, who wielded the swordlike implement. As Hoskins, dazed and battered, slumped into his chair, Chitwood stabbed him in the groin area, Hoskins told investigators.

At 9:30 p.m.—after the beating had ended—Denker arrived at the Roundhouse. The lawyer, who had been notified by Hoskins' family, was shown to a cubicle.

"When I opened the door," Denker said, "I saw one of the most horrible sights I have ever seen. Hoskins was lying on a stool, blood was coming out of his head from his right side. His hat was off. The whole side of his face from his ear section was swollen.

"The only thing I've ever seen like that," Denker continued, "was a picture of a black man hanging from a tree in Mississippi, and this is what this man's face looked like."

Medical records from Hoskins' five-day stay at Philadelphia General Hospital show that he was unable to stand when he was admitted. He had suffered severe injuries to his kidneys and was urinating blood. The left side of his body, from his shoulders to his buttocks, was swollen and bruised. He was handcuffed to a bed and placed on intravenous feeding.

At a pre-trial hearing on Jan. 20, 1976, Chitwood explained, under oath, Hoskins' injuries, but Judge Smith said he did not find the police rationale convincing. Chitwood testified that Hoskins had injured himself while answering questions.

"Did you shoot and kill Hershell Williams, also known as the Jolly Green Giant . . .?" Chitwood said he asked Hoskins.

"At this time, " Chitwood testified, "the defendant [Hoskins] started crying, putting his head down into his lap, and as he did he hit his right eye on the metal chair in which he was seated. I observed a cut over his right eye."

Chitwood went on to recount that Hoskins had given him a statement implicating Dawson and Rhone as the killers. When told that the statement would be read to Dawson, Chitwood said, Hoskins "jumped up from the chair, came at me and started shouting, 'You're going to get me killed . . .' " Chitwood also said that Hoskins punched him in the head.

Chitwood said he was then joined by Detective Strohm, who hit Hoskins in the back with a wooden nightstick.

While Chitwood was describing the altercation under cross-examination, Judge Smith interrupted his testimony and called the attorneys to the bench.

"I've heard enough," Judge Smith told Denker and Assistant District Attorney William Stevens, who was representing the Commonwealth.

After a brief recess, during which he reviewed Hoskins' medical records, Judge Smith ruled that the interrogation was illegal and threw out the statement that police said Hoskins had made.

Sources have told the *Inquirer* that Chitwood's testimony differed from the account police gave to Assistant District Attorney Clifford Haines at the Roundhouse on the night of the beating.

It was Haines, the chief of the district attorney's homicide unit, who first called for an independent investigation of the Hoskins interrogations. Haines has refused to be interviewed about it by the *Inquirer*.

Sources said that Haines, who had been told of the situation by Judge Dandridge, arrived at the Roundhouse shortly before midnight and met with Capt. Donald Patterson, the head of the homicide division, who told him that Hoskins' complaints were "nothing." Patterson said Hoskins had been taken to the hospital to "check him out." (It was unclear during the conversation with Haines, sources said, whether Capt. Patterson was aware of the extent of Hoskins' injuries.)

Before leaving the Roundhouse that night, Haines learned that Hoskins was, in fact, seriously injured. He then demanded an explanation from the police. But he got none.

Later, at around 4 A.M., Haines was awakened at home by a telephone call. A homicide lieutenant told him for the first time that Hoskins had "attacked Chitwood" and been injured in the ensuing fight.

Sources said Haines was appalled by Hoskins' injuries and promptly reported the incident to District Attorney Fitzpatrick.

Haines urged Fitzpatrick to have the detectives suspended, according to the sources. And if an investigation indicated that Hoskins had been assaulted, Haines wanted the detectives charged with crimes.

Meeting with O'Neill

Late in the afternoon of Nov. 6, First Assistant District Attorney John Morris and Haines met with Commissioner O'Neill in his Roundhouse office to discuss the Hoskins beating. Sources said Morris informed the commissioner that Fitzpatrick had decided to have his staff investigate the incident.

(Allegations of police misconduct are normally investigated by the department's Bureau of Internal Affairs.)

The investigation was coordinated by Assistant District Attorneys Robert A. McAteer and Esther R. Sylvester and county Detectives William Cole and Frank Hahn.

Three weeks after the Hoskins beating, the investigators submitted a formal report informing Fitzpatrick that there was sufficient evidence to bring criminal charges of assault against the four detectives.

At a high-level meeting, top officials of the district attorney's office debated whether to prosecute the four homicide detectives.

Haines, sources said, wanted to prosecute, and Fitzpatrick agreed.

However, other members of the district attorney's staff proposed a compromise; O'Neill should be given a choice of transferring the four detectives out of homicide or seeing them prosecuted.

Fitzpatrick was persuaded to change his position. Sources said he was concerned that a prosecution of homicide detectives would seriously undermine the close working relationship between the police department and the district attorney's office.

He also felt that it would be difficult to convict the four detectives in Common Pleas Court, sources said.

The next day, Haines and Assistant District Attorney William Stevens met with O'Neill and Levinson in the managing director's office and gave them the ultimatum: Either transfer the four detectives or face the prospect of their prosecution.

After lunch, O'Neill told the district attorney's office that the four men would be transferred.

Several months later—the *Inquirer* has been unable to learn the exact date—the transfers were rescinded, and the four detectives returned to the homicide unit.

The fact that Fitzpatrick had been considering prosecution was creating discord between the assistant district attorneys and the homicide detectives. While the city's top law-enforcement officials were negotiating the fates of the four detectives, the police staged a short-lived mini-revolt against the district attorney.

"Morale Problems"

Assistant district attorneys recall that homicide detectives "called in sick" when they were scheduled to appear as witnesses. The detectives also "forgot" to bring documents and other materials that were to be introduced as evidence.

"There were morale problems all around," one former assistant district attorney said. "Most of the people in the office just wanted to get back to normal. They wished that Haines had just kept his big mouth shut to begin with."

While assistant district attorneys were irritated by the developments, homicide detectives were infuriated. They, too, blamed Haines.

"Cliff Haines," one detective said in a recent interview, "is an egotistical ass. He was willing to sacrifice homicide detectives for three murdering hit men [the three suspects] who would have killed time and time again."

Because of the unrest, Haines called a meeting of all homicide prosecutors to "clear the air." But the rancor remained, and several assistant district attorneys said they were angry that Haines had pressed for an investigation.

"Haines lost on all counts," one assistant district attorney said. "And he was only trying to do what was right. It's really a sad situation, and unfair. This was the first time anyone in the district attorney's office ever took a strong stand against wrongdoing by a homicide detective —and look where it got Haines."

THE HOMICIDE FILES, PART IV

HOW DETECTIVES ESCAPE PROSECUTION

By Jonathan Neumann
and William K. Marimow
Inquirer Staff Writers

Every other week, on the average, a judge in Common Pleas Court rules that one or more members of the Philadelphia Police Department's 84-member homicide division acted illegally during an interrogation.

Some of the illegal acts are relatively minor. Others are not.

But no matter how serious a detective's offense might be—breaking a man's rib, beating a man until he urinates blood, or forcing an innocent man to sign a "confession" and thereby allowing the true murderer go free—the detective has always been safe.

He has been safe from prosecution that could be instituted by the district attorney's office. He has been safe from any effective action by a judge. And he has been safe from defense attorneys, who say they are powerless to stop the detectives' illegal actions.

270030

The reason is not that the illegal interrogations are a secret: Vivid examples are a matter of public record. The *Inquirer* has reported in the last three days that judges have ruled interrogations illegal in 80 cases since 1974, and that in some of those cases suspects have been shackled, kicked, blackjacked, punched, and, in one case, stabbed.

Why is nothing done?

Interviews with defense attorneys and judges show that many are aware of crimes committed in the interrogation room. But, because the practices are so deeply rooted in Philadelphia, few have tried to do anything about them.

Many in the legal community appear to have become inured to hearing testimony, almost every day, about illegal interrogations. They seem to accept such police actions as inevitable.

In theory, it is the district attorney's job to investigate and, if the facts warrant, to prosecute policemen for illegal acts in the interrogation room.

But the district attorney's office, under Emmett Fitzpatrick and his recent predecessors, has never prosecuted a homicide detective in such a case. To do so would be to risk losing police cooperation in many other serious, ongoing court cases.

Judges, when asked why policemen are not prosecuted after rulings that a suspect has been physically coerced, give a variety of answers.

Many judges say simply that it is not their responsibility. Others say that cases against police would be difficult to prove to the satisfaction of a Common Pleas Court jury.

The judges also point out that the purpose of the hearings at which interrogations have been ruled illegal is to determine whether a confession or statement shall be used as evidence—not to force the homicide division to obey the law.

. . . .

One judge who did act is Samuel Smith, who ordered the district attorney's office to investigate the beating of William Hoskins, a murder suspect who sustained multiple injuries, including severe kidney damage, and was hopitalized for five days after his interrogation.

. . . .

"We've got to stop that kind of thing," Judge Smith said recently. "You know, we can't live in a police state. I think in any case where a person is beaten up by the police—whether he's innocent or a murderer—there ought to be an investigation."

The attitude of Judge Theodore B. Smith is more representative of his colleagues on the bench.

In March 1976, Judge Smith ruled that Ronald Hanley, a murder suspect, was beaten. At that time he wrote: "Hanley was subjected to gross physical abuse, coercion, and violence at the hands of several police officers. Such violence, coercion, and abuse consisted of the sticking of a finger in his left eye and heavy blows to his face, head, and torso, heavy enough to cause his nose to bleed, his left lung to suffer a bruise discernible by X-ray 19 days later . . . and control of his bowels to be lost during part of the time he was in police custody."

Asked recently whether Hanley's beating should have been investigated, the judge said: "The district attorney's office is the one—when these charges of physical abuse rear their ugly head—that should investigate. I have no right to tell the district attorney to do anything by way of investigation."

District Attorney Fitzpatrick refused to comment on specific cases because, he said, it would "jeopardize investigations and prosecutions."

He did say in a written statement that it was his policy to investigate "when a complaint is received alleging police brutality." He added: "When the facts warrant, as in the case of any other criminal violation, prosecutions have been initiated."

Although Fitzpatrick has occasionally prosecuted policemen for other offenses, he has never pressed charges against a homicide detective for possible crimes committed during interrogations.

Assistant district attorneys explain that a prosecution would seriously undermine the close working relationship between detectives and the prosecutors, who depend on the police for much of their evidence.

Defense attorneys freely acknowledge that beatings and other crimes are committed by homicide detectives, and they agree that stopping these practices is the responsibility of the district attorney.

"I think it happens all the time," said A. Benjamin Johnson Jr., a well-known defense attorney. "I know it does. I once caught the police smacking my client. I rushed into the polygraph room when the cop was wiping his [the client's] lips clean. There was blood on the cop's hand. He pushed me out of the room with blood on his hand."

Many defense attorneys believe that only a small portion of the confessions that are taken by illegal means are actually ruled illegal in court.

Their belief is supported by the fact that suspects—even those whose interrogations are ruled legal—tell very similar stories about their experiences in the interrogation room.

. . . .

Another lawyer, Louis M. Natali Jr., assistant director of the Public

Defenders Association, said he found it implausible that police could obtain as many murder confessions as they do without using illegal methods.

"It's unbelievable that police can get confessions out of almost anybody," he said. "If you had an expert analyze the chances, you'd probably find that one in a thousand people would voluntarily waive their rights and tell police they killed somebody.

"The thing is the judge and the jury will believe the cop."

Some homicide detectives ascribe the frequent testimony about illegal interrogations to "the Holmesburg Prison Bar Association"—an informal group of prisoners who, they say, coach murder suspects in fabricating stories of beatings.

The concept of a prisoners' "bar association" is well known by prosecutors, defense attorneys, and judges.

In one recent case, Judge George J. Ivins said in chambers that he thought a defendant's testimony about beatings by police had been made up for him by the "prison bar."

During the hearing in open court, defense lawyer Joel A. Todd complained to the judge: "Your honor indicated ... you disbelieve the defendant and that you felt the statements made as to beatings were 'scripted' [by the] ... prison bar."

Judge Ivins quickly replied: "I am now telling you that you are violating a confidence of the court. ... I will hear nothing further from you on that aspect of this matter. Do not tempt me."

President Judge Edward J. Bradley of Common Pleas Court said he thought it likely that many of the suspects' claims were untrue.

"Here's a defendant fighting for his freedom," Judge Bradley said in an interview. "He might say anything to get off. This is something a judge has to keep in mind."

Judge Bradley said he believed that the 80 rulings of illegal interrogations since 1974 showed only that police acted illegally in "a small minority" of homicide investigations.

"That's not a lot," he said, "unless it's just the tip of an iceberg."

2

THE *ARIZONA DAILY STAR*

Critics frequently complain that the news media are overly protective of local institutions and prominent and powerful local people. Newspapers in small and medium-sized cities are often accused of becoming so close to the established power structure in their communities that their see-no-evil coverage resembles chamber of commerce boosterism.

There is considerable truth to such charges. Every journalist has seen editorial pages willing to take courageous stands against injustice only if it occurs in distant places, a phenomenon known as "Afghanistanism."

But such criticism fails to take into account the special difficulties faced by a relatively small newspaper when it investigates a cherished local institution. When the *Arizona Daily Star* began revealing major improprieties in the popular football program of the local university, it had to weather a public firestorm directed not against the targets of its investigation but against the newspaper itself. The reporters and editors performed their tasks in the teeth of a relentless attack on their motives and methods by the very community they sought to serve. The *Star* won the 1981 Pulitzer Prize in Special Local Reporting for its work.

We traveled to the sun-baked desert oasis to interview reporter Clark Hallas and city editor Jon Kamman. A few months later, we talked by phone with the other participants, reporter Bob Lowe, now of the *Miami Herald,* and Bill Woestendick, then executive editor of the *Star* and now editorial director of the *Cleveland Plain Dealer.*

Some information also came from published sources. Hallas and Lowe described their efforts in "Exposing Sport Scam Is a Classic Example of Following Paper Trail," which appeared in the summer 1980 issue of the *IRE Journal,* the publication of Investigative Reporters & Editors. "Reporters Tell of Stress, Soul Searching" was published in the spring 1980 issue of *The Pretentious Idea,* a "review of Arizona journalism" published annually by the students in the journalism department at the University of Arizona.

In the fall of 1979, scandals began erupting in the football and basketball programs of some of the nation's major universities. There were allegations of illegal payments to athletes, doctored transcripts, and other violations. One of the schools caught up in the burgeoning controversy was Arizona State University at Tempe.

That seemed awfully close to home to the *Arizona Daily Star* in Tucson, where managing editor Frank E. Johnson assigned reporters Clark Hallas and Bob Lowe to check out the local school, the University of Arizona. "We didn't want to be surprised on our own turf," Lowe recalled.

At first, the pair doubted anything was amiss, "perhaps because the U of A has always enjoyed a loftier image than its sister institution to the north," they would write later in the *IRE Journal*. "That image is fostered lovingly by a fiercely loyal coterie of big-spending boosters, many of whom rank among Tucson's business and civic elite. . . . Not being sportswriters, our knowledge of the university's athletic program and the rules governing college sports was that of the casual fan's and, if anything, colored subconsciously by Tucson's rose-tinted boosterism."

Hoping to tap the expertise and sources of the Star's sportswriters, Hallas and Lowe met with them and explained their assignment. "There was a pledge of support from them that they would help us," Hallas said. "But we made two or three informational thrusts at them—'Could you find out this or that?'—and we just could never get any real enthusiasm from them, so we just eventually stopped trying to use them." Wrapped up in daily game coverage, Hallas concluded, the sportswriters don't have time for investigative work. Beyond that, he said, "sports reporters tend to view things from the establishment point of view."

So they turned instead to a venerable reportorial technique: to find out what a group is doing, ask its opponents or disgruntled former members. In the case of a football team, that means approaching former players who were dropped from the team or demoted from the starting squad to lesser duties. As it turned out, there were many such players at UA, (the University of Arizona), where coach Tony Mason had demoted many regulars recruited by his predecessor in favor of transfers from Mason's former schools. This had happened so often that Arizona had been dubbed "Transfer Tech."

Hallas and Lowe met informally with some of the demoted or retired players at local bars, campus hangouts, and apartments of players and coaches. Rather than ask them specific questions, the reporters prodded them to discuss the whole range of their experience with the university's athletic program. "We wanted to make them comfortable and see what they wanted to talk about," Lowe said. "We let them know we were interested in the problems of the program."

Out of those conversations came a variety of promising leads. The reporters heard stories of athletes in academic trouble being sent to the local community college for high-grade, no-show courses; they also learned of athletes receiving money to play for the Wildcats, the university's football team. These were violations of National Collegiate Athletic Association (NCAA) rules. But other revelations interested the reporters more: some players were placed on the city payroll but performed no work, and coach Mason may have used some athletic department funds to bring non-recruits, allegedly women, to Tucson. Such misuse of public funds would constitute felonies, so Hallas and Lowe pursued these angles first and saved the other stories for later.

One player told them flatly: "The coaches are flying women around," identifying them on expense vouchers by first initial and last name only and labeling them as "recruits." That sent the pair to UA's financial records, which are open to public inspection because the school is tax-supported. From the outset, they insisted that this include the university's telephone records. City editor Jon Kamman recalled that the university balked at first but eventually concluded upon advice of counsel that the press was entitled to see the phone records. "Arizona has a good public-records law, so [UA] saw it had no recourse," Kamman said. The school sometimes took two weeks to a month to respond to the paper's requests for specific records, and the *Star* had to pay hundreds of dollars in searching and copying costs, but "push never came to shove," Kamman said. "We maintained they were public records, but we never had to fight."

Writing in the *IRE Journal*, Hallas and Lowe explained their approach:

> We checked bills charged to the university's recruiting fund for airline tickets and hotel bills for the three previous years, and then we turned to the athletic department's telephone records. . . .
>
> It took a while to pick out the first non-recruit trip to Tucson, but once we had the "m.o." down, the remainder was relatively easy.
>
> The key was the phone records. The computer printout showed, for each football extension, the date, time, duration, cost and number dialed for every out-of-town call.
>
> We took the suspect travel agent billings, which contained the date and city

of origin for each flight, and checked for calls made to the same location around the time of the trip. Then we found out who the numbers belonged to by calling or by having public library reference desks in various cities check their criss-cross directories.

In one instance, 96 phone calls had been placed to a Texas woman's home and office and we found three university-placed flights that had been made by someone using her last or maiden name and first initial.

Finally, we came up with hotel stays, plane trips and telephone calls that appeared connected to women in Canada, Nevada, California and Texas.

The story, published in mid-January of 1980, "was particularly difficult because the women wouldn't talk to us and Mason wouldn't talk to us," Kamman said. "We couldn't say 'Tony Mason is flying his girl friends to town.' And so it was worded in kind of an obscure fashion. It really was very hard to do."

The university's official reaction to the story was limited. Athletic director Dave Strack said vaguely that some of the women who had been flown to Tucson had "assisted" the athletic program in unspecified ways and were being "thanked"; he offered no explanations for some of the trips. Neither Mason nor university president John Schaefer commented publicly.

But two days after the initial story appeared, the university disclosed that there had been a string of unsolved burglaries at the football offices. Stories about the burglaries on the local television stations and in the columns of the Star's afternoon rival, the *Tucson Citizen*, implied a connection between the burglaries and what one sportscaster called the "rifling of recruiting files." One policeman told Lowe the pair were the prime suspects; he and Hallas wondered whether they might be arrested. Eventually, a retarded 19-year-old man was caught trying to burglarize the athletic offices and told police he had committed the earlier break-ins as well.

Mason and Strack met several times with Woestendick and other *Star* editors. At one meeting, "Mason broke down and cried, 'You're destroying my whole family,' " Woestendick recalled. At another session, he and Strack charged Hallas and Lowe with harassing athletes and their families, buying information, and using false identities to extract information from unsuspecting sources. Mason threatened to release sworn statements attesting to these acts if the newspaper continued to publish stories in its investigation. Schaefer, who was refusing all press interviews, told Woestendick, "You're out on a limb. You have no story."

There were other pressures as well. The president of a major Tucson industry and the head of a local bank met Woestendick for breakfast one morning at the airport and asked him to stop the articles. " 'Every-one cheats on his expense account,' they told me," Woestendick said. " 'Why hold that against [Mason]?' "

One automobile dealer sent a message to Woestendick through one of his reporters: "Tell your boss we're going to run him out of town." "There were a lot of ugly letters and one telephoned bomb threat," Woestendick recalled, in which the caller said Woestendick would meet the same fate as Don Bolles, the investigative reporter whose probe into organized crime in Arizona ended when he was killed by a bomb placed in his car.

The city's auto dealers stopped advertising in the paper for two months; Woestendick said that in Tucson, as in other cities, there were close links between the auto dealers, who furnished courtesy cars to coaches and athletes, and the university's athletic teams.

All in all, "it was the ugliest thing I've ever been through," Woesten-dick says. "The pressures were really tremendous. It was an all-out effort; they pulled out every stop. But we had a good story going and there was no way anyone was going to stop us. We were out on a limb, but I talked to my guys [Hallas and Lowe], and they convinced me" the story was legitimate and important.

The drumfire of criticism of the *Star* and its reporters forced the paper to respond. Managing editor Frank Johnson declared in a public statement that "Information set forth in the *Star* article of Jan. 13 was accurate and truthful in every respect. All documents relied upon in compiling the story were public records obtained through the proper university channels."

The hostile reaction of the university and of the community surprised Hallas and Lowe. "[The] university administration . . . . seemingly could care less about integrity," Lowe told *The Pretentious Idea*. "An insti-tution supposedly dedicated to the pursuit of truth which seems totally unconcerned about the performance of [its] staff is something I can't understand." Hallas described the university's response to the revela-tions as "flackery at its best. We went to the university with the infor-mation we had accumulated before it was published and were naïve enough to think they would be interested in cleaning their own closets."

Later they concluded that part of the explanation lay in the tradi-tionally cozy relationship the UA enjoyed with the area media. "I think the university, particularly the athletic department, used to view the local papers as their own private house organ," Hallas said. "And most of the coverage was toy department coverage, sports coverage for en-tertainment. They're not used to a lot of public scrutiny."

Similarly, public support for Mason and the athletic program seldom wavered as the revelations continued. Describing the relationship between the community and the university as a "love affair," the *Los Angeles Times* observed that the community was hurt by the Star's stories. "It was akin to a brother being caught stealing, a sister being mugged, or your father being charged with income tax evasion. It was family."

Even the other news media in Tucson rallied to the university's side, questioning the veracity and significance of the Star's findings and the methods used to obtain them. Woestendick objected so strenuously to a TV sportscaster's innuendoes about the possible complicity of Hallas and Lowe in the burglaries that the station broadcast a formal retraction. "It was extremely disappointing to us to see the rest of the media try to discredit us," Lowe said. "We didn't necessarily need them to agree with us, but we felt an added pressure and stress from people supposedly in the business for the same reasons we are." Lowe recalled being angry with a local TV reporter who followed him in hopes of an interview as he walked away from a press conference with Mason and Strack instead of trying to talk to the university officials. "We had worked hard and dug deep and needed some support. . . . His following me instead made me angry. Fortunately I've learned to channel my anger and didn't say anything too brash."

All of this pressure and community hostility took its toll on the two reporters. Hallas stopped attending UA basketball games. "It sounds paranoid," he admits, "but I really felt threatened and didn't want to be in a position where I could be framed." More seriously, they wondered whether their paper would continue to support the investigation. "All this happened when we weren't sure about the Star's commitment," Lowe said. "The paper had never taken on an institution of equivalent power that was willing to fight back."

Lowe agreed with John Carroll, former city editor of the *Philadelphia Inquirer*, that such fears are an occupational hazard of investigative reporting (see Chapter I). "You start feeling you're fencing in the shadows," he explained. "You imagine conspiracies. You do get paranoid and hypersensitive. But it isn't just paranoia. Editors sometimes wilt in the face of pressure and pull the rug out from under their reporters."

Lowe was also concerned because "we didn't have a law enforcement agency saying 'We're going to get to the bottom of this.' We sensed a little bit of panic on the part of our leadership [at the *Star*] and some of it was directed at us. We didn't know who the deluge would fall on—us or [UA]."

As the brouhaha generated by the January 13 story continued, Hallas and Lowe began checking out tips from two sources that no-work jobs with the city had been provided for UA athletes. One informant urged the reporters to check the city of Tucson's Parks and Recreation Department. Poring over three years of payroll records, they recorded the names of athletes that they recognized, inasmuch as they didn't have a complete list of all UA players for that period. They checked those names against university records and found that some of the players listed as working for the city were ineligible to do so under NCAA regulations.

Trying to establish that the players did no work in return for their paychecks was more difficult. A check of payroll records yielded six suspicious entries, so the reporters began contacting the players. "We hit [them] by surprise," Hallas and Lowe reported in the *IRE Journal*, "reaching them on the phone and beginning each interview by asking whether they had ever worked for the city. The first three said 'No.' By the time we got to the other three, the word was out and they maintained they had worked for their paychecks." As they did throughout the investigation, Hallas and Lowe taped all of these conversations.

One night at a local watering hole, a former athlete told Hallas that he had been recruited with promises that he and his wife would be given city jobs for which they would not have to work if he agreed to play for the Wildcats. It was this anonymous source who identified Herb Reeves, a prominent Wildcat booster and former city official, as the man who made the arrangements. It was impossible to tape this conversation, but city editor Kamman insisted Hallas get the admissions on tape. "It's very difficult to talk to these people because sometimes they were monosyllabic and quite hostile and terribly defensive," Kamman said. "They thought we were tearing down the whole football program and their careers were on the line, and it took an awful lot of cultivating these people to get them to admit" their role in the scheme. But after patient questioning over the phone with the tape recorder running, Hallas got what he needed. "Clark was kind of stumbling around trying to get this guy to fill in the blanks," Kamman recalled. "He says, 'Well, we want to get the story about people having these parks and rec jobs' and finally this guy comes across with 'Yeah, I have this job but I'm not doing any work.' . . . So we had it on tape."

In seeking to determine whether there was a pattern of such illegal activities, Hallas and Lowe found a source who told them about star tailback Larry Heater. Another visit to the city's payroll office produced records showing that checks to Heater totaling more than $3,000 were being mailed to the home of assistant coach Karl Singer. They also learned that the player was in Las Vegas when he was supposed to be working for the city.

The story, published on February 3, prompted more than denials: the city and the university began investigating. Athletic director Strack and a UA lawyer questioned Heater, who confessed his role in the scheme and explained how the payoffs were made. Hallas and Lowe obtained a tape recording of the session—they have never explained how—and published the story on February 16 without naming Heater.

But the university took no action against Mason or any member of the coaching staff. At this point, Lowe and Hallas began working on a tip they had received soon after the first story was published: the coaches were using phony airline tickets and hotel receipts to collect reimbursements for recruiting trips they had not made. This was to be the revelation that brought Mason down.

It took nearly two months to pin down this elusive story, but during that time a series of lesser but significant news breaks kept the controversy simmering. And for the first time, some of the work was done by the *Star*'s previously skeptical rival, the *Tucson Citizen*. The *Star* was glad for the competition. "It eliminated us as the primary target," Hallas said. "It put pressure on the university to answer the questions more seriously because they could no longer paint a single villain. It became an all-out media thing and the TV stations started doing their little stories. The tone was starting to become different, from one of skepticism to 'The *Citizen* said this yesterday' and 'The *Star* said this."

Public reaction remained negative, however. "The people had already made up their minds," Kamman said. "Either you love the university and it can do no wrong or you don't care all that much. . . . All we were hearing was the criticism; we weren't getting an awful lot of pats on the back. Occasionally a few people would call or we'd get a letter saying that the whole state of college sports today is disgraceful and 'keep at it,' but these were few and far between."

Meanwhile, the travel-voucher story was turning out to be particularly difficult. Lowe, Hallas, and Kamman pored over stacks of vouchers for 10 coaches over a three-year period. Some of the trips were well-documented, with restaurant and car-rental receipts as well as airline receipts; others had only the airline receipt. Some of the restaurant and car-rental receipts were legitimate, phone checks by the reporters determined, but others were not; apparently the coaches had gotten blank receipts from some of the restaurants and rental agencies they patronized. But it was the airline receipts that puzzled the trio; they had the ticket agent's validating stamp and appeared authentic.

Still, there were intriguing discrepancies. Recruiting is normally done between December and March, and some of the trips were taken at other times. When the tickets were matched up with the telephone records for the same periods, no calls had been made from the cities where the coaches supposedly had gone. This seemed curious because the coaches normally keep in close touch with their office and homes during these trips. And the serial numbers on the tickets added another element to the puzzle. Some issued months apart were surprisingly close numerically.

Eventually, the three men singled out about 20 of the 300 travel vouchers that seemed particularly suspicious, all of them from American Airlines. At the Dallas–Fort Worth headquarters of American, officials stalled the reporters for weeks, then explained that it would take months to check the tickets; besides, they said, such information could be released only in response to a subpoena or a request by the passenger. After several other approaches failed, a *Star* columnist who had helped a reader obtain a refund some months earlier suggested a call to American's ticket-control center in Tulsa, where a secretary, unaware of the company's policy, agreed to check out the suspicious tickets. They were mailed in, and ticket control called back a few days later saying it had no record of having sold the tickets, which were considered "still outstanding." The list sent to Tulsa included several tickets that looked legitimate mixed in with the suspected bogus tickets; when American confirmed that the legitimate ones had been used, "we felt confident in running the story," Hallas said.

Mason resigned a week later, and the university did not renew the contracts of any of the assistants named in the flights-to-nowhere story. Three months after Mason resigned, he and six former assistants, along with an American Airlines employee, were indicted by a state grand jury. They were accused of 88 felony charges involving $13,000 paid to them by the university over a two-year period. Meanwhile, Tucson police stepped up their probe of the parks-and-rec payroll scheme and found abuses beyond those exposed by the *Star*. And the NCAA began its own investigation into possible rules violations by UA.

Although there were more disclosures to follow, notably the exposure of bogus community college credits, the flights-to-nowhere story and the subsequent resignation of Mason represented the high-water mark of the *Star* investigation.

If Watergate was the epitome of the glamorous side of investigative reporting, the work of Hallas and Lowe must surely occupy the opposite end of the spectrum. Instead of dramatic, dangerous, late-night interviews in parking garages with shadowy sources, the Arizona reporters put in long hours poring over vouchers and computer printouts or downing beers with reluctant athletes in Tucson bars. "They worked themselves ragged," Kamman said.

Crucial to their success was the chemistry between the 45-year-old Hallas, a seasoned political reporter who had joined the staff a year earlier from the *Detroit News*, and Lowe, 26, a graduate of Stanford who had been with the *Star* for three years, much of it covering the state legislature in Phoenix. Although they had never worked together previously and were from different generations, they were "practically inseparable for five months," Hallas said, yet he could recall "no major conflicts. There was a certain symbiosis there. You don't always have that."

Their desks in the newsroom were close together, they ate together frequently, and they spent part of every day "reassessing" their progress. They often went out on interviews together, which was sometimes an inefficient use of their time, because they were constantly groping for a handle on the complex project and felt it was important that "we always knew what each other was doing all the time," Hallas said. "I've been on projects where one guy may have a piece of [this or] that and you never do catch up. The tendency is, 'OK, I'll let him handle that,' and you never do get the nuances of what he has."

Kamman thought the personalities of the pair "complemented each other. Bob Lowe, even though he's low-key, is something of a combative personality. He really does enjoy going for the jugular. In some respects, he needs a little bit of restraint. He needs to be reminded that you have to give the other person the benefit of the doubt. You cannot jump to a conclusion. Bob is a pretty good point man for blood and guts, and Clark has got plenty of experience and has handled so many stories in so many different circumstances that it was good to [have] his experience and maturity. . . . Occasionally, Bob would be out there spurring the horse on and Clark would be saying, 'Yeah, but what about this?' Bob would get discouraged because he couldn't put the sword in all the way and Clark would tone him down just a little.'

"I was more aggressive in the pursuit of the whole thing," Lowe said. "I provided more of the raw energy, getting up every day and getting back into the battle—and after the first story it really was a battle— taking all of the garbage and going after them again, getting back into the ring." But Lowe rejected any suggestion that he needed to be restrained. "I wasn't reckless or overzealous. I didn't do anything to endanger the story or the paper."

For his part, Hallas objected to being cast as the "elderly restrainer.

I think too much has been made of the 'generational' difference. I suppose the difference in our ages makes the Mutt-Jeff comparison inevitable, but in actual practice there wasn't any dramatic difference in our reportorial styles and in the way we 'thought' the project. Complementary adrenalin probably was a more important element in our relationship than offsetting 'restraints.' This is a fairly common phenomenon on long-term team projects. No two reporters can expect to feel the same every day, and what often happens is that one person may feel a bit discouraged or frustrated at a given point, and the partner may pick up the adrenalin slack for a short period of time, and vice versa. This happened with us, too, and I think the fact that each of us was able to pick the other up on occasion added to the success of the project."

Overseeing the pair throughout the investigation was city editor Kamman, who helped solve the puzzle of the bogus airline receipts by suggesting that they be run through the office computer to look for suspicious patterns. A shirt-sleeve editor, Kamman pitched in and helped Hallas and Lowe work the computer for several hours. "I did some of the work, yeah. I don't want to imply that I was out beating the bushes; they would be out and come back with some basic information. 'We know this is going on. How are we going to [prove] it?' Keep trying is basically the idea. And then we hit on the idea of putting [the vouchers] into the computer. I looked around, it was late at night, and I figured, 'Oh, hell, I'll do it myself.' You get close to something and you feel anxious about it."

Although Kamman tried to keep close tabs on his reporters' progress and sometimes participated in brainstorming sessions with them ("If you don't keep up on a regular basis, you get lost"), he left them largely in control and felt free to concentrate on other duties as well. "In an awful lot of cases it was simply a matter of 'Well, OK, good work, now let's go a little bit further. I'm not even sure what to do but you guys will work it out.' And I did have a number of other things to do at the same time, and I'm sure they were distressed from time to time that I wasn't paying enough attention to them. I would say, 'Hey you guys, that's great.' 'Hey, you're going to work it out, I know.'"

When he did confer with them, Kamman challenged all of their findings to make sure they were sound. How do you know this happened? Who told you? Do you have it on tape? Do we have this cold, so that no one can deny it? He said he would sometimes let the pair "go for a week or 10 days without an editor's intervention. I knew what they were doing and what they were trying to get. ... It was a particularly exhausting period for all of us, so I didn't mess with them if they really didn't need some decision-making or if I didn't need to be updated on what was happening."

Kamman also kept his superiors informed so they could respond to the "flak" they were receiving in the community.

Although Lowe said that "there were times, moments, when we thought the support of some of the editors was qualified," they mostly felt reassured that Kamman, managing editor Johnson, and executive editor Woestendick were behind them. "You need to know there's someone ready to go to the wall for you," Lowe said.

Kamman and his two reporters worked together intensely in writing the stories, a process that sometimes tested their patience with each other. "You're all pulling in the same direction and you realize how hard each of them is working, and you don't want to alienate them by saying, 'Hey, this story just doesn't make it,'" Kammam explained. "There were times when we were all exhausted, there were times when something was expressed-back-asswards and I would want to re-do it or I would feel that an element in the middle of a story would need to be moved up. And then I think that if these two guys hadn't been as cooperative as they are naturally, it could have gotten to be a personal problem. In any management job you get into the personality conflicts. 'Well, go away, this is my job, I'm going to do it my way, the hell with you. I've got the information; I'll write the story however I see it.' I think most of the time we did everything by consensus. . . . We had a few clashes, but I never got exasperated with them. . . . You've got some prima donnas who think 'I am the world's greatest writer. I am the world's greatest investigative reporter. An editor is just going to muck up this story. Please get away from it and leave it alone.' [If that happens] you're in trouble."

The first story in the investigation produced more in-house problems than any other. It was originally scheduled to run in late December, but it was postponed at the last minute while Kamman was away in California on personal business. "Management came to the conclusion that we should wait until after the Fiesta Bowl because we were already beginning to get some feedback, even though the story hadn't appeared, that it might hurt the team's performance in the game and it might destroy their concentration and preparation for the game," Hallas said. "That wasn't terribly popular with the reporters," Kamman conceded. "But if we run a story which is derogatory or casts the university football program in a bad light and the team goes to the Fiesta Bowl and loses the game, we are never going to live this down."

Kamman supported the decision to hold the story for another reason as well: Mason and Strack had been refusing to talk to Hallas and Lowe, claiming they were too busy preparing for the game and promising to sit down with the reporters afterwards. "We certainly couldn't do the story without [Mason] being able to give us his undivided attention, " Kamman said. Beyond that, "a newspaper can't operate in a vacuum. You have to be aware of what's going on in the community and the pressures that are naturally being applied to the institution that you are trying to report on. If it were City Hall, I'm not sure whether we would have held off during the last-minute negotiations on the police contract, or something that was governmentally related."

The very nature of the revelations in that first story also raised ethical problems. "We felt a little gritty when we got into the telephoning and found out that the people on the recruiting vouchers were women," Lowe recalled. "We found ourselves hoping we would find someone who would turn out to be a real, live player, or at least a man." The reporters "weren't interested in getting into a personal scandal or hurting anyone, " Hallas said. "But there is a fine line between what is private and what is public when it comes to personalities. We looked at Mason as a public official, using public funds."

They did decide, however, to withhold the names of the women because they could not establish that the women knew their travels were paid for by the university.

Kamman said that as the subsequent stories got away from the principals' private lives and could be expressed in a more "clear-cut" fashion, "there was less and less foreknowledge of exactly the way we were presenting them on the part of the other editors." And the decisions to publish these later installments were made more quickly because they were breaking news stories and the *Star* was racing competition from the other media.

There were a few other ethical questions as well. "We don't have an awful lot of qualms about using unattributed sources," Kamman said, as long as the information could be adequately checked out. Some of the players contacted during the investigation were willing to discuss such matters as the no-work city jobs only on condition that they not be identified.

The reporters felt equally justified in using the athletic department's telephone records because UA is tax-supported and the printouts were used not to invade the privacy of a phone conversation but to look for patterns of calls to particular cities and individuals.

We noted earlier that this investigation was marked more by drudgery than by drama. Even so, the denouement here—for a long time, anyway—was stunningly anticlimactic.

For one thing, a Tucson jury in 1981 acquitted Mason of any wrong-doing, even though he admitted the charges leveled in the *Star* stories. Mason's attorney, Hallas said, portrayed him as "a victim of the system." Mason wept on the witness stand, Kamman said, insisting he had put more money into the football program than he had taken from it. "It was quite a theatrical performance," Kamman observed. "One would assume that the jury would have sympathy for Tony because he had lost his job, he had suffered enough, his dirty linen was being aired in public. . . . [The jury] saw him as being persecuted for trying to field the best football team that the University of Arizona ever had."

The prosecutors concluded that if they could not win a conviction against Mason, it would be unfair, and probably futile, to bring his former assistants to trial at all. The Arizona attorney general's office declined to prosecute Mason and his staff on the basis of the revelations about "flying women around," according to Hallas, "because they could not determine to their satisfaction that public money" was involved. The newspaper assumed throughout the investigation that alumni contributions funneled through the boosters to the athletic department became public money, but "it never was an issue that was totally resolved legally," Hallas said.

All of the coaches agreed to reimburse the university for the bogus trip expenses.

In May 1982, Larry Heater, by then a member of the New York Giants of the National Football League, pleaded quilty to charges that he had defrauded the Tucson Parks and Recreation Department. He was placed on two years' probation and fined $9,000.

Herb Reeves, the Tucson parks official who arranged the no-work city jobs for the players, also was placed on two years' probation and ordered to pay more than $11,000 in restitution for his role in the scheme.

But it was not until May 1983, more than three years after the *Star*'s initial story was published, that the major result of the paper's dogged investigation occurred: the National Collegiate Athletic Association banned the UA football team from playing any bowl game or appearing on television for the next two seasons. The NCAA said the university committed "quite serious" violations of rules governing intercollegiate athletics in 18 categories between 1971 and 1980. The university said it would not appeal the sanctions.

"More severe penalties would have been imposed if the case had involved current staff members," the NCAA said. (One year after the departure of Mason and his coaches, athletic director Strack stepped down to become professor of physical education.)

The NCAA investigation was triggered by the revelation at Mason's trial that the Wildcat boosters' club had operated a secret "slush fund" that funneled $35,000 to UA players and coaches between 1973 and 1978.

The *Star* was proud of its role in helping to generate what Hallas described as "a national debate on reform in athletics. It was our investigation that got the official investigation going; we weren't feeding off leaked NCAA reports. We truly exemplified what is meant by investigative reporting."

For Kamman, the principles at stake were fundamental: private individuals are not supposed to cheat on their expense accounts, and those responsible for handling public funds must abide by the same rules. "Somebody's got to mind the store, and we showed that the university was not," he said, adding that the paper's work "may also serve to show other people that no particular area is immune. Since then we've looked into the expense vouchers of the state narcotics-control police agency, which was sort of the equivalent of a state CIA. [This] resulted in the resignation of the director, one of the state's top cops, [who] was caught cheating on his expense vouchers. It serves notice."

Still, some bitterness remains. We asked Hallas whether he felt like a pariah in Tucson during the early going. "Oh, yeah," he replied. "In fact, I still do. It still is there. There's still a lot of resentment."

And in Cleveland, the *Star*'s former executive editor, Bill Woestendick, reviews the entire controversy and concludes: "In view of all of our work, it's a sad commentary. It says something about our system of ethics and justice. They got away with it. Nobody was really punished for serious crimes. The entire community was against us. That was the bottom line of their attitude: 'So what?' "

The real victims, he believes, are the athletes lured into college sports by promises of glory "and all they get is an education in deceit and trickery. It disturbed me a great deal then and it still does now."

Woestendick warned that a newspaper should not approach an investigation expecting to "clean things up. It doesn't work that way. People have to get mad." In the end, was it worth the effort? "I would do it again tomorrow. I was very proud of the way we stood our ground."

UA SPENDS FOOTBALL RECRUITING MONEY ON NON-RECRUITS

By Bob Lowe and Clark Hallas
© 1980 The *Arizona Daily Star*

Football coach Tony Mason used University of Arizona recruiting funds at least six times to bring non-recruits to Tucson, billing the UA once for a resort stay by the owner of a California massage studio, the *Arizona Daily Star* has found.

The visit of the California woman a year ago, several trips made by one or more Houston women, plus a trip from Toronto by another person were among 12 Mason-approved recruiting expenditures totaling nearly $3,000 that the *Star* has asked university officials to examine.

UA Athletic Director David Strack has confirmed that at least three recipients of the trips were not prospective football players, although they were identified as recruits on university documents accounting for the expenditures.

In written explanations of several of the trips, Strack— in consultation with Mason—has justified the expenditures as being connected with the UA football program. The *Star*'s findings conflict with Strack's explanations, however. Among the discrepancies are:

• Strack said several university-paid flights from Houston were made by different persons, indicating that three were made by different sisters from a family that has helped Mason recruit in the Houston area.

The *Star* learned from Houston court records and family members, however, that there are only two sisters in the family. The husband of one sister says she has not been in Tucson since Mason took over coaching duties at the UA in December 1976.

• According to Strack, another Houston trip was made by one sister's son, who played football under Mason before the coach came to the UA. The son was being interviewed for a job as a graduate assistant, Strack explained.

However, the father of the former University of Cincinnati football player has told the *Star* his son never finished college—a requirement for holding the graduate assistant job—and maintains his son hasn't been to Tucson for at least several years.

• The California woman's flight was a justifiable "thank-you" visit given by Mason out of gratitude for her assistance in recruiting on the West Coast, according to Strack. She was entertained by both Mason and his wife, he said.

Approximately a month ago, however, the woman denied to reporters that she knew Mason. She said the Tucson visit was made by her stepson, but her explanation was later refuted by the man she described as her former husband.

Ordinarily, the recruiting funds—donated to the university by the Wildcat Club booster group—are used for coaches' recruiting trips and to bring authentic recruits to the UA campus for up to 48 hours. Wildcat Club donations also provide athletic scholarships.

Recruiting practices in intercollegiate athletics are tightly controlled by the National Collegiate Athletic Association.

The UA's paying for airplane flights and accommodations for the non-recruits could be contrary to NCAA regulations, according to the official in charge of enforcing the organization's rules.

The expenditures also could be grounds for an inquiry by the Arizona attorney general, state officials said.

Strack has confirmed that at least six trips were made by non-recruits, although expense vouchers and billings sent to the university and approved by Mason for five trips incorrectly list the persons entertained as recruits. Documents for three of the trips bear the notation "recruit" or "prospect," apparently in Mason's handwriting.

In a review of five of the cases, Strack has said that "from the facts now known" it appears the expenditures were properly connected with football recruiting activities.

Strack did not say whether the sixth, a trip from Toronto made by "a person who has helped us in our public relations," was a proper university expenditure. The visitor was "not in any way involved in recruitment of prospective student-athletes," he said.

Mason has repeatedly refused to be interviewed about the use of recruiting money for non-recruits' visits, including the six trips for which the university paid more than $1,800 in air fare and accommodations. In a Jan. 3 letter, Mason acknowledged that he had received written questions, submitted by reporters a week earlier, but said he would rely upon Strack to "communicate with you further."

Mason's claim on hotel and travel-agency billings that the 36-year-old massage studio owner was a UA football recruit was discovered during a *Star* examination of the UA's football program. On Mason's authorization, the university paid a total of $259.55 for her round-trip plane fare from Monterey and her Jan. 3–4, 1979, stay in a private cottage at Skyline Country Club.

University documents identify the woman only by first initial and last name.

Because the *Star* found no indication that she or other recipients of university-paid trips knew the UA paid for their visits, their names are not published here.

UA records also show that the athletic department was billed for 23 telephone calls to the California woman's home during a five-month period from December 1978 to April 1979, including one made from the Stouffer Inn in Denver, where Mason was staying the day the call was made.

The *Star* also found that in a one-year period, the UA Athletic Department paid for 90 telephone calls to the home and office of a Houston woman whose maiden and married names match those on billings for four airplane trips to Tucson.

Travel-agency billings and one of Mason's expense vouchers show the Houston woman's first initial and name on documents accounting for four visits since 1977, Mason's first coaching season at UA.

Her first initial and maiden name was on billings for one trip from Cincinnati (Sept. 20, 1977) and two from Houston (Sept. 1, 1978 and Aug. 24, 1979). The billing for another trip from Houston (July 14, 1978) carried her first initial and married name.

The *Star* has been unable to determine whether four other persons flown to Tucson as recruits under Mason's authorization were athletes. Documents for all trips listed first initial and last names.

The telephone calls to Monterey were to a home owned by the woman who listed a massage studio for her business address on a 1977 traffic ticket. California corporation records indicate she owned the business until its sale last August. She has since moved to Florida.

On an invoice from the Hyways and Byways Travel agency billing the university for a $170, round-trip ticket from Monterey to Tucson for the California woman, Mason apparently signed his name, marked it "OK" and, in the same handwriting, wrote "Recruit."

Similarly, Mason appears to have signed the $89.55 Skyline Country Club bill, which included a $31.79 room-service charge for a steak dinner for two, with the words "Recruit ... OK ... Tony Mason."

That billing to the university is marked "revised billing" and charges the school for the Jan. 3–4 stay of the supposed recruit identified only by first initial and last name. The billing bears the notation, "Cottage guest—per Tony Mason."

The room listed on the billing is a private cottage known as the "executive parlor." A Skyline employee said it probably rented for more than $70 a night at the time of the visit last January, although the billing was for only $25 per night. The cottage consists of a sitting room, two double beds, a dining area, a kitchen, and large porch.

Strack characterized the woman's visit as a "thank you" for her help in UA's recruiting efforts and said she was entertained by both Coach and Mrs. Mason during her two-day stay. He said Mason knows the woman's father, as well.

"The woman lived in California after her marriage and Coach Mason asked her for help in connection with recruiting," Strack said. "At that time she was connected with a restaurant and had relatives in the trucking business.

"Her help was instrumental in obtaining off-season jobs for football players and in providing transportation and entertainment facilities in connection with [UA] recruiters traveling on the West Coast," Strack wrote.

Earlier, the woman herself gave an entirely different explanation of the trip.

"I personally don't know Tony Mason," she told a reporter Dec. 11 in a telephone call from Florida.

She claimed that the person who traveled to Tucson was the son of her ex-husband.

The woman said the prep star has been heavily recruited by UA and "a school in Colorado." She could not recall where he played high school football.

According to the woman, the first time she met the young grid star was when he came to live with her temporarily in Monterey during the period the recruiting contacts were made. She said she believed the calls were made by a UA assistant coach.

She also told the reporter she was in Florida to obtain emergency medical treatment for her 6-year-old son before returning to Montego Bay, Jamaica, where she would be inaccessible by phone.

However, two days later, a reporter reached the woman's former husband and his first wife, who is now a lawyer. Both denied the existence of the purported football-star son.

Later, the first wife said she contacted the California woman in Florida and confronted her about the story.

The lawyer later told the *Star* that the woman said she had fabricated the story given to the newspaper, and actually made the January flight to Tucson herself.

"She told me that she had known Tony Mason for 20 years, that she was from the same town in Ohio where he had coached," the lawyer said. (Mason coached at Niles McKinley High School in Ohio from 1958-63 before moving into the college ranks.) "She said she had talked to Tony about this."

In connection with the Houston trips, the *Star* found that from July 1978 to last June at least 62 calls were made to the accounting office of a labor union in Houston. Another 28 calls were made during that period to a private residence in a Houston suburb.

According to a person who answered the phone at that residence, it is the home of a woman whose first initial, along with her maiden and married names, match names listed for persons who made three university-paid trips from Houston and one from Cincinnati. The Houston woman also has worked in the union's accounting office. Acquaintances describe her as a divorcee in her 40s.

Repeated attempts to interview the woman, including a request submitted to her attorney, have been unsuccessful.

The four 1977–79 flights authorized for persons with the woman's maiden and married names cost the university more than $900, and UA paid at least one bill for lodging—$21.50 at the Plaza International Hotel.

Reporters also asked university officials about a person of another name who was listed as a recruit and flown to Tucson from Houston on Nov. 16. 1978, at a cost of $208.

Strack, in an apparent reference to the five Houston and Cincinnati flights, said, "Three of the names which were questioned are those of three sisters whose father was a close friend of Coach Mason."

He said the son of one of the sisters was flown to Tucson to interview for a graduate assistant's job and that the son had played for Mason before Mason came to UA.

"One of the others who was flown in was a prospective football recruit," said Strack.

According to Strack, the entire family, while not actually contacting prospective recruits, aids the UA football program in other ways, such as helping to find off-season jobs for players, providing UA recruiters with transportation, and "numerous other activities."

February 3, 1980

CITY PAID UA PLAYERS FOR JOBS THEY SAY THEY DIDN'T PERFORM

By Clark Hallas and Bob Lowe
© 1980 The *Arizona Daily Star*

Three University of Arizona football players and one player's wife have been issued checks for nearly $6,000 in city funds for jobs they say they never performed.

Officials say the payments to all four, plus checks issued to three other players, appear to have violated National Collegiate Athletic Association regulations.

Paychecks from the Tucson Parks and Recreation Department averaged close to $100 a week.

Total amounts paid varied widely among the six players who either did not work or whose work would have violated NCAA rules. One player's checks totaled more than $3,000; another had only $260, the *Arizona Daily Star* found. The wife of one athlete was paid more than $3,000 over a 10-month period, but her husband says she did no work.

The checks spanned a period from September 1976 to August 1978.

Three players appear to have been paid when they were enrolled at the UA under full athletic scholarships. Such employment during the school session, as well as receiving unearned pay, violates NCAA rules, association officials say.

Among the players issued paychecks are:

*Star tailback Larry Heater, who completed his collegiate career last season. According to city payroll records, Heater was issued more than $3,000 in paychecks through most of 1978. Checks were issued during the entire spring semester of that year while Heater was on scholarship. He could not be reached for comment on whether he actually worked.

Records indicate that at least some of the paychecks were mailed to the home of assistant football coach Karl Singer.

• Robert "Boot" Robertson, a heavily recruited junior-college running-back star whose last season was in 1978. Robertson said neither he nor his wife, Stephanie, performed any work for the city, although payroll records indicate they received nearly $5,000 between February and December of 1977.

• All-American tackle Cleveland Crosby, a senior last season, who maintains he has never worked for the city's recreation program but who is listed as having been issued two paychecks during the summer of 1978 that total about $300.

• Former offensive guard Willie Tompkins, who last played in 1978 and who says he received at least one summer paycheck in 1977, although he has never worked for the city.

The athletes' jobs were set up by former city recreation official Herb Reeves, a Wildcat supporter who is close to several players. He has flown with the team to games.

Reeves acknowledged hiring the players but maintained they all worked for the money they received. "They are lying if they say they didn't," he said.

One player who was paid, however, told the *Star:* "I never knew what kind of job I had, because I never had to show up for work."

City Parks and Recreation Director Jim Ronstadt said his office was unaware of any payroll improprieties. He said the city will investigate the *Star's* findings.

UA spokesman Hugh Harelson said Athletic Director David Strack would have no immediate comment.

Heater, last season's starting tailback, was issued his first Recreation Department paycheck for more than $200 in late January 1978, shortly after transferring from Dixie Junior College in St. George, Utah, on an athletic scholarship.

The biweekly paychecks continued through mid-August of that year and totaled more than $3,000, according to city payroll records. Heater was hired as a "Sports Official II" at the Southside YMCA at a starting hourly rate of $3.92, and was listed as working an average of 25 hours a week over the seven months. In July, Heater received a 24-cent hourly cost-of-living increase.

Roughly $1,600 of Heater's paychecks were issued by the city during the spring semester of 1978, when the player was on scholarship at the UA.

The portion of Heater's 25-hour-a-week employment with the Recreation Department during the summer of 1978 coincides with a full-time job he held with the City of South Tucson, according to officials there.

City payroll employees say they believe records indicating that Heater's paychecks were sent to Singer's home are accurate.

Telephoned at home Friday, Singer declined to say whether Heater's checks were sent to his address or if he knew the player was being paid while school was in session. "We'll have to talk about this in my office on Monday," he said.

Robertson's wife, Stephanie, was put on the city payroll shortly after he transferred to the UA in January 1977 from Garden City Junior College in Kansas, where he was the nation's leading rusher.

Like Heater and several other players, Robertson was befriended by Reeves. In April of 1977, Robertson was put on the department's payroll.

Records show that Robertson and his wife—his fiancee at the time of her hiring—received 27 Recreation Department checks totaling almost $5,000 between February and December 1977.

Robertson was listed as a $3.74-an-hour baseball official at Estevan Park, and Stephanie Lotharp was recorded as a $3.40-an-hour basketball official at Apollo Junior High School.

Asked by the *Star* about the payroll documents, Robertson said he and his wife never worked for the recreation program.

The NCAA also prohibits arrangements which give an athlete's relatives or friends extra benefits not available to the general student body.

City payroll records indicate that two Parks and Recreation paychecks totaling about $300 were issued to Crosby in the summer of 1978, but Crosby told the *Star* he has never worked for the department.

Crosby said his summer employment that year was with a development company and a cement firm. He said that only his wife had worked in recreation.

His wife, Angelia, said she worked occasionally for the Parks Department the year before, shortly after Crosby transferred here from Purdue, but she declined to discuss details of her employment

Recreation Department records indicate Mrs. Crosby worked as a $3.40-an-hour softball official at Santa Rita Park between November 1977 and January 1978, receiving four paychecks totaling about $700.

Former offensive guard Tompkins told the *Star* he received at least one paycheck from the Recreation Department in 1977 but had never reported to work. Tompkins, a former junior-college teammate of Robertson's, said Reeves arranged the job for him after he transferred here from the Kansas school.

Department records indicate two paychecks totaling more than $300 were issued to Tompkins in the spring of 1977. He was listed in parks records as a $3.40-an-hour baseball official at Mission Manor Park.

Tompkins, who said he had "no idea" what his job was, recalled receiving only one check, however. "They suddenly stopped arriving, and I assumed it was because someone found out and put a stop to it," he said.

A current UA player, Darrell Solomon, a junior middle guard last season, said he worked for the city Recreation Department for a short time one summer and received only one paycheck.

City records indicate he was issued two recreation paychecks totaling about $400 for work performed between Jan. 29 and March 4, 1978.

If the city records are accurate, Solomon, who was hired as a $3.92-an-hour sports official at the Southside YMCA, apparently violated NCAA rules by working while school was in session.

Solomon, who has a year of eligibility left, said he would not have worked for compensation while school was in session, because he was aware that to do so is against NCAA rules. He said the city records are not accurate.

Obra Erby, a linebacker who last played for the UA in 1976, also appears to have violated NCAA rules by working for pay while school was in session, according to payroll records.

Erby said he worked at the Recreation Department only during the summer and school holidays, but records show that two of his paychecks, amounting to about $260, were apparently for work performed early in the 1976 fall semester and during the spring semester of 1977. Erby says he was on scholarship both semesters.

Reeves has been described by one of the players as a "good-hearted man" who liked to do things for UA football players, including lending them his car, providing them jobs and food, and accompanying them on local outings with visiting recruits.

"I did that on my own," Reeves said about entertaining players. "There were no funds from anybody. . . . It was my bucks. I paid for it."

Reeves, who has occasionally flown with the football team to games and who described himself as a good friend of some of the assistant coaches, was sports coordinator for the Recreation Department until his suspension last June after an arrest for an alleged $4,000 heroin sale. He is awaiting trial.

Told that some players say they performed no work for the recreation pay, Reeves said: "That's a lie."

"I'm not saying we had a person to watch them every minute of the day, but for the time they were scheduled, they were there," he said. "I know I would think . . . I'm sure they put in the time.

"These people worked, you know. I deal with the public, the city. I can't have those people if they weren't working. There'd be no way."

One former player said that although he and others showed up for work at a 1977 summer recreation site, they put in only part of the hours they were supposed to work and still got full paychecks.

"We'd get there late in the morning, put in a little time before lunch, then leave early in the afternoon," said the player, whose last season was in 1977. He said he and the other players understood that "we wouldn't have to work too hard."

Asked what his recreation job entailed, he said, "Our function was . . . there was no function at all."

Ronstadt said: "It's nice to find out what, in fact, was going on, because that type of thing is not in any way, shape or form condoned by the City of Tucson or this office.

"If this in fact did occur, it was done very underhandedly. If this office had been aware of it, it would have been terminated.

"Whatever allegations are made by the paper, the city will make a legal investigation of it. If they are true, we would do everything necessary legally to recoup."

Gene Reid, Ronstadt's predecessor during part of the period that players received the city paychecks, said, "We were very careful about checking time cards, and there were a number of checks and balances to prevent this type of thing from happening."

He said roving supervisors would visit each city recreation site to pick up time cards and to ensure that employees actually were working. The time cards were checked again when they arrived at the central recreation office, according to Reid, who is now retired.

Reid acknowledged, however, that "because of the high number of part-time employees we hired, something like that [unearned payments] could have slipped through."

NCAA enforcement chief Dave Berst said student athletes on full scholarships are prohibited from receiving pay for employment while school is in session and that such employment is grounds for declaring a player ineligible. Players are allowed to receive compensation for work performed during school recesses and summer vacation.

The *Star* obtained information on the players' employment from Tucson Recreation Department payroll records, which indicate how much the department instructed the city's main payroll office to pay the athletes during each two-week pay period.

Berst said discovery of NCAA-rules violations by players who have used up their eligibility may still result in a university's being penalized.

"You would have the question of whether the institution has the responsibility to bear for the violations that have occurred, so it's usually a two-pronged question," he said.

"First, how is the student-athlete involved, and how is his eligibility affected? Secondly, why did it occur, and how responsible is the institution for the violation?"

February 16, 1980

FOOTBALL STAR SAYS SOME COACHES KNEW OF UNEARNED CITY PAYCHECKS

By Bob Lowe and Clark Hallas
© 1980 The *Arizona Daily Star*

A University of Arizona football star who confessed to university officials that he regularly received city paychecks without doing any work also told officials more than a week ago that at least two members of the coaching staff were aware of the payments, the *Arizona Daily Star* has learned.

The payments, which may have violated state laws as well as National Collegiate Athletic Association rules, were promised by a volunteer recruiter as an inducement for the athlete to enroll at the UA, the player reportedly told officials.

He identified the recruiter as Herb Reeves, a former sports coordinator for the Tucson Parks and Recreation Department who has acknowledged hiring several UA athletes for part-time city jobs.

Reeves was suspended by the city last June after his arrest on heroin-sale charges. He is awaiting trial.

Shortly after the player enrolled at the university, the player told Athletic Director David Strack, Reeves delivered a stack of blank time-cards for him to sign. The player said he and Reeves were in the office of an unidentified assistant coach, who had left the room.

"I really wasn't aware what was happening, so I signed them," the player told Strack.

The player was one of several Wildcat football players interviewed by Strack and Tucson lawyer Stanley Feldman after the *Star* published a copyright story Feb. 3 in which three UA players and the wife of one were identified as receiving a total of nearly $6,000 in city funds for work they said they never performed.

The interviews were held in Strack's office. Feldman explained to one of the players that the purpose of the interviews was for Strack to determine whether UA coaches took part in the payroll arrangement, and "whether they did right or whether they did wrong."

Strack declined to comment yesterday, according to UA spokesman Hugh Harelson. Reeves told the Star, "I'm not in a position to say anything."

Feldman said he would have to contact university officials to see if they wanted to respond.

The player who described the payroll scheme told Strack and Feldman that he never worked or showed up at the Parks and Recreation Department work sites listed on his timecards.

The biweekly checks began arriving soon after he enrolled for his first semester at the UA, the player said. The checks continued to be sent for several months—even for a 30-day period when he actually was vacationing out of state.

According to the athlete, sealed envelopes containing the paychecks were mailed to the home of Assistant Coach Karl Singer every two weeks, and some were deposited in the player's savings account at a Tucson bank when he was out of town.

"Somebody knew I was getting the checks," he said.

The player, who explained he didn't know who deposited his paychecks, said he had never discussed with Singer what was in the envelopes or whether he had actually performed work for the city.

Singer, reached by telephone at home last night, said he would comment only in a personal interview. Attempts earlier yesterday to arrange an interview were unsuccessful. Messages left by the *Star* at his office were not answered.

The player also told Strack that he did not know whether Head Coach Tony Mason had knowledge of the payment arrangement, saying, "Coach Mason wasn't hardly around." But he added that there were "a couple of coaches . . . who were aware of this situation." He refused to identify them.

He told Strack the paycheck scheme had been going on for several years at the UA, and involved many other players.

According to the player, Reeves—whom he had not yet met—first contacted him at home by telephone before he visited the UA campus. At the time, he planned to attend another university, and in several calls Reeves tried to talk him into enrolling here, the player said.

If he decided to play football for the Wildcats, he'd "have it made," the player said Reeves told him. The player said he thought Reeves mentioned in one call that he was phoning from a coach's office at McKale Center.

When the player said he did not know how Reeves had obtained his name and home number to make the initial recruiting calls, Strack reportedly told the player the information "obviously" must have come from the coaching staff.

Strack explained that it is a normal practice for coaching staffs to provide recruiters with such information so they can encourage athletes to enroll.

The player said he then met Reeves at McKale Center when he made his recruiting visit to the UA. While other recruits toured the campus on foot, Reeves drove him around in his car.

The player said Reeves promised during one conversation he would receive "such and such" every two weeks.

Asked what the player meant by "such and such," he explained that soon after he enrolled at the UA, Reeves brought the blank timecards over to McKale Center for the athlete to sign.

An assistant coach left his office while the player signed the timecards in the room with Reeves at his side, the athlete said.

"He [Reeves] did whatever from there," he added, and the paychecks began arriving at Singer's home shortly after that.

City police are investigating the *Star*'s reports of alleged payroll irregularities involving UA athletes to determine whether any laws were broken.

The NCAA also reportedly has questioned players on the payroll allegations. NCAA regulations prohibit student athletes from receiving compensation for work not performed.

In addition to the unearned pay, the *Star* reported that several UA football players apparently violated NCAA rules by working at the parks department while school was in session. Athletes on full aid are permitted to work only during summer and semester breaks. The *Tucson Citizen* later named additional athletes and quoted Strack as confirming that NCAA rules had been broken.

March 30, 1980

MASON, STAFF REIMBURSED FOR APPARENT FLIGHTS TO NOWHERE

By Bob Lowe and Clark Hallas
© 1980 The *Arizona Daily Star*

The University of Arizona paid head football coach Tony Mason and several of his aides more than $3,300 last year for plane trips they apparently didn't make, *the Arizona Daily Star* has found.

The coaches obtained the money from UA by submitting personal expense accounts showing they had made recruiting trips. They attached American Airlines passenger receipts reflecting that they had paid for the air travel.

But ticket officials at American Airlines' central accounting office in Tulsa said the company has no record of having sold nine tickets the coaches submitted to the university.

"It means the tickets are still outstanding," said Les Barnes, ticket-control supervisor for American. "There's no record of anybody purchasing or using them."

Barnes said that when a passenger boards a plane, the airline retains the flight coupon from the ticket as proof that a ticket was used. The flight coupon, as well as the ticket's sale coupon, are forwarded to the airline's data center, he said. The passenger retains the other part of the ticket, the passenger coupon, as his receipt.

Serial numbers on the nine passenger's receipts submitted by the coaches failed to match any flight or sales coupons in American's computer system, indicating the tickets were neither purchased nor used, Barnes said.

"If there was any usage, we'd still have the records" for the flights in question, he said.

Barnes added that the airline had no record of anyone having been given a refund on any of the tickets.

The tickets, which the airline checked at the *Star*'s request, were submitted to the UA for reimbursement by Mason and associate football coaches Tom Yelovich, Bob Davie, Bob Shaw, Tony Roggeman, and Robert Valesente.

On their UA expense forms, the coaches said the air coupons— ranging in value from $190 to $476—represented recruiting trips to Chicago, Philadelphia, Tampa, St. Louis, Atlanta, San Francisco, Minneapolis, and Pittsburgh between May and October 1979.

The nine no-record coupons included two each by Yelovich, Shaw, and Davie and one each by Mason, Roggeman, and Valesente. The coaches received a total of $3,154 for the air fares and an additional $227.50 for meals and other costs they said they incurred on the following trips:

• Yelovich, last year's UA offensive-line coach and now a member of the coaching staff of Tulane University in New Orleans, claimed expenses for an Oct. 5–7 recruiting trip to Tampa and an Aug. 8 flight to San Francisco. He submitted air receipts totaling $628.

• Davie, defensive-end coach and recruiting coordinator last season, submitted airline coupons totaling $904 for a Sept. 21–22 trip to Pittsburgh and an Aug. 24–26 flight to Philadelphia.

• Shaw, defensive-end and linebacker coach, turned in airline receipts amounting to $735 for a July 2–3 flight to Philadelphia and June 2–3 trip to Chicago.

• Mason submitted a $303 air receipt for an Oct. 3 flight to Minneapolis, also claiming $40 for meals and lodging.

• Roggeman, defensive-line coach last season, turned in a $270 air coupon, and charged the UA $33 for meals for a June 30–July 2 trip to St. Louis.

• Valesente, defensive-back coach, submitted an airline receipt for $314 for a June 4–6 flight to Atlanta, where he said he did recruiting and visited the Atlanta Falcons office.

The nine purported trips inspected by the *Star* did not appear to be as well documented as other recruiting-trip vouchers turned in by the coaches.

In all but Valesente's case, coaches produced no expense receipts for the nine reimbursements other than an American Airlines passenger's coupon. In addition to an air receipt, Valesente turned in one $3.50 restaurant tab, which he said was for entertaining an Atlanta recruiter.

The other coaches claimed expenses for some meals and, in Mason's case, lodging, without documentation.

For most recruiting trips, coaches typically submit hotel, restaurant and sometimes car-rental receipts, as well as airline tickets, UA records reflect.

Mason, Yelovich, and Valesente could not be reached for comment.

Davie, when asked if he had made the Philadelphia and Pittsburgh flights, replied, "Well, obviously both of those are in my recruiting areas." The flights were difficult to recall, he added, because "I made an awful lot of trips back there."

Shaw declined to answer whether he had made all of the trips for which the university has reimbursed him. "I won't even get into that question," he said. "Everything's turned in to the office here—you'll have to ask them."

Roggeman did not return phone calls to his office Friday, and declined to comment when reached at home.

American's Barnes said the airline probably will ask its security department to look into the matter.

"If someone is pulling tickets and giving them out without any record, that would be a matter of concern to us," he said. "There could be an internal problem."

Barnes said it does not appear that American is "out any money" on the mystery flights, as there is no record of sale, usage, or refund. The only apparent record of money changing hands was the amount disbursed to the coaches by the university.

He said the tickets all appeared to have been issued at the American Airlines ticket counter at Tucson International Airport, rather than through a travel agency.

Mike Riley, American Airlines ticket-supervisor at the airport, said it would be unusual for a used ticket to slip through the airline's ticket-control system, because gate agents tear out the passenger's flight coupon and staple it to his boarding-pass stub. The coupons are then pouched and sent nightly to the airline's data center, he said.

Asked how common it would be for the airline to be missing records of nine randomly selected tickets, an official in Tulsa said, "About as common as me or you being hit by a car walking out of our office."

George Boiko, manager of services for American in Tucson, could offer no theories on why the nine tickets did not show up in Tulsa records.

"I don't know anything about a coach's expense account," Boiko said. "If we sold him a ticket, we sold him a ticket. If he used it, fine. If not, he didn't.

"The revenues that are derived from a ticket sale are reported. If you're telling me somebody in Tulsa says it's not there, I cannot explain that here locally. That's something for the ticket-control people to explain."

Patricia M. Myers, head of the Arizona Board of Regents' auditing staff at UA, said that auditors participating in the university's current internal investigation of Athletic Department expenditures had not spotted the apparent ticket discrepancies. "However, this is something we're going to look at," she said.

UA spokesman Hugh Harelson reported Friday that the internal investigation is nearing completion but that Athletic Director David Strack has not made his report to University President John P. Schaefer.

The *Star* asked university officials Friday for assistance in verifying whether the coaches had made the nine out-of-town trips for which they were reimbursed.

Harelson said he turned a list of the trips over to Strack. The *Star* was unable to reach Strack Friday or yesterday at his office. Reached at home late yesterday, Strack refused to talk to a reporter.

Coaches' recruiting trips are financed through the UA Athletic Department's intercollegiate football account. The account, which is separate from the Wildcat Club booster account used to support campus visits by prospective athletes, is supported by stadium gate receipts.

April 3, 1980

MASON ADMITS UA BILLED FOR NON-TRIPS

By Bob Lowe and Clark Hallas
© 1980 The *Arizona Daily Star*

University of Arizona head football coach Tony Mason admitted yesterday he and other members of his coaching staff billed the university for airline trips they did not make.

UA President John P. Schaefer immediately expressed disapproval of the practice. He said he will wait for a report from Athletic Director David Strack before deciding whether to take any action.

Mason conceded that he and some of his assistants were reimbursed by the university for some non-existent recruiting flights and reportedly said he would explain later why the false documents were filed.

Mason would not respond to phone calls from *Arizona Daily Star* reporters yesterday but admitted the reimbursement practice to other media.

The *Tucson Citizen* quoted him as saying that funds received for the non-existent trips were "not used for personal profit." They were used to reimburse the coaches for out-of-pocket expenses they had incurred but for which they had not been paid, the newspaper said he explained.

Mason's admission came after the *Star* published copyright articles Sunday and yesterday reporting that Mason and assistant coaches Tony Yelovich, Bob Davie, Bob Shaw, Tom Roggeman, Robert Valesente, and Karl Singer had collected more than $3,500 for air fare and living expenses for 10 recruiting trips they apparently did not make.

Yesterday's story also pointed out that Mason had double-billed the university for some travel expenses purportedly incurred on two July 1977 trips.

"What you've written is essentially true as far as I can see," Schaefer said. He still is awaiting a full report on the affair, he said.

If coaches submitted false claims because they were insufficiently reimbursed by the university for legitimate travel, Schaefer said, "It's not the smartest way of dealing with a very understandable problem.

"I understand their [the coaches'] problem, but I don't approve of the method they used to deal with the problem," Schaefer told the *Star* yesterday.

Schaefer said that until last fall, coaches' per-diem allowance for out-of-state travel was $40, a rate he characterized as being unrealistically low.

"As anyone knows who does any traveling, it's pretty hard to get a hotel room [and] take care of three meals and other expenses on $40 a day," he said.

"And when you're not making all that much money, as some of those assistant coaches aren't, you wind up in a pretty big hole in a hurry."

Schaefer said the per-diem rate was raised to $70 a day last fall, but added, "even that isn't enough to get you by in a place like New York City."

Later, however, UA spokesman Hugh Harelson said he checked the university per-diem rates at Schaefer's request and found that the president had made a mistake in reporting the allowable rate. Since September 1977, the per-diem rate for university employees' out-of-state travel has been $40 without receipts and $75 with receipts, Harelson said.

Schaefer said he was unaware that Mason and the other coaches were using the air-ticket reimbursement method "until [the *Star*] raised the issue. And I got people on it right away."

He said an internal investigation of athletic-department expenditures being conducted by Strack and university lawyers probably will be completed by tomorrow or Monday. He said the timetable for completion was delayed by the *Star*'s story Sunday.

Schaefer said he would issue a statement on the findings of the investigation.

"I do want to read the report thoroughly and evaluate its findings before commenting," he added.

Asked if Mason had explained how coaches obtained the air coupons from American Airlines and why they used that method for reimbursement as opposed to proper filing of expenses, Schaefer said, "I don't want to go into those details at this moment." He added:

"As a matter of fact, I don't know all the facts myself. I don't know how that will be touched on in the report. I haven't dealt directly with Coach Mason on the issue.

"This is Dave Strack's responsibility—it's his department—and I'm relying on him and the attorneys to conduct the investigation and to look into the matter and evaluate the facts as they see them."

Harelson said Mason made his report to Strack at the athletic director's request yesterday. In it, Mason reportedly explained the airline-ticket reimbursements and other matters involved in the university's investigation into the expenditure of athletic funds.

The *Citizen* reported Mason said his report to Strack would refute many allegations made in the news media against him over the past four months.

Mason reportedly spent yesterday morning in a meeting with his lawyer.

In addition to the university's internal investigation, city police, the Arizona Attorney General's Office, a subcommittee of the Arizona Board of Regents, and the National Collegiate Athletic Association are looking into various aspects of the UA athletic program.

April 8, 1980

MASON OUT, CLOUD REMAINS—UA TO HOLD TIGHT REIN ON SUCCESSOR

By Bob Lowe and Clark Hallas
The *Arizona Daily Star*

University of Arizona head football coach Tony Mason resigned yesterday but remained, with his football program and most of his coaching staff, under a cloud of multiple investigations focusing on alleged widespread financial abuses.

University officials immediately began a search for Mason's successor and admitted the need for "certain administrative changes." They left the fate of Mason's assistants in limbo pending decisions based on the outcome of the UA's nearly completed investigation of the football program.

UA President John P. Shaefer said the UA's head football coach will be given strict guidelines on the spending of university money to avoid repeating the problems of Mason's regime.

"I hate to make a mistake once, and I'm sure as heck not going to make it twice," Schaefer said shortly after announcing his acceptance of Mason's resignation.

"I've said many times I want an athletic program above reproach and above suspicion," Schaefer added. "My concern is that we have the type of program that can stand the light of day. If we don't we've got to make the appropriate changes."

Mason's resignation came one day after Schaefer received a preliminary draft of the still-undisclosed findings of an investigation headed by UA Athletic Director David Strack. The internal investigation was touched off by articles in the *Arizona Daily Star* since Jan. 13 spotlighting apparent improprieties in the school's $4.5 million athletic program.

"I have no quarrel with any factual material in the *Star*," Schaefer said, adding he has a "real quarrel with regard to some inferences you've made."

Mason could not be reached by the *Star* yesterday. He reportedly left with his family on a vacation. One sportscaster who talked with the 50-year-old coach soon after he submitted his resignation described Mason as "jovial."

Other reports quoted Mason as saying his story involving the financial irregularities "has never been told."

"They [UA officials] have a complete written report," Mason was quoted as saying. "They're going to make a release and cover every one of the allegations and let the people make a decision.

"If they [the news media] give it as much attention as they did all the allegations, they'll know what I did [his resignation] was for the university. It was not for any guilt feeling."

Mason, who refused for four months to talk to the *Star*'s news reporters, said, "There's two sides to every story, and I never had mine told."

Conceding that his resignation might be construed as an admission of guilt, the coach added, "It may, but I can't help that. I resigned because of my sanity and because of my family. I think they [the media] were taking on the university too much."

Schaefer and Strack said they did not pressure Mason to resign. Despite the coach's admission last week that he and some of his assistants had received reimbursement for non-existent plane trips, Strack remained silent yesterday on whether he believes Mason had acted improperly.

Of the resignation, Strack said, "I, of course, recognize the pressure under which he has been for many, many months. And he's withstood it very well."

Mason's short resignation letter said:

"In view of the events of recent days, I have decided that it is in the best interest of the university and of my family that I resign as head football coach.

"Please accept this letter, then, as my resignation and my request that it be accepted at once."

Mason will receive the remainder of his $41,318 annual salary through June 30, the expiration date of his one-year contract.

The coach's resignation ended a colorful, three-year coaching stint at the UA. He accumulated a 16-18-1 record, climaxed last season by a season-ending, last-minute victory over rival Arizona State University and a Fiesta Bowl appearance—a 16-10 loss to the University of Pittsburgh.

Renowned as a quipster par excellence and one of the nation's top coaching-clinic speakers, Mason seemed to divide UA football fans into loyalists and detractors.

Mason also seemed to inspire division within his squad—players who were fiercely loyal to him and those who considered him arrogant and insincere.

In beginning the search for Mason's successor, the UA yesterday created a six-member screening committee for applications to be received by April 15.

The effect of Mason's resignation on a banner crop of new UA recruits, who could change their minds about joining the Wildcats, remains to be seen.

Strack said, "I think it's incumbent on us to try and get the proper information to the recruits."

The athletic director also canceled spring football practice for the rest of this week. He said he will pick one of Mason's assistants to take charge when the team returns next week.

The fates of the assistant coaches remained in doubt yesterday, although UA officials hinted that the "housecleaning" that often comes with the appointment of a new head coach might make the question moot.

In copyright stories last week, the *Star* reported American Airlines had no record of the sale or use of airline tickets submitted for reimbursement by Bob Davie, Robert Valesente, Karl Singer, Tom Roggeman, Bob Shaw, and Tony Yelovich. Yelovich recently was named an assistant coach at Tulane University.

Although Mason admitted that he and some assistants had received reimbursement for non-existent flights, Strack indicated yesterday he has not tried to question the assistants about the purported trips.

"They, as you well know, have an attorney," he said. Asked whether the assistants have refused to answer questions, Strack said, "They've never refused anything."

Strack would not say whether the assistants face disciplinary action.

"We are . . . preparing a report which will address all of the allegations that have appeared in the papers," he said.

"No decision has been made at this point," Schaefer said of the assistant coaches, adding that they had been asked to continue running the spring practice.

"No one will try to sweep that under the rug," he said. He indicated however, that determining the propriety of assistant coaches' travel reimbursements "is obviously not a priority," and the search for a new head football coach is among the first orders of business.

Schaefer, who said "no deals" were involved in Mason's resignation, added that the former coach and others may be asked to pay restitution.

"Where there's an indication funds were obtained improperly we will make every effort to recover those funds," he said. "There's every indication that won't be an issue with the individuals involved. They have pledged their full cooperation."

Referring to allegations that some UA players may have broken National Collegiate Athletic Association rules by accepting city of Tucson paychecks without performing any work, Shaefer said:

"On the basis of what I've seen, we may receive a [NCAA] reprimand, but I don't think it will be more serious than that."

He and Strack indicated that they believe coaches sought reimbursement for non-existent trips to compensate for out-of-pocket expenses involved in setting up a recruiting network and in entertaining alumni, recruiters, and other supporters.

"Mason said no money was used to line their pockets or to personally enrich themselves, and we have not found anything to contradict that statement," Schaefer said.

Schaefer said he has resisted establishment of a booster group outside the university that could help defray recruiting expenses.

Informed that UA football coaches are routinely reimbursed through a special booster-financed account for entertaining recruiters and alumni, plus other recruiting-related expenses, Schaefer said, "You know more about that than I do."

Among various coaches' expenses which have been picked up by the university are a $90 restaurant tab in Houston for several "alumni" entertained during a recruiting trip. Mason also has been reimbursed by the UA for floral arrangements sent to UA supporters, their relatives, and at least one member of the Tucson media.

Schaefer said the report into allegations of financial irregularities may not be made public. The report will be submitted to the Arizona Board of Regents subcommittee on intercollegiate athletics when it is completed this week.

He revealed, however, that the investigation has turned up no major irregularities beyond those exposed by the media.

The preliminary report contains no indication of coaches' "complicity" in several former players' employment in the city's Parks and Recreation Department, he said. Some players have told the *Star* they performed no work, although they were paid as much as $3,000. Last year's star running back, Larry Heater, told Strack in February that at least two coaches "were aware of the situation."

Schaefer yesterday denied a Tucson legislator's allegations of a "cover-up" in the UA's handling of the athletic inquiry.

"There was no cover-up, and I resent the implication that there was," he said. Schaefer added that UA vice president Gary Munsinger in mid-February passed along to Strack information concerning coaches' non-trips. Strack then wrote auditors asking them to examine coaches' travel records to see if the travel reported actually occurred.

Strack's letter, however, made no mention of falsified airline tickets, although the coaches' method of collecting the travel pay was reportedly detailed to Munsinger.

Regents' auditor Patricia M. Myers would not comment on the Feb. 15 letter other than to say, "It was pretty general."

April 10, 1980

EX-WILDCAT SAYS COACHES PAID HIM

By Clark Hallas and Bob Lowe
© 1980 The *Arizona Daily Star*

A former University of Arizona football player has told the *Arizona Daily Star* that coaches gave him money and free plane rides home during the two years he played here under recently departed head coach Tony Mason.

The player, who asked not to be identified, said the payments and free trips—both prohibited under National Collegiate Athletic Association rules—were fulfillments of promises made by Mason when the athlete was being recruited by the UA.

"Tony Mason offered me a lot," the player told the *Star*. "He said I could fly home any time I wanted. Mason told me I'd start the first game. He also promised money."

He added, "That's how Mason worked. If he wanted a blue-chipper, he'd get him. People get paid here [at the UA] if they're blue-chippers. I was one of the highest-paid players on the team, even though I wasn't playing much. I know others who were getting paid but I don't want their names to come from me."

The player said Mason used a personal check at least once to pay him, but "most of the time he [dealt] in cash."

"If you needed something, you'd go into the office and he'd say, 'Be back here at 5 and I'll have it for you.' It wasn't a regular thing, but you'd go in there when you were hurting for cash."

The former UA athlete said he disliked having to go to Mason for money, but added, "There were times when it was necessary.

"I'd go in there when my rent was due and I couldn't pay it, or if my electricity was going to be cut off," he said. "He also gave me money to make a car note."

The player recalled that Mason gave him at least one personal check. "I think it was for $125," he said.

He said an assistant coach gave him $500 cash soon after he had enrolled in school so that he could pay a deposit and two months' rent for an apartment.

Asked how much money he received over the two seasons, he said, "I don't know, but I was always on the take when I wasn't working."

He said the amount of the alleged payments depended on "the player's situation—whether he was married or whatever."

"But it was nice. Just put it that way. I'm struggling now. Those were the best years."

He said he made at least three free flights home while he was on an athletic scholarship.

The athlete said he didn't know where the coaches got the money for the payments and plane trips. However, a source close to the team, told the *Star* that he was told some coaches obtained money for players by submitting false vouchers for recruiting trips they didn't make. (See accompanying story.)

Mason, who coached the Wildcats for three seasons, resigned Monday in the wake of *Star* reports that he and six assistants had been reimbursed by the university for recruiting trips they apparently did not make.

Mason later admitted the false airline-ticket billings, saying the money didn't go to line the coaches' pockets but was to recover expenses.

Mason was out of town yesterday and unavailable for comment.

When informed of the player's claims of being paid and given free trips home, UA President John P. Schaefer said, "It's absolutely improper if it took place, and it won't be tolerated. It's a violation of regulations."

Another former UA football player told the *Star* that he also received a university-paid trip home, but said he believed it was allowable under NCAA rules because he had not used the return leg of a round-trip ticket he got when he visited the campus during recruiting time.

The player said that instead of returning home after visiting the UA campus, he enrolled in school and later counted his university-paid flight home as the return leg of his recruiting flight. He added that he paid for his return flight to the UA.

NCAA rules, however, state that an athlete's round-trip recruiting ticket must be used during the official campus visit.

April 10, 1980

NON-TRIPS REPORTEDLY USED TO PAY PLAYERS

By Bob Lowe and Clark Hallas
© 1980 The *Arizona Daily Star*

A source close to the University of Arizona football team says he was informed that some of the university funds obtained by coaches for nonexistent plane trips went to pay players.

The source said he was told that when some coaches needed money for players, they would "take a trip," meaning file a travel voucher for a fake trip.

In addition to being reimbursed for non-trips, coaches also occasionally would book players' flights in their own names to conceal the trips, he said he was told. Such trips by players would violate National Collegiate Athletic Association rules.

Meanwhile, American Airlines officials said yesterday that they are investigating how former UA head football coach Tony Mason and at least six of his assistants obtained passenger receipts from tickets for which the airline has no record.

The passenger receipts—one of the pages in an airline ticket—were submitted to the UA for reimbursement. Mason has admitted he and some coaches were paid for non-existent trips.

Bill Stringer, head of American's regional security office in San Francisco, confirmed that the airline is investigating the matter. He said out-of-town investigators for the company are involved in the inquiry, which centers on Tucson.

The authentic-looking passenger receipts appear to have been validated with seven different Tucson ticket agents' stamps.

On Friday, the *Arizona Daily Star* sent local American officials a letter asking them to explain how 10 passenger receipts were obtained when the airline's ticket-control office in Tulsa has no record of their purchase or use.

The airline also was asked for assistance in determining whether it has any record of 10 additional passenger receipts.

Art Pickell, general manager of American in Tucson, said the airline probably will reply to the *Star*'s letter and "state our position" in a week.

July 24, 1980

MASON AND 7 OTHERS INDICTED IN FELONIES

By Bob Lowe, Clark Hallas, and John DeWitt
The Arizona Daily Star

A state grand jury has indicted former University of Arizona head football coach Tony Mason, six assistants, and an American Airlines employee on 88 felony charges, claiming they bilked the university and a booster group out of more than $13,000 over two years.

The 52-count indictment, returned Tuesday but made public yesterday by Arizona Attorney General Bob Corbin, accuses the coaches of filing false airline receipts for 17 phony trips. It also alleges that Mason claimed expenses for four fictitious trips to Tucson supposedly made by football recruits.

Charges contained in the indictment were theft, conspiracy, tampering with a public record, participating in a fraudulent scheme or practice, and filing false claims. Some charges carry a 10-year maximum prison term upon conviction.

Mason, 52, was indicted on 25 counts, including 15 counts of theft.

American Airlines freight supervisor Michael E. Hoffman, 34, was charged with 20 counts of theft and one count of conspiracy.

Both Mason and Hoffman were named in some counts involving trips by assistant coaches Robert Shaw, 49; Thomas Roggeman, 49; Robert Davie, 25; Tony Yelovich, 40; Robert Valesente, 40; and L. Wayne Jones, 41.

Arraignment for the eight has been set for next Thursday in Pima County Superior Court.

Corbin credited an investigation by the *Arizona Daily Star* earlier this year for prompting the Department of Public Safety probe that resulted in the indictment.

He said in a Phoenix press conference that another investigation is continuing into reports by the *Star* that former UA players received a total of at least $9,000 from the Tucson Parks and Recreation Department for work they didn't perform.

Mason resigned April 7, a week after the *Star* detailed the coaches' collecting of reimbursements for flights they did not make.

Of the assistant coaches named in the indictment, only Roggeman remains on the football staff. He is the squad's strength coach under new head coach Larry Smith.

At the press conference, Corbin identified only Mason, Hoffman, Shaw, and Roggeman as having been charged. He said the other men, whose identities were learned independently by the *Star*, had not been notified of the indictment.

According to the indictment, Mason and his six assistants requested and received false airline receipts from Hoffman from mid-1977 through last fall. The coaches, when submitting the receipts on their expense accounts, stated they were for university-related travel.

"The [assistant] coach would, sometimes after consulting with Tony James Mason, obtain a false American Airlines ticket receipt from Michael Eugene Hoffman," the indictment said. "Such ticket was neither paid for, nor used, but was issued for the sole purpose of creating an official-looking ticket receipt."

Mason was charged with billing the university for fictitious trips dated in October 1977 to San Francisco and Minneapolis, and one he claimed he took in July 1977 to Dallas and Detroit.

In addition, the indictment says Mason received payment in 1978 for four bogus trips to Tucson by recruits he identified as J. Zimmer, J. Collier, Fred Sams, and L. Busby, who supposedly flew in from various parts of the country. Reimbursement for the purported recruiting trips was from funds donated by the Wildcat Club, a UA booster group, said the indictment.

Mason was indicted on one count of conspiracy, three counts of fraudulent schemes and practices, 15 counts of theft, three counts of filing false claims, and three counts of tampering with public records. Some of the theft counts involved fake receipts turned in by his staff.

Shaw, a linebacker coach under Mason, was charged with collecting university funds for three fake trips—in July 1979 to Philadelphia; August 1978 to Dallas; and June 1979 to Chicago.

He was indicted on one conspiracy count, two counts of fraudulent schemes and practices, three counts of theft, one count of filing a false claim, and two counts of tampering with public records.

Roggeman, who was the Wildcats' defensive-line coach under Mason, was charged with receiving university funds for three phony trips—in June 1979 to St. Louis; July 1977 to San Francisco; and August 1977 to Atlanta.

He was indicted on one conspiracy count, one count of fraudulent schemes and practices, three counts of theft, two counts of filing false claims, and one count of tampering with public documents.

Davie, formerly Mason's strength coach and now at the University of Pittsburgh, was charged with collecting UA funds for two bogus trips—Philadelphia in August 1979 and Pittsburgh in September 1979.

He was indicted on one count of conspiracy, and two counts each of fraudulent schemes and practices, theft, and filing false claims.

Valesente, defensive-backfield coach under Mason and now defensive coordinator at Mississippi State University, was charged with receiving payments for two fictitious trips—June 1979 to Atlanta and August 1978 to Dallas.

He was indicted on two counts of theft, and one count each of conspiracy, fraudulent schemes and practices, tampering with public records, and filing false claims.

Yelovich, Mason's offensive line coach until he resigned in March to join the Tulane University staff, was charged with collecting UA funds for two non-trips—August 1979 to San Francisco and October 1979 to Tampa.

He was indicted on one conspiracy count and two counts of theft, fraudulent schemes and practices, and tampering with public records.

Jones, a local salesman who coached quarterbacks and receivers for Mason until December 1978, was charged with collecting UA funds for two bogus trips—July 1977 to Houston and February 1978 to Memphis, Tenn.

He was indicted on two counts of theft and one count of conspiracy.

All of the coaches except Jones were identified by the *Star* in March as having been reimbursed for the bogus trips. Former assistant Karl

Singer also was named in one article, but was not mentioned in the indictment.

Phillip J. MacDonnell, director of the attorney general's special-prosecution division, said, "There are allegations against other people and certain aspects of the case are still under consideration."

MacDonnell did not rule out the possibility of more indictments in connection with the phony airline tickets.

Corbin noted that the DPS will cooperate with Tucson Police Department's "parallel" investigation into the city payroll allegations.

3

THE *LONG BEACH INDEPENDENT,*
PRESS-TELEGRAM

Reporters, especially those doing investigative work, are a cynical lot. And when they are looking into a story, nothing will arouse their suspicions more than a source suggesting they should be checking out something else.

So when several doctors in Orange County, Calif., told John Fried, the new medical writer for the *Long Beach Independent, Press-Telegram* (I,P-T) early in 1980 that he should investigate something called "patient dumping" in neighboring Los Angeles County, his initial reaction was skepticism. "My instincts are that when somebody tells me what I really should be doing, my mind kind of turns off," Fried explains, "because they're either trying to divert attention from what we're talking about or they're probably referring to something that has been covered by the press. I just somehow pigeonhole it."

But while Fried wanted to do a story about how Orange County had developed a trauma center system, the doctors he contacted told him his attention was urgently needed elsewhere. Although L.A. County's Emergency Aid Programs (EAP) supposedly guaranteed emergency medical care to the critically injured, the doctors told him, many indigent victims were dying or suffering needless complications because participating private hospitals were treating them inadequately and hastily transferring them to county facilities.

Fried remained unconvinced. Casting about for a story on a slow Monday, he spotted an item in a routine report from the Centers for Disease Control: surgical wound infections in the United States had declined for the first time in many years. Sensing a "nice, upbeat story," Fried began calling surgeons and professors of surgery for an explanation of the development. His first contact gave Fried the information he sought, then said: "Listen, why don't you stop screwing around and do something important?"

"Like what?" Fried asked.

"Why don't you look at the way emergency patients are treated in L.A. County by private hospitals?"

"I thought, 'Well, OK, somebody's trying to tell me something,'" Fried recalled. Agreeing to look into it, the reporter arranged to visit the physician, who worked at a county facility.

In what turned out to be the first of many such meetings, the physician (whose identity Fried has never revealed) described the problem but hesitated when the reporter asked for his help in investigating it. "Well, I don't really know you. We'd have to spend a lot of time getting acquainted to see if I can trust you." Fried, a veteran of the medical beat who well understood the close-knit profession's fierce aversion to publicity, agreed. "We set up a couple of more talks and after that he said, 'OK, let's see what we can do,'" Fried said.

The physician had been gathering information for the past two years on the effect of high blood pressure on trauma (bodily injury) victims. In the course of this study, he had accumulated case histories on thousands of patients who had been brought directly to his hospital or transferred there by a private hospital. "I've got all this up there," he told Fried, pointing to a set of loose-leaf notebooks on his shelf.

By now intrigued, Fried approached Gerald Merrell, the paper's special-projects reporter. Merrell had never covered medicine nor heard of "patient dumping," but he told Fried it sounded like a "hell of a story" and he ought to go after it.

Later that day, Fried filled in the assistant managing editor, Ladd Neuman. Although the story clearly would require months of research by two full-time reporters, Neuman approved it "after I talked to him for all of a minute and a half," Fried recalls. "He said, 'Goodbye and good luck—come and see me when you have something.'"

He also asked Neuman if he could work with Merrell on the project, and Neuman agreed. Fried had not asked Merrell if he wanted to participate, but "he knew me well enough to know that I'd jump at that," Merrell said. "By that afternoon, we both had been assigned to it."

This relaxed informality contrasted sharply with a larger paper such as the *Philadelphia Inquirer*, where established procedures must be followed before such a long-range commitment could be made. Fried believes he won approval for the project so easily because Neuman trusted the two veteran correspondents. Fried, 39, had been a reporter for *Life* magazine, the *Detroit News*, and United Press International; he had also written eight medical and science books. Merrell, 36, had worked for newspapers in California, Arizona, and Nebraska and had served as an aide to a congressman in Washington for three years. "So Ladd knew what he could expect," Fried says. "These things depend on a great deal of chemistry. Two other reporters might have walked in and been told 'no.'"

During the three-month investigation that followed, Fried and Merrell were subjected to minimal editorial supervision. After they had done considerable preliminary legwork, they sat down with city editor Mark Ivancic for about three hours and outlined the areas they would go after and how they would proceed; after that, they checked in about once a week. "They are experienced pros," Ivancic explained. "We knew what direction they were going, what they were doing. Making them report in every day would be infantile. I didn't need to know how often they went to the bathroom or if they took a 2½-hour lunch." In the end, Ivancic said, the final product turned out "remarkably close" to the original outline.

Even though Fried and Merrell were not general-assignment reporters (they contributed mostly to the Sunday paper), freeing them for an indefinite period worked hardships on the staff. "We never had enough [reporters] even with Fried and Merrell," Ivancic said. "This is not an overstaffed paper. But we all agreed we should strive for such a series. We made a conscious decision not just to do car wrecks and the latest shooting. We sought to build a solid Sunday package each week, to put something in the paper on Sunday that no one else had. So we decided to bite the bullet for those three months. We had to call on other reporters who had other responsibilities. There was some staff resentment and jealousy. Other reporters had ideas for series, but I had to tell them they would have to wait their turn."

One reason the paper may have been willing to "bite the bullet," Ivancic said, was to improve its reputation. Late in 1976, its arch-rival, the *Los Angeles Times*, published an extensive series charging that top *I,P-T* executives worked so closely with local officials that few major decisions were made in the city without the newspaper's approval; at the same time, the *Times* alleged, the paper "shielded much of the city's business from public view." Coincidentally or not, the newspaper executives named in the articles were replaced soon afterwards, and their successors, Ivancic said, were eager to "achieve some respectability."

For several weeks, Fried and Merrell pored through the patient records in the physician's office. For each case, the file contained the patient's name, a diagnosis of the injury, the treatment he had received, the result of that treatment, and whether he had insurance or other financial support. For patients who had been transferred to the hospital from private facilities, the records indicated how long they had been kept at the private hospital and what treatment had been administered there.

The reporters were keenly aware that their source was hardly disinterested. He believed that community hospitals were routinely transferring patients to county hospitals, often endangering their lives, if a check of their financial status (known as a "wallet biopsy") showed they could not pay for treatment. This physician had studied and taught at several of the nation's top medical institutions, Fried noted, "but he could be a nut" trying to use the press for his own ends. "You start out with that in your mind," Fried said. "On the other hand, he didn't say, 'Here's this case and this case and this case.' He said 'There are the books. Go through them.'" So if the evidence contradicted the physician's hypothesis, the reporters would probably find out.

What they found, Fried said, was that the community hospitals surrounding the county facility where the physician worked "were doing a very, very good job of taking people who were black, Hispanic, or very old and rather than giving them treatment, dumping them on the county hospital."

But this was only a small part of the picture, which included four county institutions and 73 community hospitals participating in the EAP. Was the situation they found in this one corner of the county indicative of the countywide situation?

Fried and Merrell had learned that the EAP program allowed participating hospitals to bill the county for emergency services rendered to indigents. The hospitals' contract also allowed them to transfer an indigent patient to the nearest county facilities—at county expense—if treatment was unavailable at the community hospital and if the patient's condition was stable. (In sprawling L.A. County, such a transfer could mean a trip of 20 or 30 miles.) The county's privately owned ambulance companies also took part in EAP. They had contracted to move patients from the scene of an accident or injury to the closest EAP emergency room and to transfer them to the nearest county hospital if necessary.

But Fried, who had joined the *I,P-T* only a few months earlier, had not yet developed sources at the other hospitals who might provide them with the kind of sensitive information they had about the one county institution. The most straightforward approach would have been simply to ask for the records from the L.A. County Department of Public Services, "but we were afraid to do that because we thought they would stall and contact other officials and we would not get the information," Merrell recalls. "Just because it's public doesn't mean you can get it quickly."

"So we sat around talking," Fried said, "and decided that if there was a county program, the county had to be paying bills to the hospitals and to the ambulance companies. So we said to each other, 'Let's go see who's making what kind of money on this.'"

This tactical decision opened up what turned out to be the second major aspect of the series: the financial and administrative side of EAP. "John never really cared so much about the administration of the program," Merrell says. "Were funds being wasted? Were there adequate safeguards? He was interested in safeguards as they related to patient care. He was interested, and given his background it would make sense, in what was happening to the patients. I didn't know anything about medical reporting, but I've had a good deal of experience looking at various programs and reading budgets, looking at figures and trying to make sense out of all that."

The *I,P-T*'s county-beat reporter sent them to the auditor and controller's office to find the ambulance-company bills. Fried and Merrell asked to see the records for four or five of them, the names of which the reporters plucked at random from the telephone directory. "We had two objectives in mind at that point," Fried remembers. "One was we'd be able to say 'So-and-so's making a lot of money shoveling patients around,' but we also wanted to find out which ambulance companies were doing the bulk of the transportation. And we felt that if we go talk to those people they'll be able to confirm that patients are transferred appropriately or inappropriately from other facilities. In other words, we were looking for sources."

The official brought the reporters several thick folders of bills. It took them three days to go through the bills and record the information on index cards, one for each patient, the same approach they used with their physician-source's case studies. The billing records reported where the patient was picked up, where he was taken, and how much the county paid the ambulance company for the transfer.

Then Fried and Merrell asked to see the bills submitted by five EAP hospitals. "And that's when we hit pay dirt," Fried said. When the official brought them the records, the reporters found individual bills for every EAP patient treated by each hospital for the period covered by the file. In each case, the record included the patient's name, diagnosis, treatment, and final result of treatment, plus whether he was transferred and, if so, to what hospital. The bills itemized everything from the most expensive surgery to a 25-cent item. "But the important thing," Fried said, "was that all of a sudden we realized that we had data for more than 65,000 patients because they had the files there for three years."

To get those files, the reporters devised a stratagem. "John and I deliberately made a request that we thought was going to be too large for them to handle," Merrell explained. "What we were hoping for was that they would throw up their hands in despair and say, 'It would take up too much staff time, so you guys do it.'"

And that's exactly what happened. They told the official they wanted to see the billing records for the remaining 71 EAP hospitals. "He said, 'You want to do it, do it yourself,'" Fried recalled. "'There are the file cabinets over there.' Gerry and I just looked at each other. How many times do you run into a situation where a bureaucrat tells you that the files are open?"

These records were far more important than the ambulance-company files. "We didn't care too much about the money, although that became part of the story," Merrell said. "But the money itself wasn't going to tell us anything. What we needed to know was what the hell they were doing to the patients." The hospital records, Merrell said, "were much more valuable than we ever envisioned. We never thought we would get the patients' names on a public record, but thinking back on it, it's not all that surprising because if you didn't have the patient's name, if you didn't itemize the services, I don't think any auditor would ever allow the county to pay for the services. We were hoping there would be a lot of detail, but there was more detail than we thought there would be. I am absolutely convinced that had they known what we were looking at, they would have locked those files on us."

This wealth of raw information created two immediate problems: the reporters could not devote months to examining every patient file, nor did they have the expertise to determine whether a patient had received adequate medical care. They resolved the first matter by selecting 125 cases for close scrutiny. The selection was random except that they wanted as broad a distribution as possible among the 76 EAP hospitals and they limited the cases to those in which the patient had been transferred.

To deal with the second point, they decided to ask emergency-care experts in the county to examine the data they had assembled, which now included 317 cases of patient transfers: 125 chosen at random from county files and the rest from the study compiled by the physician who encouraged Fried to do the story in the first place. During these weeks of poring through records, the reporters had also been interviewing many experts in emergency medicine, because they had felt from the outset that if they could not get adequate documentation about patient dumping they might have to tell the story simply on the basis of interviews, clearly a last resort. They asked every source they interviewed to suggest names of others they should see; past issues of the newspaper yielded more names.

Out of this pool, an emergency-medicine panel was created. In addition, Fried and Merrell consulted a number of specialists in particular areas to help interpret some of the data. "For example," Fried said, "we went to a leading vascular surgeon in Long Beach who had no connection with patient dumping, who didn't treat emergency patients. We said, 'What kinds of patients would you not transfer?' 'Well, I wouldn't transfer a patient with a penetrating knife wound to the chest; I wouldn't transfer one with penetrating trauma to the abdomen.' And we went back and we counted in the 317 cases we had, how many patients had been transferred who had stab wounds to the heart, stab wounds to the stomach."

Fried relied on his knowledge of narrow specialization among doctors in consulting these "satellite physicians" to supplement the panel. "Doctors really pigeonhole themselves," he explained. "We would take the cases to an internal-medicine man and he'd look at [them] and tell us everything that had been done right or wrong between the neck and the pubic bone. But then we took the same cases to a neurosurgeon, and she couldn't tell you a thing about what was wrong between here or here, but boy, she could tell you what was done right or wrong in terms of anybody who had a head or spinal injury. And it even went beyond that. We happened to come upon one guy who pointed out what problems there were with patients who had hip fractures and what happened to you when you broke a leg. Nobody else bothered to point out, for example, that if you fracture your leg, one of the great dangers is that if you're lying around in the emergency room for six hours without having the fracture set, it compromises the circulation to the leg [and] you might eventually lose use of the leg."

The physicians participating in the study insisted that none of the hospitals or doctors whose work was being evaluated would be named. "I agreed to that," Fried said. "I couldn't put anybody in that position." The panelists were not identified either.

By the time the panelists and the ancillary physicians had examined the material, the conclusion seemed clear: between 10 percent and 30 percent of the patients transferred from private community hospitals to county facilities had received inadequate or inappropriate care. But Fried and Merrell were concerned that the medical establishment had not been heard from sufficiently. They had conducted interviews with

county officials, EAP administrators, and officials of the Hospital Council of Southern California, so the viewpoints of EAP's defenders would
be included in the story, but none of them had seen the data. So the
reporters told the Hospital Council about the data and asked it to
choose an emergency-room expert to look at the records and offer an
interpretation of the care rendered to the patients, but it refused. So
did the L.A. County Medical Association. "At this point we were kind
of stuck," Fried said, "so we talked about it and I said, 'Let's just pick
out a doctor, an emergency-room physician from one of the hospitals
that has an EAP program.' So we arbitrarily chose the head of emergency room in one of the hospitals that did a moderate amount of
transferring. And we asked him, 'Will you look at these things?' And he
said, 'Sure.'"

The reporters worried about the impact on their story if his assess-
ments differed sharply from those of the other participants, but they
agreed in all but a handful of cases. "So once we had that," Fried said,
"we started running."

No aspect of this investigation differentiates it from the others in this
book more vividly than the reporters' need to break down the walls of
silence erected by the medical profession. Merrell said he had never
encountered such a closely knit, tight-lipped profession with the exception of higher education. And the reporters were asking physicians
to do what they found most distasteful to do: pass critical judgment
on the work of their professional peers.

"It's a tremendously touchy area," Fried said. "We had to talk to a
lot of doctors with whom we didn't have the opportunity to build up
a relationship. And there were people who were just shaking in their
boots." Fried recalled one physician's reaction in particular: "He baldly
lied to me. It was one of the few times in my career as a reporter where,
when I told this guy what I was doing, I could see him just absolutely
disintegrate. The touchiness of it was just incredible."

One result of the wariness of so many of their sources was that Fried
and Merrell had to allow many of them to speak anonymously. On
many occasions, they would sit for hours in a physician's office, listening to him describe one instance after another of seriously injured
patients being transferred despite their condition, but then he would
refuse to speak on the record. "We went to numerous physicians who
were really concerned [but] they did not want to criticize another
hospital, another physician," Merrell said. "Many of them said, in effect,
'If you look hard enough you're going to find dirt at our place.' There
were mistakes. Physicians make mistakes, hospitals do, and they just

weren't going to blow the whistle on one of them. It bothered [us] and it bothered the editors. But I don't know how you break that down, and we tried."

The reporters risked losing their sources entirely if they insisted on proper attribution. "We didn't push them to the wall because in many cases the interviews were lengthy and a great deal of that time was just trying to break them down to say anything," Merrell recalled. "We would go into someone's office or meet him someplace and we were getting zilch. We might get a cup of coffee and that was it. And slowly they would drop this and then they would drop that, and then finally they would start talking more about it. And to push them at that point, 'Well, Christ, we have got to have your name. That's the only way we can take it,' well, we would have been out the door. That's one of the judgments you make. We did not go into it saying we're going to have everyone off the record. But once you're sitting down with someone you can tell whether or not you're going to lose that person if you insist upon the name."

Fried insisted that the heart of the story lay in its well-documented facts and figures and that the unattributed statements merely "enriched" it. "We never used anonymous sources to impugn the reputation of a physician or hospital," he said. "They were used only to discuss the emergency care system itself." Even so, he acknowledged, using unidentified sources for any reason leaves journalists on "shaky ground."

The investigation turned up a number of physicians who had begun keeping their own records about inappropriate transfers. They would use these files to register private complaints to the facility responsible, but they preferred to work within the system in hopes to improving it rather than to make their objections publicly to a reporter.

Dealing with one such physician proved particularly frustrating to Fried and Merrell and illustrated a major difference in their reportorial techniques. Fried is a patient and persistent man who believes that sources require slow, careful cultivation. He will spend hours in apparent idle conversation with a source, stopping by his office frequently just to chat, hoping to win his confidence. And when he found this source and learned of his study, he spent a great deal of time with him in hopes of prying information loose. But the physician stoutly resisted, insisting that he could improve the system from within but not by publicly airing its problems. "I'd say 'OK,'" Fried recalled, "and then I'd go back to see him in about 10 days or two weeks and his bowels would be in an uproar because something had just happened which had confirmed to him that basically the bureaucracy didn't want to move, and he would be outraged. And for two hours we'd talk and I would get very good information. I would never be able to look at his study, but he would back what was emerging as the basic principles of our story. He would document them at least in quotations, but he wouldn't do it on the record."

This cat-and-mouse game infuriated the more volatile Merrell. "John's approach is softer," Merrell said. "Mine is, if there is a roadblock, try to go over the person; do what you have to do to get the damn information. When people were really jacking us around who had information but were afraid to talk, my instinct was just to go after them and do whatever we could to put them in a corner so that they would have to give us the information. John's approach was to work on them little by little and to keep giving them the benefit of the doubt. And I would be standing with John screaming, 'Screw the guy. Let's go after him.'"

Fried remembers Merrell being so angry at the physician's continued refusal to show them the study that "Gerry said he was leaving the building and he was going to rip his lungs out. I don't know how much he was kidding, but I had to stop him and say, 'No, let's just play him along a little longer.' " Although he had nothing so violent in mind, Merrell said that he did want to "give [the physician] an ultimatum. We had given him weeks and weeks and weeks. I don't know how many times we had gone to him and just said, 'We're not horsing around. We are talking about life and death. You give us all of this gobbledygook off the record. We know you've got the figures, we know you've got a study. We're going to say you've got it.' It wasn't blowing his cover. Everyone in the county knew he had a study. The only thing he was doing undercover was talking to us. But he wasn't giving us anything; he was giving us nonsense. I would never suggest that we blow someone's cover if he is working with a reporter. What I was saying is that he's got information that county officials ought to have, that the public ought to know. Why hold it to himself?"

Merrell agreed to wait awhile longer, and, as it turned out, the physician did eventually release some of his material, but not before the *I,P-T* began publishing the first installments of the patient-dumping series. The initial stories prompted demands for a county investigation of EAP. "The county investigation took 60 or 90 days," Fried recalls. "Essentially it was conducted by the department we wound up criticizing, and they issued a report saying that the incidence of inappropriate dumps was 6/10ths of 1 percent."

When Fried contacted his sources for reaction, they were "outraged" by what they saw as a whitewash, including the reluctant physician.

Fried asked him if he was finally willing to divulge some of the findings of his study, and he agreed. In fact, the county study proved a boon to the reporters because several other physicians who had previously refused to reveal what they knew now came forward, convinced at last that it was the only way to bring about changes.

The dispute over the physician and his study was one of the few to mar the smooth collaboration of Merrell and Fried. Their most vocal disagreement (Fried called it a "minor tiff," but Merrell described it as a "hell of a fight") concerned a major ethical dilemma: whether to identify the hospitals accused of inadequately treating their indigent patients. Fried argued that the series was intended to look at the EAP system as a whole. "We were dealing not with faulty care by one or even 10 hospitals but a system that was shot through with problems. That system was predominantly responsible for what was wrong." If a hospital were named in one or even several cases of questionable transfer, he maintained, the implication that its treatment of indigents (and, by extension, all of its patients) was frequently negligent would be strong, yet there would be no way to ascertain whether such incidents were typical. Beyond that, Fried was not primarily interested in pointing fingers: "Naming names has become a journalistic machismo, to prove what a tough guy you are, but it's got nothing to do with what you're trying to do: expose a situation that is inimical to the public good."

Merrell contended, however, that even though the focus of the series was the EAP, the program was inseparable from the hospitals participating in it. He felt that failing to name them detracted from the credibility of the series and encouraged readers to draw conclusions about individual hospitals that might not be warranted—tarring all of them, in effect, with the same brush.

Besides, he argued, he wasn't advocating bushwhacking them. He wanted to show each hospital to be identified the information about it that was going to be published and to give it a chance to comment. "There was no question that we had the goods on the hospitals," Merrell said. "We had done our work. We weren't publishing something that we had to be worried about backing off of."

When the two reporters could not resolve the issue, they took it to the editors. City editor Mark Ivancic wanted to identify the hospitals, but managing editor Rich Archbold, assistant managing editor Ladd Neuman, and editor Larry Allison decided against it. They agreed with Fried that they did not have enough information to establish patterns of negligence at any one hospital. Ivancic suggested that the investigation be extended until they had examined enough records to draw conclusions about individual hospitals, "but if we did that we would have been on this for two or three years," Archbold explained. "We're a daily newspaper. We had a lot of time invested in this and we wanted to get it in the paper."

Archbold also seconded Fried's point that the purpose of the series was not to isolate villains. "Our goal was not to investigate every hospital in California. We felt we had enough really good solid information to make a contribution to the community. We were not trying to put people in jail."

Nevertheless, Archbold said, "It was a close call. We all had our doubts. It was not an easy decision; we went round and round for hours."

Merrell never entirely reconciled himself to the decision. "It came as a real surprise to me. I never contemplated that we would not name the hospitals. I am not sure that I would have been a part of it had I [known], going into the assignment, that we would not name them."

A related question involved the conflict between the patients' right of privacy and the public's right to know. All of the patients' names used in the series were fictitious. Fried and Merrell wanted to interview some of the patients, but most were transients who vanished back into the black and Hispanic ghettos and could not be traced. What if they had located one of them?

"If you were a patient, had we been able to track you down, do we tell you that we think you got screwed by such-and-such a hospital?" Merrell asked. "We weren't sure how to handle that, because we could see you immediately filing suit based upon what we said, not based upon what anyone else told you. On the other hand, we really wanted to talk with some of the patients."

Merrell detected a certain irony here: if the fact that most of the patients were indigents made contacting them virtually impossible, it may also have helped the reporters in dealing with the medical establishment. "I think that the physicians would have been even more reluctant to cooperate had we been dealing with middle-class anglos," Merrell said. "I don't think they would have touched it."

A final question concerned not ethics but methodology. Since Fried and Merrell, like most reporters, were not trained in statistics and social-science research, how could they be sure that the random-selection method they used was valid? Fried conceded that he could not vouch for the validity of the method or of the conclusion it produced (10 percent to 30 percent of the EAP patients received questionable care), but he insisted that what was important was not the precise numerical incidence of negligence or dumping but the fact that the problem existed. "You have to be satisfed that you're doing a good job with the broad-brush kind of approach," he said. "That's all you can do. If it turns out that your theory is correct in its broad outlines, then it really doesn't make much difference whether a scientific study would have revealed a 9 percent incidence of something, whereas in using the rougher principles you came up with a 20 percent incidence."

Fried had always seen patient dumping as only part of the story. He knew that studies done in Orange County before it developed a trauma-center system indicated that victims of accidents or injuries who were taken to emergency rooms, whether they were indigents or fully insured, middle class victims, were in great danger of death because the hospitals lacked proper facilities. He wanted to know what such a study would show in L.A. County. The story had to take a back seat to patient dumping, but he began work on it soon after the latter was completed.

With the help of the doctor who conducted the Orange County study, Fried put together a panel of experts who studied a scientifically selected sample of patients who died in emergency rooms in the county in 1978 and 1979. The study concluded that 59 percent of the deaths could have been averted. The report was published in December 1980, six months after the patient-dumping series.

Fried, who did this story without Merrell, who had gone on to other projects, had little difficulty lining up six medical authorities to serve on the panel; in fact, none of those approached for the story declined, and all agreed to be identified in the story. That result seemed clearly attributable to the patient-dumping series. "People saw that it wasn't just a hatchet job or a cheap, dirty project," Merrell said.

About six months after the patient-dumping series appeared, the L.A. County Department of Health Services launched a new system of controlling patient transfers. Henceforth, the county was able to monitor inappropriate transfers, and doctors and hospitals guilty of such actions would be referred to the district attorney for prosecution.

The follow-up study about emergency care problems in Los Angeles County for all trauma victims had less immediate effect. It predicted—accurately—that changes in the system would be slow in coming, but in 1983 L.A. County got its own trauma-center system.

For their work, Fried and Merrell won Sigma Delta Chi's Distinguished Service Award and the Clarion Award of Women in Communications, Inc. They also were finalists in the competition for the Pulitzer Prize and the Robert F. Kennedy Award for reporting on problems of the poor.

July 6–16, 1980

PATIENT DUMPING

POOR ARE OFTEN VICTIMS OF COUNTY PROGRAM TRANSFERRING ILL, INJURED

A Los Angeles County program designed to guarantee emergency medical care to the critically injured or ill is endangering the lives of the very people it is supposed to help, a three-month *Independent, Press-Telegram* investigation has revealed.

Some patients who might have survived have died as a result of their encounter with the Los Angeles County's Emergency Aid Program (EAP): some because they did not receive adequate treatment and others because the program causes long delays before they receive definitive care.

An estimated 24,000 indigent men, women, and children are treated each year for emergency problems in 73 community hospitals participating in the county's EAP.

But because they don't have medical insurance or money to pay hospital bills, nearly all of these patients are eventually transferred or "dumped"—as county officials, hospital administrators, and doctors refer to the practice—into four county hospitals and UCLA Medical Center.

Even patients who have money or insurance but cannot prove it— because they are unconscious, unable to communicate, or simply without proper identification for the moment—find themselves "dumped."

As a result of the transfer process, an estimated 10 to 30 percent of these patients—between 2,400 and 8,000—receive questionable medical treatment.

In its investigation into the program, the *I, P-T* found that in violation of conventional medical practice:

• A substantial number of patients who are hemorrhaging are being moved from private hospitals to county-operated institutions even before the extent of their bleeding is defined or the bleeding is fully brought under control.

• Many victims of accidents resulting in serious head injuries are moved, although little or no effort is made to assess the extent of their injuries or to determine if the ambulance ride to the county hospital will compound the injuries' effects.

• Many of these patients are moved even though they are in shock or in comas.

• Badly injured or seriously ill patients who should be admitted quickly to intensive care units are first kept waiting, often for four to 12 hours, in emergency rooms until arrangements are made to shunt them over to a county hospital.

For many of the patients, the substandard care will mean prolonged, unnecessary complications, extended hospital stays, and even stormy periods of recovery.

And some patients, as one noted emergency medicine expert believes, "are dying needlessly because the system is not operating anything like the way it is supposed to."

Most of those who fall under the EAP program are the poor—many times the elderly and the young, but most often the county's Mexican-Americans and blacks.

"If you are black or Chicano or have no money, you get one type of treatment; if you have insurance or funds, you get another," says one expert who has had a firsthand view of the program.

But because the system includes hospitals scattered throughout the county—from desert hospitals in the Antelope Valley to institutions deep in the inner city to hospitals catering to the affluent areas on the county's west side—medical problems in the EAP are detectable everywhere.

Thus, says Dr. Rodney White of Harbor–UCLA Medical Center, even the fully insured could find themselves swept into medically risky situations.

"It doesn't matter who it is," says White. "The president of the Bank of America could be in an automobile accident, go to an emergency room, and not be able to tell them who he is because he is unconscious.

"And, if in the process of taking care of him, someone cuts off his pants and throws them in the trash, there goes his identification.

"So it's not as though you are protected just because you work and have identification. We wind up with people here and we may not know who they are for three or four days.

"Everyone's care is only as good as the system is."

And a ranking law enforcement official who has dealt with medical malpractice problems in emergency room treatment of indigents adds:

"I used to think that once a patient went through the emergency room doors you could sigh a sigh of relief—knowing that everything was all right and that whatever could be done would be done.

"Now I know differently. When you send someone to a hospital, you have to worry about the quality of that hospital because you may be putting the patient in real jeopardy."

Virtually everyone officially connected with the EAP denies that private hospitals—which in the last two fiscal years collected $12.4 million for the services they did render to indigents—are providing inadequate care or that the program is riddled with problems.

"One inappropriate transfer is one too many," says Robert W. White, director of the Department of Health Services. "And while we don't know how many inappropriate transfers there are, there does not seem to be a large number."

Administrators of hospitals participating in the program agree.

"The number of incidents identified are minimal if indeed they exist," says Richard A. Norling, administrator of California Hospital, one of the largest hospitals participating in the program.

"Sure, one can take a specific case and blow it up, if one has a cause to celebrate. There are people out there who like to do that."

Similarly, Hospital Council of Southern California officers—who often work hand-in-hand with officials of the county's medical care bureaucracy to deal with assorted medical crises—say that they are convinced that care dispensed under the emergency aid program is satisfactory.

"Each time it is really looked into, you find very minute numbers of patients who might have experienced that kind of a problem," says one council officer.

But the *I,P-T* investigation indicates that the EAP is not marked only by the occasional medical mishap or the one case that will cause a spectacular splash on the front page of a newspaper.

Rather, the *I,P-T* found in its examination of patient cases and in discussions with observers of the program, that the hallmarks of the EAP are thousands of patients who receive inadequate care that puts them at considerable risk but who—precisely because they don't make for spectacular illustration—simply escape official attention.

While hospital administrators and emergency room directors emphasize that *their* institutions offer only the best of care to indigents brought to their emergency rooms, the *I,P-T* found instances of questionable practices in many hospitals.

Moreover, the *I,P-T* found that virtually every hospital in the EAP will, at one time or another, treat its indigent patients with less than complete medical attention.

The *I,P-T* obtained access to medical histories of 317 patients treated under the EAP program. Among these were 100 cases that the *I,P-T* submitted to several experts for detailed comment.

The experts included:

• A nationally known surgeon with extensive background in the medical needs of critically injured patients.

• A physician who specializes in emergency medicine and who is studying care given to indigent patients treated under the EAP.

• The director of the emergency room in one of the 73 hospitals participating in the EAP.

"In this case," said the physician who specializes in emergency medicine, pointing to written details of one patient's care, "St. Francis [Medical Center in Lynwood] did a good job of stabilizing him and taking care of his problems.

"But then, St Francis has a good reputation for this sort of thing."

He then turned his attention to the next case submitted to him by the *I,P-T.*

"This patient," he went on, "was in no way stable for transfer. They just did not handle him well."

The expert then looked to see the name of the hospital involved.

It was St. Francis, the institution he had just praised.

Official denials that the EAP is malfunctioning come not because hospital administrators, county officials, or physicians are determined to hide medical malfeasance, but because they don't really know what is going on within the program.

Observers in the public health field—including two researchers at the UCLA School of Public Health—have alluded, as far back as 1972, to the medical hazards inherent in the EAP.

Although the EAP has been in effect for well over 30 years, an intensive and officially-sponsored study of its medical effectiveness has never been made.

And when questions do arise about medical care dispensed under the EAP, the official answers are often contradictory.

"We keep a monthly record of those transferred, but we don't break it down into appropriate and inappropriate transfers," a high-ranking official in the Department of Health Services told the *I,P-T.* "We don't know how many inappropriate transfers there are."

The answer was different when, in March 1979, L.A. County Supervisor Peter Schabarum asked the Department of Health Services to investigate charges that private hospitals were transferring accident and sudden illness victims to county facilities without first giving those patients appropriate care.

Seven weeks later—on May 14—Robert W. White, director of the department, reported that "we do not have specific data indicating a significant number of inappropriate transfers."

Given the way the department conducted its survey to answer Schabarum, it is little wonder it could find no "specific" data on inappropriate transfers.

The department made no attempt to carry out a scientifically acceptable study—for example, to pick out a large number of patients transferred to the county and to compare their rates of death and complications with those of patients with the same illness but who had not been shunted about.

Instead, officials of the department simply picked up their phones, called the directors of the various emergency rooms at the county facilities, and informally asked them if they thought medically unwise transfers were taking place.

Whatever the answers might have been, they would have allowed White to report that he had no "specific" data about questionable transfers.

Certainly, the shoddy treatment often dispensed under EAP seems to be well known within the medical community, especially among emergency room physicians.

"The people I know who work for the county and who work at the county hospitals tell me that frequently patients are transferred [there] who were really not appropriately stable for transfer," says Dr. Marshall Morgan, medical director of the emergency department at Santa Monica Hospital Medical Center.

"There are hospitals notorious for transferring out unstable patients, patients with the knife sticking out of his belly, his blood pressure at 60 and both feet sticking out to freeze," says Dr. Jerry Hughes, director of emergency services at Long Beach Community Hospital.

Information that "inappropriate" transfers do take place is not merely secondhand.

There are hospitals that do treat indigent emergency patients adequately, says Dr. Daniel Whitcraft, medical director of the emergency department at Long Beach Memorial Medical Center, who also is on the staff at the University of Southern California–L.A. County Medical Center.

"But there are some that do very little for a patient," he adds.

Following leads provided by trauma and emergency medicine experts—men and women also readily available to county officials—the *I,P-T* undertook its own investigation of the EAP.

In its three-month investigation, in addition to the 317 patient histories it obtained, the *I,P-T* also searched through coroner's reports and hundreds of official county documents.

We also interviewed more than three dozen medical experts, hospital administrators, state and county officials, as well as law enforcement officials who have had firsthand experience with the EAP.

We found widespread abuses in the program and that, despite claims to the contrary by the county, many critically ill or injured patients are indeed being shunted from private hospitals to county-operated facilities without first being properly treated.

Thirty-three years ago, Los Angeles County became one of the first local governments to establish formal links with ambulance companies and private hospitals in an attempt to insure quick and definite emergency treatment for the public.

In the last 13 years, moreover, the EAP has evolved into a massive network to guarantee that no one—"prince or pauper," as one county official put it—would ever be denied emergency medical care.

"The basic purpose of this is to make sure that everybody who needs emergency care will get it promptly with no questions asked," says the chief of the EAP, Marion Diamond. "We'll settle all the financial questions later."

The program consists primarily of two parts:

• Formal contracts with ambulance companies to guarantee transportation of a seriously ill or injured patient to the nearest emergency room.

• Contracts between the county and 73 private hospitals who agree to provide emergency care to all patients brought in to them under the program and to give all necessary care to bring the patient's injuries under control before sending the patient to a county facility.

The ambulance companies and hospitals are obligated to try to collect their fees from the patients or from the patients' insurance carriers.

But the county agrees to pay the medical bills of indigent patients served by the EAP—those who cannot pay themselves or who are not covered by medical insurance.

Moreover, under the program, hospitals are authorized to keep an indigent EAP patients for up to 24 hours. After the first full day, hospital officials may call the county and obtain approval for extended hospitalization.

"Normally, that authorization is to be renewed every 72 hours," Mrs. Diamond says. "So it is usually issued three days at a time."

The EAP, however, also allows the private hospitals to transfer patients to one of the county hospitals—Los Angeles County–USC Medical Center, Harbor–UCLA Medical Center, Martin Luther King Medical Center, Olive View Medical Center—if, in medical terms, the patient is stable.

That, in theory, is how EAP is supposed to work.

But the spirit of the program is abused because various pressures seem to force transfer of indigent patients.

It is difficult to find private surgeons and physicians who will attend to these patients. Many hospitals, especially in the more affluent parts of the city, don't want, as one expert put it, "a clientele that won't mix well with its regular patients or leave graffiti all over the walls."

And hospital administrators, with an eye on balance sheets, often pressure emergency room physicians to transfer out patients who will not pay their way.

As a result, patients by the thousands are put into ambulances for yet another ride down the freeways, their lives at risk.

HOSPITAL DIDN'T GIVE THIS VICTIM A GOOD CHANCE

Early in the morning of a recent September day, 25-year-old George Santiago, wearing a "I'd rather push my Harley than Drive a Rice-Eater" T-shirt, was roaring down a Los Angeles street, anxious to get home and go to sleep.

Suddenly a car pulled out of a side street.

Santiago tried to stop, but couldn't. Within a few minutes, paramedics were at the scene, put Santiago into their ambulance, and drove him quickly to the nearest hospital with a basic emergency service.

Barely two hours later he was put into another ambulance and moved to L.A. County–USC Medical Center.

In the *Independent, Press-Telegram* investigation of Los Angeles County's Emergency Aid Program, the treatment accorded Santiago emerged as a direct challenge to an oft-repeated official contention: That the program works well to serve the indigent emergency patient and that only an occasional case—and then only one provided by disgruntled doctors in training at a county facility—can be dredged up to show otherwise.

In the course of its investigation, the *I,P-T* gained access to medical accounts detailing care given to thousands of patients transferred from private hospitals to county facilities.

From the records available, the *I,P-T* randomly selected 100 cases.

These were chosen to meet two main criteria:

—To obtain a cross-section of medical problems for which indigent patients were taken to private hospitals.

The range was wide: From a man who had somehow managed to cut his chin on a lawn mower blade, to a man who had accidentally shot himself in the stomach, to a child who had fallen out of a third-story window, to a young woman who had tried to end her own life with an overdose of pills.

—To obtain a representative sample of hospitals involved in the program. The cases included patients taken to 22 of the county's leading transferring hospitals.

Cases were then presented to several experts for review.

Among the cases drawn at random was George Santiago.

To the casual observer, the list of procedures performed for him is impressive:

X-rays were taken of his chest and abdomen. His blood was typed and cross-matched with blood in the hospital's blood bank. He was given fluids intravenously as well as extensive medication, including steroids.

But one expert, a director of the emergency room in a hospital participating in the EAP, was straightforward in his assessment of the case: "You don't transfer a patient who is that sick."

Another physician, a man who has made a specialty of emergency medicine, was irate.

"The diagnosis says skull fracture and intra-abdominal hemorrhage," the expert pointed out.

"If indeed he was bleeding into his abdomen, they should have done a peritoneal lavage, a procedure in which a catheter is put into the abdomen under the umbilicus to draw out fluid and see how much blood it contains.

"And if they weren't going to do the lavage, then he should have gone into the operating room immediately.

"But nothing they did do for the man was reasonable and they did little to really stabilize him.

"There is no way, the chances are less than zero, that he should have been transferred. He could have bled to death in the ambulance."

Intrigued by the expert's willingness to state that Santiago might have bled to death during the transfer to the county, the *I,P-T* checked coroner's records.

George Santiago, these records revealed, died fourteen hours after he had been dumped into the ambulance for transfer to L.A. County–USC Medical Center.

Moreover, a review of the autopsy report shows that Santiago probably did not die an easy death: Among other things, he had suffered cuts and bruises, fractures of the right clavicle, the right ribs, and the bone of the upper left arm.

He also had numerous and severe internal injuries, including a lacerated liver and a cut of the thoracic aorta.

Given his serious injuries, could Santiago had been saved if hospital officials, rather than wash their hands of him because he had no insurance, had insisted that surgeons on the hospital's staff come in and operate on him?

To find the answer, the *I,P-T* submitted notes detailing care given Santiago in the emergency room and copies of the coroner's detailed autopsy records to a fourth expert, one of the Southland's leading surgeons, a man who also has made a specialty of treating the critically injured.

"This was a very tough case and he might have been lost anyway," this expert said.

"But they [the transferring hospital] didn't handle him well at all. They did not give him a good chance."

EMERGENCY ROOM TREATMENT SEEN AS "PIT-STOP" MEDICINE PERILING LIVES

Driving south on La Cienega Boulevard in the heart of Los Angeles, the motorist who comes to the junction of La Tijera Avenue is suddenly face-to-face with a imposing sign: Daniel Freeman Hospital. 24 hr. Emergency Service. An arrow points off to the left.

Hundreds of similar signs dot the Los Angeles County landscape—and to most laymen, they are a comforting indication that quick, dependable emergency care is just around the corner.

For many accident victims or for those taken suddenly ill, the sign may indeed point to life-saving help.

But for thousands of men, women, and children—in large part those who are the county's Chicano, black, or poor citizens—the assumption that the basic emergency room around the corner offers hope in a medically critical situation often ends in a rude, and often dangerous, surprise: That their "medical" care will include only a quick stop at the emergency room—a "medical pit-stop," one emergency care physician calls it.

What will come hard on the heels of that "medical pit-stop" will be another ambulance ride from the emergency room to one of the county's four publicly supported hospitals or to UCLA Medical Center, because the first hospital could not or would not provide the patient with the required medical care.

And for thousands of patients each year, that ride may result in substantial medical risks, including incomplete recovery from the injury or illness and, in some cases, even death, a three-month investigation by the *Independent, Press-Telegram* has found.

The transfer of indigent patients from private hospitals to public facilities is part of a 33-year-old Los Angeles County program designed to guarantee proper emergency care for those who cannot afford to pay their own medical way.

But medical and court records as well as extensive interviews with medical experts indicate that many hospitals either cannot or will not provide the rudimentary care that will insure the patient's survival until specialized care can be provided.

Almost 24,000 patients come under the county's program—officially known as the Emergency Aid Program (EAP)—each year, official figures show.

But between 10 and 30 percent of these patients, according to these different experts in the delivery of emergency care, are given inadequate and often even dangerous care.

Recently, for example, officials at the UCLA Medical Center agreed to receive two EAP patients a day whom private hospitals wanted to transfer out of their emergency rooms.

The UCLA experience with these patients, says one ranking medical official at the center, has not been good.

"Twenty percent [of the patients sent to UCLA] should not have been transferred," the official says.

"And 10 percent deteriorated en route. [In these cases] you could predict that there was a reasonable chance they would deteriorate during the transfer process."

One measure of the disregard for patient welfare under the EAP is the manner in which indigents are transferred from private to county hospitals.

Many of the 24,000 transferred patients have only relatively minor medical problems like broken bones or face cuts—the *I,P-T* survey even turned up one patient who was transferred with a sprained finger.

But thousands are seriously injured or ill men and women.

Many of these patients, experts say, should be transported only in ambulances equipped with paramedics—the men and women who would be able to respond quickly to any emergencies that might arise on the way to the county hospital.

But time after time, critically ill and injured patients arrive at various county facilities in ambulances staffed only by the driver and a technician, experts say.

And a survey of transportation records confirms that transfer patients are not moved with proper precautions.

As part of the EAP, the county pays private ambulances to transport patients when the county's own ambulances are too busy to keep up with the demand for transfers.

The ambulance companies have trained paramedics and will send them with the ambulance—when the transferring hospital requests them.

And when the paramedic is assigned, the county pays the ambulance company $25.74 above the regular fee paid for use of the vehicle.

The *I,P-T* surveyed charges submitted by two of the county's leading ambulance companies for transportation of tens of thousands of patients. The additional $25.74 charge was seldom evident.

In February 1980, for example, the two companies participated in the transfer of at least 308 patients.

But only 18 patients, according to the bills examined, had a paramedic at their side during the trip from the emergency room to the county hospital.

The men and women transported included patients taken from California Hospital in the downtown Los Angeles area to Harbor–UCLA Medical Center in Carson, a distance of almost 30 miles; from Marina Mercy Hospital to Harbor, a distance of approximately 20 miles; from Dr. David Brotman Memorial Hospital in Culver City to Harbor, also a distance of some 20 miles.

"People are arriving in garden variety ambulances," says the administrator of one county-affiliated hospital that receives transfer patients.

"They arrive without breathing even though it is recorded that they [left the other hospital] with respiration.

"One lady arrived with tachycardia [an abnormal and potentially dangerous heart beat] even though the transferring hospital said she was stable.

"Another man arrived with a dissecting aneurysm [a weak spot on an arterial wall about to burst].

"The kind of patients we see transferred without paramedic support is unacceptable. Just unacceptable.

"They should not have been transferred.

"And if they had to be [transferred] due to extenuating circumstances that were not just economic, they then definitely should have been transferred with paramedics capable of communicating with a doctor [via radio] and able to change things en route."

The practice of transferring patients whose conditions have not been stablilized is exacerbated by the distances many ambulances have to travel during the transport of indigent patients.

Ideally, experts say, if a patient must be transferred from a private hospital emergency room, he should be taken to the closest county hospital.

But because the closest hospital may not have a bed for the patient, he is often transferred to a county facility that does have room for him.

Thus, patients in critical condition are often placed in ambulances and driven, sometimes up to 20 to 30 miles, to the place where they will finally be treated.

It is not unusual, for example, to find patients transferred from Hollywood Presbyterian—in the Hollywood area—to Harbor–UCLA Medical Center in the South Bay area.

"Say someone rolls into an emergency room with a ruptured spleen, a broken leg," says an expert who has studied the system.

"Their blood pressure [seems adequate] so they start an IV, load him into an ambulance because he looks fine, and transfer him to Harbor, which is 45 minutes away.

"The ambulance gets in a traffic jam on the freeway and the ride is actually an hour and fifteen minutes. Meanwhile the guy continues to bleed, goes into shock, and dies.

"It happens."

That transfers are often conducted with little or no regard for the patient's welfare can also be seen in the number of transferred patients who need the specialized care available only in an intensive care unit.

"If we have somebody here, if this guy needs hospitalization, how do we decide whether he is stable enough to transfer?" says Dr. Marshall Morgan, director of the emergency room at Santa Monica Hospital.

"Well, you use a whole lot of criteria, but one of the criteria we have found useful is that any patient who would go to the ICU if he were to stay here is not stable enough to be put into an ambulance and sent across town," he says.

But in many of the 73 hospitals that have agreed to participate in the EAP, the indigent never reaches the intensive care unit.

Instead, after rudimentary efforts are made to give the patient some care, the emergency room physician will arrange for an ambulance to come for the patient.

The *I,P-T* obtained access to the medical histories of almost 200 patients transferred to one county facility.

Of these patients, 74—or 37 percent—were diverted to the county hospital's intensive care unit. Some were placed in the ICU after undergoing surgery. But many patients were sent directly from the county hospital's receiving dock to the intensive care unit.

Moreover, of those 74 transferred patients, 18 had to be placed on ventilators—machines that had to supplement or completely sustain their breathing.

Officially, hospital administrators and emergency room physicians say that they transfer patients who need intensive care only if their own intensive care units are full.

However, many of these hospital administrators admit—and independent physicians confirm—that the fully-insured patient will not be transferred even if the ICU is full.

Strenuous efforts are made to find an ICU bed for that patient in the private facility.

"First, they will try to find a bed in other units where [continuous] monitoring is available," says one prominent physician who has seen the transfer system close at hand.

"If there is no room there, they will call doctors who have patients in the ICU and find out if one of their patients can be moved out.

"And finally, if they have to, they will open an ICU bed and call in the nurse for one-on-one care."

Emergency medicine experts stress that patients eligible for admission to an intensive care unit are not the only ones who should not be subjected to a second ambulance ride before they are given definitive care.

The patient who is hemorrhaging—or who has injuries that could lead to hemorrhage—should not be dumped into the transfer system.

"The classic example of a patient [who should not be transferred] is the [one where] there is evidence that he is bleeding internally," says Dr. Morgan.

It is particulary important, say several medical experts consulted by the *I,P-T*, that car accident victims or others who have internal injuries not be subjected to irrational transfer.

Many car accident victims, the experts point out, may have suffered a ruptured or lacerated spleen, an injury that could lead to massive hemorrhage and death.

"When you first see them, they might be stable," says one leading emergency room expert. "Their blood pressure is OK, their pulse is not too fast, they are breathing OK, and there is no evidence of trouble.

"But if you figure someone is going to have to wait an hour, two hours, whatever, just to get the ambulance there and they are going to be in the ambulance for up to an hour and that their condition during transfer may or may not be monitored by a paramedic . . . these people could deteriorate significantly in route.

"They could then arrive [at the county facility] and are not resuscitable or [in a condition] that makes resuscitation more difficult.

"The complication rate is higher, it reduces their chances of survival or survival without complications [and increases] the cost to the individual, which may be his life."

Nevertheless, the *I,P-T* found that patients who are bleeding or who are in the midst of hemorrhages are routinely transferred out of private hospitals.

According to the 317 records and patient histories obtained by the *I,P-T*, 124 transferred patients were actively bleeding when they were put into ambulances for transfers.

In several instances, notations made in the private emergency room show that the patient's bleeding was "uncontrollable."

Moreover, tranfer times noted on patient records show that many of them were not held at the first hospital long enough to allow doctors to determine if the bleeding posed a threat to the patient's life, experts consulted by the *I,P-T* point out.

Many of the records for the 124 bleeding patients do not show the time the patient arrived at the first hospital or the hour at which the patient was transferred.

But those records that have complete information reveal that 72—more than half—of the bleeding patients were in and out of the transferring hospital in less than three hours.

A key diagnostic tool that can help determine if a patient is bleeding internally—and if that bleeding is potentially serious—is the hematocrit test, emergency medicine experts consulted by the *I,P-T* say.

The test, which determines the percentage of red blood cells in a blood sample, should be repeated several times at intervals of several hours, the experts add, if a proper picture of the patient's blood volume is to be obtained.

However, experts point out, hematocrit tests were of little value to the patients who were transferred after only short periods of stay in private emergency rooms. Many patients, they say, were probably out the door before the results of the first hemotocrit test came back.

Nor were these patients around long enough to allow doctors to obtain a repeated hematocrit test.

A study of emergency room procedures performed on hemorrhaging patients with suspected bleeding discloses that 49 received only one hematocrit test.

In at least 29 cases, the emergency room personnel did not even bother to order the crucial test.

In only one case, records show, was a patient given more than one hematocrit test.

The dangers posed to EAP patients with bleeding problems are compounded, experts point out, because many of them are gunshot or stab wound victims.

And the man or woman who has been shot or stabbed in the stomach or chest, the experts say, should be a candidate for immediate surgery—not a drawn-out transfer process.

In many gunshot blasts to the body, experts point out, there is high risk that the heart or other major organs or blood vessels are affected.

"In gunshot wounds to the chest or belly, most surgeons operate on these people right away and they are not candidates for transfer," Morgan says.

Other surgeons agree: A patient who has a penetrating stab or gunshot wound to the chest or abdomen should not be transferred, says Dr. John Rosental, a Long Beach surgeon, because all too often there "is potential for disaster . . . even if the patient is stable."

Yet, the *I,P-T* investigation found the 317 transferred patients included 54 patients who had serious chest and abdomen wounds. Some of these patients also suffered hemorrhaging.

Among the transferred were:

• A 22-year-old man who had been shot in the chest and who, according to hospital notes, may have suffered a heart wound.

Although he was held at the receiving hospital for 3 hours and 15 minutes and even though his blood type had been determined, he apparently was not given a blood transfusion.

Nor was an EKG done to determine if the bullet had damaged the heart's electrical conduction system.

Instead, he was transferred to UCLA–Harbor Medical Center.

A patient with a gunshot wound to the heart needs all the help he can get, a noted emergency medicine expert who reviewed the case for the *I,P-T* says.

"You take him to the operating room immediately. But transferring him . . . well . . . "

• One patient with a penetrating stab wound near the heart. The patient needed, and received, blood transfusions. Nevertheless, he did not receive surgery and was transferred out after a little more than one hour in the emergency room.

• A 30-year-old man who was stabbed in the chest.

Emergency room notes say that he had "uncontrollable bleeding."

He was given some fluids to keep his blood pressure up. Yet, even though emergency room personnel had sufficient presence of mind to check his blood type, he was apparently not given any transfusions.

After 1 hour and 40 minutes, he was shipped out to USC–County Medical Center although, as one expert who reviewed the case says, "he needed to go to the operating room because you don't put a person with a stab wound and uncontrollable bleeding into an ambulance."

Administrators of hospitals participating in the EAP routinely claim that, in many cases, they would like to take care of indigent patients who come to their emergency rooms with serious problems.

But they cannot do so, they claim, because often neither the physicians nor the specialized facilities needed to treat these patients are readily available.

Experts say that these assertions are rationalization, that, in the final analysis, many hospitals in the EAP are capable of rendering all the care indigent emergency patients require—but that, often these hospitals just simply don't want to be bothered.

SOME SPECIALIST SHIRK THEIR DUTY WHEN IT COMES TO TREATING INDIGENTS

Late on a recent summer evening, 30-year-old David Carmell was driving home. At about 10 P.M., somewhere along Sepulveda, he fell asleep at the wheel, ran off the road, and hit a tree.

An ambulance was called and Carmell, unconscious, was taken to a local hospital.

Because most tests showed that Carmell was not critically injured—even though it took awhile for him to come to in the hospital—emergency room personnel went on to concern themselves with the other patients who were clamoring for attention.

Eventually, someone made arrangements for an ambulance to pick up Carmell and take him to a county hospital for treatment of the major injury he had suffered—a dislocated hip.

"They kept that man for eight hours without doing anything for the hip," says one of the surgeons who treated Carmell.

"And the longer a hip is left dislocated, the longer the blood supply to it is cut off.

"And that means the chances are good that the fracture head of the leg bone that fits into the hip will die, that he'll lose the hip and need an operation to replace it sometime in the future."

As transfers of indigent patients go, Carmell's case is not dramatic.

Nevertheless, Carmell's brush with Los Angeles County's Emergency Aid Program (EAP) is, in a way, representative of one of the system's major weaknessess.

He came away with a ruined hip as a painful and lifelong legacy because, the surgeon who ultimately treated him believes, Carmell's status as an EAP patient blocked his access to a specialist: an orthopedic surgeon would not come to the hospital in the middle of the night and treat Carmell because the physician knew that his fees would not be paid.

Thus Carmell—albeit belatedly—was transferred to a county facility where salaried physicians stood ready to minister to his problems.

County officials who designed and implemented the EAP, for all their original good intentions, undermined their own program by failing to provide for physician payments, experts point out.

It is an oversight that has never been corrected.

And to a large extent, medical experts agree, that lack of funds for physician fees is a major flaw in the EAP.

Moreover, these experts often point out, the inclusion of hospitals with limited backup facilities—with no holding areas for drug overdose victims, or no specialized care for head trauma victims—is also in large part responsible for the dangers inherent in the EAP.

However, the *Independent, Press-Telegram*'s investigation of the EAP revealed, the lack of physician reimbursement and specialized facilities all too often serves only as an excuse for the failure of hospitals to provide even the minimal support they are required to give victims of medical emergencies.

"They [the EAP] do not pay the doctor, and under those circumstances, we have a hell of a time sometimes finding a doctor who is willing to work for nothing, who is willing to come in on a complex, time-consuming, physically and emotionally draining problem," says Dr. Marshall Morgan, director of the Emergency Department at Santa Monica Hospital.

And the problem, hospital administrators admit—but only off the record—is compounded when an indigent patient with multiple injuries or problems is brought into the emergency room.

"In the case of true major trauma, a total body crunch in which you need a urologist, a neurosurgeon, an orthopedic surgeon, a general surgeon to head the team, you are not going to get these guys to come in and accept the patient for essentially free," says the administrator of one large hospital.

"You can push and impose on these guys and if they have loyalty for the organization they will [come in]. But you can only do that up to a point."

Theoretically, every hospital has the wherewithal to force physicians on its staff to treat indigent patients with immediate medical needs.

"Every hospital in this country has bylaws that say that every patient who needs emergency care will receive it from someone on the staff," says one physician. "And every hospital has a roster of physicians who must render care in [an emergency] situation."

Directors of most emergency rooms maintain that, in many cases, they can prevail on physicians to respond to uninsured emergency patients.

But most hospital administrators—even if they want their institutions to provide full medical coverage for every critically injured emergency indigent patient brought to their facilities—cannot "push" their specialists, experts point out, because all too often the hospital depends on the specialist to fill their beds with paying patients.

"If a hospital tries to put heat on an orthopedic surgeon to come in the middle of the night to treat for free people who don't have money, he'll just pack up and go to the hospital down the street and take his paying patients with him," says one physician.

Although "if-physicians-don't-get-paid-we-can't-treat-patients" is an often-repeated litany to rationalize the transfers of indigent emergency patients, some physicians point out that a handful of hospitals committed to dispensing care to all patients do insist that specialists on their staffs treat indigents who need emergency care quickly.

"St. Luke [Hospital of Pasadena] is very serious about rendering good care," says one physician who has worked in a county facility and who is now in private practice at another hospital.

"When a physician arbitrarily punts a patient down to county because he doesn't want to be bothered, they [hospital administrators] land on that doctor hard.

"It's not a rich hospital but they take their responsibility to the patient seriously. Other hospitals in my experience don't."

But by in large, experts say, many physicians do not live up to their responsibility for taking care of indigent emergency patients.

"There are plenty of doctors who do come in, who have been up all night operating on some guy and have never gotten a nickel out of it," says one prominent physician.

"But private physicians on hospitals have had a soft ride. They use their hospital's emergency room to [take care of their] own patients if they have a problem after hours.

"But they have not had to dirty their hands, to take their fair share of unfunded patients."

The unwillingness to pressure specialists into caring for indigent emergency patients has its greatest impact on the victim of a serious head injury.

Many of these patients, experts say, should not be moved after they have been brought to a private hospital—especially if they are unconscious or show other indications that their mental condition has been impaired.

Nevertheless, in its survey of the records of more than 300 patients, the *I.P-T* found that 54 patients with head injuries had been transferred, often after only short stays in the emergency rooms of private hospitals.

Many of these patients, the *I,P-T* found, were moved even though their injuries were severe—including patients who had been shot in the head, who had stopped breathing, were in comas or in "altered" mental states, or who had also suffered other severe internal injuries.

And because it is virtually impossible for most hospitals to recruit neurosurgeons to provide care to indigent emergency patients, experts familiar with the transfer system confirmed that these patients are often shipped out with little or no regard for their ability to withstand the move.

"At least 20 to 30 percent of the patients with severe head trauma sent to the county were unstable," says one neurosurgeon who recently left a county facility to establish private practice.

"Some were not breathing and were not intubated [to provide oxygen]. Some were bleeding and did not have functioning IVs [to give blood or other fluids] or only had small IVs when massive [support] was needed."

While some hospital administrators argue that lack of specialist cooperation prevents them from extending full emergency care to indigents, others say that their transfer policies are dictated by lack of key facilities needed to treat some of the indigent emergency patients brought to them.

Drug overdose patients must be transferred, many administrators and some emergency room physicians argue, because many of these men and women are combative or need intensive psychiatric care—psychiatric care beyond the capabilities of their institutions.

Emergency medicine specialists, meanwhile, point out that patients who have taken an overdose of drugs need, first and foremost, close medical scrutiny—especially if they cannot tell the physician, because they are unconscious or because they do not know, the nature or quantity of the drugs they took.

Even the fully conscious drug overdose patient, many experts say, should not be transferred quickly.

"If the patient is sleepy and looking at you, should you transfer him?" asks one well-known expert who has scrutinized the EAP closely.

He answers his own question:

"No. Because you may put them into the ambulance and they are alert and breathing.

"But what may happen is that as they are getting a tour of the city, the drug takes more and more effect and by the time they arrive at the receiving hospital they are without respiration or blood pressure and may need vigorous resuscitation and may even die.

"And yet, overdoses get transferred all the time."

In its survey of the EAP, the *I,P-T* found that the transfer of overdose patients is common—including the transfer of patients who have dangerously combined tranquilizers with alcohol, patients who have taken several drugs, and patients who are deep in comas.

In one case, for example, a 20-year-old woman was taken to a private hospital emergency room because she had taken an overdose of drugs and was in a coma.

The patient survived her ordeal.

But according to a medical expert who reviewed the case for the *I,P-T,* she was probably lucky to do so: The private hospital, the expert points out, failed to take an electrocardiogram even though it is common medical knowledge that many drugs affect the heart rhythm and could lead to fatal heart attacks.

Moreover, according to all indications, the hospital did not make an attempt to pump her stomach to insure that any remaining drugs would not be absorbed into her body. Nor was she given medication to help her fight off the effects of the overdose.

She was transferred to a county facility within five hours of her arrival at the hospital—though most drug experts say that an overdose patient should be monitored for at least 12 hours.

Finally, the expert points out, no provisions were made to support her breathing while she was on the road to the county hospital.

"The woman," the expert concludes, "was not handled right and should not have been transferred."

The rationalization that lack of specialized facilities prevents them from extending care to emergency patients who could just as well be treated at a county facility extends also to problems involving the heart.

A patient should not be transferred, experts say, if there are indications that he is having a heart attack.

"You have to assume that someone you think has an acute myocardial infarction or unstable angina is not transferrable just because percentage-wise they can get into trouble with an arrythmia in which they can go from perfectly normal to no pulse in a matter of seconds," says Dr. Robert Fitzgerald, an emergency room physician at Dr. David Brotman Memorial Hospital in Culver City.

"To transfer someone with an acute myocardial infarction is not standard community practice."

Adds another physician with long-standing experience in emergency medicine:

"If you walk into an emergency room and say I have a crushing chest pain and [if the doctor writes down] this person has a high probability of myocardial infarction, medically that person should not be transferred.

"That person should be in the coronary care unit immediately because the mortality rate is between 50 and 60 percent. Moreover, if they are going to die, it is going to be within the first four hours."

And yet, though experts are adamant that heart attack—or even suspected heart attack—patients should not be shunted about, the practice seems to go on.

Moreover, many medical experts say, patients whose physical state indicates that they might be on the verge of a major heart attack can—and should be—watched even if a bed is not immediately available in a coronary care unit.

"You have to find a corner to put that patient in, hook him up to a monitor, and [have] a nurse sit there and watch him," one emergency specialist says.

But rather than take the trouble, experts say, many hospitals simply transfer out heart attack victims.

In several instances, one expert with EAP experience says, patients have been transferred from private hospitals even though there was clear medical indication they were in danger of developing a full-blown heart attack.

"Work-up time and transfer time eats up most of the four hours [during which the patient is in danger of dying]," the expert says. "And there is no way to adequately monitor a patient and respond to their needs if they are going to be rocketing around the county in an ambulance."

The experience of one 53-year-old woman seems to be typical of suspected heart attack victims who are transferred from private to county facilities.

She was brought by ambulance to a small emergency room because she had suddenly developed severe chest pains. The admitting physician suspected that she had been working up to a full-blown heart attack.

He ordered, among other things, that an electrocardiogram be administered. And because an EKG is often inconclusive, he also ordered that a specialized test—a blood test for certain enzymes released by heart muscle when it is injured or killed during a myocardial infarction—be performed.

The order for the specialized test—known as a CPK—demonstrated that he was seriously concerned about the woman, an expert consulted by the *I,P-T* points out.

Yet, despite this apparent concern, the woman was transferred out of the hospital after only one hour and fifteen minutes—even though a laboratory cannot complete a CPK test in less than "several" hours.

"By and large, it makes no sense to transfer this patient," the expert says.

In fact, say many experts, no one whose heart has been compromised in any fashion—including assault victims who have been stabbed or shot in the chest or the car accident victim who, among other things, has suffered a chest injury because he has slammed against the car's steering wheel—should be subjected to a transfer.

"If I just got into a car accident and hit my chest on the steering wheel," says Dr. Robert Rothstein, director of the emergency room at Harbor–UCLA Medical Center, "that's a serious injury . . . as serious as a myocardial infarction.

"A lot of people do fine, but a lot develop arrhythmias and die. That is an unstable patient who should be admitted to a coronary care unit for 48 to 72 hours before he has been proven to be stable."

And yet, transfers of patients suspected of having suffered myocardial contusions are not at all uncommon, an examination of transfer records shows.

One Long Beach man, for example, was involved in a serious automobile accident in Compton in March 1979. He was taken to an emergency room. The physician who saw him there suspected that he had suffered "possible cardial contusion."

In this case, however, only an EKG was done. Without the benefit of additional tests, he was, after only one hour and 11 minutes, placed in an ambulance and shipped to Martin Luther King Medical Center.

Another man, 45, was stabbed in the chest in the early hours of a June morning and rushed to a hospital near the Iglewood area.

The physician who examined him suspected that the knife used to

assault the man had struck his heart and may have caused a tampon-
ade, a condition in which blood accumulates in the pericardium, the
membrane that contains the heart.

And yet, despite this diagnosis and despite the fact that the man had
no blood pressure when he was brought into the emergency room, he
was not given the immediate surgery he should have had.

Rather, he was held for nearly 10 hours before he was transferred to
a county hospital where he was rushed into the operating room.

LONG WAIT IN EMERGENCY ROOM NEARLY FATAL

It had been a routine soccer practice. But during one of those free-for-
alls so characteristic when six-year-olds are involved, Robert Boyd had
fallen and had been kicked in the head.

Though a bit shaken, he assured his coach he was all right, finished
practice, and went home.

But two hours later, he began to complain of headache and dizziness.
His parents drove him to the local hospital, the one with the big "Basic
Emergency Service" sign.

Robert was checked over quickly, patted on the head, told to rest.

Within minutes, however, he slipped into unconsciousness. Hour by
hour, as the boy lay in an examining room, the coma deepened.

Not until six hours later—when the boy was close to death—did the
emergency room physician call an ambulance and have him transferred to USC–L.A. County Medical Center.

By the time the ambulance company arrived at the medical center,
Robert was no longer breathing.

"We didn't even take his clothes off or wait for his parents to get here
to sign a release," one of the neurosurgeons recalls. "We just rushed
him into the operating room. He had a blood clot between the skull
bone and the brain."

Robert survived, though he required physical therapy at Rancho Los
Amigos, one of the country's leading rehabilitation centers, to overcome
nerve damage which, the surgeon believes, was probably attributable
to the long delay before surgery was performed.

EAP SUFFERS FROM LACK OF QUALITY CONTROL, USE OF INADEQUATE HOSPITALS

The official stand—taken by virtually everyone associated with the
Emergency Aid Program—is that every one of the 73 hospitals participating in EAP is well qualified to handle critically ill emergency
patients.

"All [the hospitals participating in EAP] are licensed, have passed inspection by the Joint Commission on the Accreditation of Hospitals," says Douglas Steele, a deputy director of the Department of Health Services.

"It seems to us that that is prima-facie evidence they are operating within the requirements of the law and are acceptable."

But medical experts disagree.

Many of the hospitals participating in the EAP, these experts say, are ill suited to handle critically ill or injured patients.

"The system takes seriously injured patients and puts them in institutions not prepared to take care of them," says Dr. Kenneth Waxman, a surgeon at Harbor–UCLA Medical Center.

To a large extent, medical experts say, hospitals with less than 150 beds often do not have sufficient facilities to provide support for critically injured or seriously ill patients and often do not hire physicians trained in emergency medicine to work in their emergency rooms.

"When you get down to 100 to 150 beds, you are more likely to be in a motel-like hospital which functions 9-to-5, five days a week," says Dr. Jerry Hughes, director of the emergency room at Long Beach Community Hospital.

"A 150-bed hospital is not likely to have the volume or revenue [to draw specialists who can deal with emergency care]."

The result, says a physician who worked in a county facility and is now in private practice, is that the EAP is seriously compromised by the participation of these small institutions.

"Risks cannot be avoided when there are so many emergency rooms that do not have full medical services and surgical backup," this physician says. "The patient is only a little better off in that emergency room than he was in the street."

Yet, of the 73 hospitals participating in the EAP program, 18 have fewer than 150 beds.

During calendar year 1979, all EAP hospitals transferred 19,821 patients.

The 18 hospitals with less than 150 beds transferred more than 4,000 patients to the county—almost 20 percent of the 1979 total.

And of the small hospitals, Morningside Hospital—an institution with only 124 beds—transferred out 1,217 patients. Greater El Monte Community Hospital, with only 115 beds, transferred 675 patients.

Although the inclusion of small hospitals in the EAP program is, in the eyes of many experts, a serious flaw in the system, it is by no means the only barrier to the delivery of adequate medical care.

Hospitals—large and small—in the EAP are essentially given free rein to do as much or as little as they want for the indigent emergency patient because there are few, if any, "watchdogs" to monitor the system effectively.

The EAP office, for example, has formal responsibility for monitoring the manner in which the hospitals carry out their medical duties.

Much—if not all—of the monitoring is carried out by a registered nurse.

County officials say that the nurse—who, among other things, looks over a log maintained in each emergency room, talks with the emergency room nursing supervisor and the medical director, inspects the emergency room's hygiene and medical supplies—visits each hospital four times a year.

But because the nurse has other responsibilities—she must also spend four hours at her desk, waiting for those hospitals that choose to keep indigent patients to call for county approval of charges—she only has four hours a day in which to carry out her inspections.

Thus, because there are 72 hospitals she must visit quarterly (the 73rd is on Catalina Island and is usually not inspected more than once a year), she can only spend an average of 3.4 hours per hospital per year—travel time to and from each of the institutions in the 4,000-square-mile county notwithstanding.

County officials, moreover, admit that the nurse, even if she should find that a hospital is not providing adequate care for indigent patients, has no power to order changes but can only "make strong suggestions for improvement."

The county's only other attempt to infuse the EAP with a semblance of medical rationality came in the mid-1970s with the formation of the Medical Alert Center (MAC) at the USC–L.A. County Medical Center.

The alert center was organized, in large part, to give the county a better way of responding to large-scale disasters, to muster and coordinate medical response to earthquakes, fires, bombings.

But it was also charged with responsibility for coordinating transfer of indigent patients from private hospitals to one of the four county hospitals.

Before MAC was established, the transfer of patients was carried out when the physician at an emergency room in a private hospital called one of the county facilities and asked if physicians there were prepared to accept the patient.

Because the physicians at the county facilities were—and still are—largely overworked residents and interns who did not relish the idea of receiving an unending stream of critically ill patients, sources say, phone conversations about transfers all too often deteriorated into screaming matches.

Thus, many private hospital emergency room physicians, rather than call the county, would simply put a patient, stable or not, into an ambulance for transfer.

MAC, it was thought, would stop the transfer of unstable patients: Physicians would be able to talk to a dispassionate dispatcher who, rather than argue with the doctor, would concentrate on finding a bed for the patient in one of the four county facilities.

And physicians in private hospitals, realizing that the county would accept the patient in any case, would take more trouble to insure that the patient was being transferred in as sound a condition as possible.

And to some extent, various health experts say, MAC has brought some order to the chaotic EAP transfer system.

"MAC is helpful ... because they have speeded up transfers and locating beds in burn centers when you have a burn patient," says Steven Hirsch, assistant administrator of Marina Mercy Hospital.

But like everything else about the Emergency Aid Program, MAC's role in the transfer of patients often seems better in theory than in practice.

Many hospitals, sources say, still do not bother to call MAC to discuss the transfer of patients.

"Our use of MAC is minimal," says Dr. Stephen Shea, director of the emergency department at St. Mary Medical Center in Long Beach. "Unless we know Harbor–UCLA Medical Center is overloaded, we call them directly. We always have and we have never been told to do it otherwise."

Although MAC is staffed by specially trained personnel and even though two physicians—Dr. Gail Anderson, director of the emergency department at USC and Dr. Gerald C. Crary, the associate director of the department—are on call to help make decisions in difficult cases, physicians say MAC's ability to bring medical rationality to transfers is limited.

"If you talk to MAC, you may not be talking to someone qualified to ask questions," says Dr. Shea. "It is more appropriate to have physician-to-physician contact or valuable information is lost."

MAC's greatest shortcoming, however, is that its personnel is not, as one expert puts it, "on the firing line."

When someone from a private hospital calls to say that a patient needs transfer, experts say, a MAC dispatcher can ask the proper questions to make sure that the patient is stable for movement.

"But there is no question you can fool them," says one emergency room physician. "I can take someone who has gastrointestinal bleeding and looks terrible and tell them that his vital signs look fine."

MAC dispatchers, moreover, have only limited opportunity to review firsthand the patients whose transfer they approve. Only a fraction of the scores of patients whose transfers MAC arranges are brought to USC–L.A. County Medical Center, the operation's headquarters.

"You call the center and say I have a patient, he is stable, but we can't handle him because we haven't got a surgeon here and MAC says, 'OK, this is where the next bed is available,'" says one emergency room director. Most of the time, if not all of the time, that person will not be aware of the status of the patient when he arrives.

"So if the patient is described as stable and having all his bodily parts and then arrives with three limbs missing and no blood pressure, he [the MAC dispatcher] won't even know it."

Even that old workhorse of medical practice—the medical record— fails to bring any rationality to the transfer system.

Under the provisions of the EAP, a patient transferred from a private hospital must be accompanied by a full set of records—results of laboratory tests, a summary of procedures performed, copies of X-rays taken.

But even in defending the EAP and stoutly denying that wholesale inappropriate transfers occur, county officials admit that in at least half of the transfers, patients arrive at the county hospital without adequate records.

And some physicians charged with supervising the care of critically ill or seriously injured patients passed on to their institutions say they are wary of using records provided by a hospital that obviously has no interest in treating the patient thoroughly in the first place.

"If the patient was transferred [in unstable condition] in the first place, you have to wonder who the hell this person is who would transfer him," says one expert with intensive and long-standing familiarity with the transfer system.

"What I know is that the patient who arrived is [according to records that come with him] not the patient who left, that they get here considerably worse off than when they left the first institution.

"You might question if the records have been carefully filled out not to reflect the instability of the patient."

More than anything, however, discussions with critics of the program reveal a deep-seated pessimism, a feeling that little or nothing can be done to bring about the delivery of rational care to indigents under EAP.

Although many hospital administrators say they could live without EAP patients, it is obvious that participation in the system is advantageous to their institutions.

Hospitals that belong to the EAP are guaranteed a steady flow of emergency patients—a number above and beyond those that would normally trickle into their emergency rooms—simply because public and private ambulance companies know these institutions are officially sanctioned to receive these patients.

"If you are not in the EAP network, none of these patients are brought to you and no ambulance will come except ambulances that are ordered by private physicians," says Dr. Morgan.

"Hospitals have very high fixed overhead costs and the marginal improvement in their financial picture with increasing number of patients is great. So if you have a drop in your patient census, it becomes more and more difficult for you to make ends meet.

"Also, frankly, the people who come in under EAP are people who are badly injured or who have significant problems since they are so ill. These people require more care and the more care you deliver, the more you have to do for them and the more you bill."

Once all patients brought in under the EAP are in the emergency room, the hospital has the luxury of sorting them out: to keep those whose insurance coverage will help guarantee a healthy balance sheet and then ship out to the county those who would contribute nothing.

"Some people would say the community hospital is, in a sense, a private enterprise and that the present system works fine because God made county hospitals to take care of patients who don't have insurance," says Dr. Fitzgerald.

Although most EAP hospitals transfer out those patients who do not have insurance, some do keep a few—if only for public relations reasons.

But, according to some critics, even when a hospital does keep an EAP patient for full and intensive treatment, there often is an ulterior motive.

Several of the hospitals in the EAP program, the critics say, are accredited as teaching institutions.

"If a patient comes in who looks to have teaching value, they'll admit him and he'll get first rate care through the house staff training program," says one physician.

"If the patient does not look to be an educational treat, then the patient goes down to the county."

Thus, say some critics of the EAP, any attempt to modify the system is likely to meet with opposition.

Moreover, many critics say, the system has stumbled along largely unchallenged because its magnitude simply inhibits would-be reformers.

"The transfer of the unfunded, unwanted, unmanageable patients is of such order of magnitude that people who [are forced to deal with them at county hospitals] are doing everything they already can by simply taking care of these patients on a daily basis," says a former high ranking county official who grappled with the EAP for years.

"Beyond that, they have not been able to go beyond that and [ask themselves] 'My God! How can all this happen.'"

And even if someone within the county wants to do something, this official says, it seems to be a person who perceives him or herself as only a cog in a massive wheel.

"They think they are not the right people, that they don't have power. They perceive themselves only as functionaries in the system. And that goes right down to and includes the doctors."

A CLOSER LOOK AND MEDICAL REVIEW OF 26 PATIENTS DUMPED BY HOSPITALS

A 20-year-old woman, deep in a coma, is put in an ambulance and, at the height of rush hour, is transferred 15 miles to a county hospital. A 42-year-old man, seriously injured in an automobile accident, is allowed to linger on a community hospital's emergency room table for nearly two hours before an ambulance is summoned to move him 21 miles to L.A. County–USC Medical Center.

A 62-year-old woman with a serious head injury is given a tetanus shot, some intravenous fluids, and transferred out after an hour and half.

In its investigation of the Emergency Aid Program, the *Independent, Press-Telegram* gained access to the medical details of treatment accorded to 317 patients who received emergency treatment under the EAP.

In its attempts to determine whether the program is meeting the needs of those it allegedly serves, the newspaper asked medical experts to review dozens of medical histories.

The woman in the coma, the accident victim, the 62-year-old woman—and the other patients whose confrontation with EAP are detailed today—are people, who, in the opinion of these experts, were mishandled in the emergency room to which the patients were first taken.

The experts included:

• A surgeon with extensive background in treatment of critically injured patients.

• A physician who specializes in emergency medicine and who has analyzed care given to some patients under EAP.

To insure that all possible viewpoints were represented, the *I,P-T* asked the Hospital Council of Southern California to choose another expert to review these cases.

Council officials pointed out that the organization deals largely with administrative problems of concern to its members but agreed to ask several hospital administrators to nominate a physician.

The hospital administrators contacted by the council declined to participate.

As a result, the *I,P-T* sought out the emergency room director of a hospital that participates in the EAP and which transfers a moderate number of patients to county facilities each year.

The physician agreed to comment on the cases presented him, provided his identity not be revealed.

In its investigation, the *I,P-T* obtained names and medical histories of patients treated at the following facilities:

Little Company of Mary Hospital, Hawthorne Community Hospital, St. Mary Medical Center, Hollywood Presbyterian Medical Center, San Pedro Peninsula Hospital, La Mirada Hospital, Centinela Hospital Medical Center, Queen of Angels Hospital, California Hospital.

Morningside Hospital, St. Francis Medical Center, Santa Teresita Hospital, St. Joseph Medical Center, Santa Monica Hospital Medical Center, Dominguez Valley Hospital, Baldwin Park Hospital, Santa Maria Hospital, Greater El Monte Community Hospital, and Dr. David M. Brotman Memorial Hospital.

In some instances, cases came from institutions that some experts believe render adequate, and often excellent, emergency care to indigent patients.

Moreover, some hospitals not included in this list were often cited by some medical experts as institutions with a serious disregard for the welfare of emergency patients.

To respect patient privacy, names of the men, women, and children involved in these cases will not be used.

In the summaries below, the term "consultant" refers to the surgeon and the emergency room specialist. The E.R. physician is the director of an EAP hospital emergency room.

1. *Patient:* 20-year-old man who nearly drowned in a neighborhood pool and suffered severe heart failure as a result.

Emergency room action: Blood tests given. Some intravenous fluids administered. Patient held 2½ hours and transferred approximately eight miles to Los Angeles County–USC Medical Center.

Consultants: Patient was in "great trouble," and needed aggressive medical help but did not receive it. Records show patient given medication usually administered when circulatory system is failing and patient is close to death.

Yet, despite evidence patient critically ill, an electrocardiogram to determine extent of heart damage was not done. Kidneys also suffer from oxygen deprivation in a near drowning, but no tests were done to determine if his kidneys had indeed been affected. No X-rays performed to determine if lungs affected.

Transferring E.R. physician: Agrees that transfer was inappropriate. "They saw that he was seriously ill. He could have gone bad quickly."

2. *Patient:* 26-year-old man stabbed in abdomen.

Emergency room action: Intravenous fluids given. Tetanus shot. Blood tests. Blood typed but no blood given. Patient held two hours and transferred 11 miles to Harbor General–UCLA Medical Center.

Consultants: The patient should not have been transferred because it is unwise to move someone with an abdominal stab wound. If transfer absolutely necessary patient should have been held at least six hours— and possibly overnight—to make sure he was indeed stable.

E.R. physician: A questionable transfer. They were worried enough to set aside four units of blood for him, but transferred him out within two hours.

3. *Patient:* Six-year-old boy with open skull fracture suffered when he was struck by an automobile.

Emergency room action: Oxygen given. Intravenous fluids administered. Spine and skull X-rays taken. Patient held 36 minutes, transferred six miles to LA–USC.

Consultants: It makes no sense to transfer someone with an open skull fracture. The child should have been taken to the operating room as fast as possible.

E.R. physician: This is not a patient I would transfer. An open skull fracture is a significant trauma.

4. *Patient:* 20-year-old woman in coma as a result of drug overdose.

Emergency room action: Blood tests performed. Apparent steps to deal with heart beat irregularities. Intravenous fluids given. Urinalysis tests. Patient held 5½ hours then transferred 15 miles to LA–USC.

Consultants: A comatose patient should not be transferred. If absolutely necessary to move patient to another hospital, it should be done only if action is taken to help support the patient's breathing—for example, by placing an endotracheal tube in the mouth to keep airway open.

In this patient's case, nothing was done to insure that the patient's breathing could be sustained during the 15-mile transfer, which began at 5:30 P.M., the height of rush-hour traffic.

Transferring hospital personnel did not adminster electrocardiogram to determine if heart was affected by drugs she had taken. No attempt was made to wash out patient's stomach. No medication was given to counteract effects of drug overdose. No X-rays were taken to determine if patient had, while unconscious, breathed contents of stomach into lungs.

E.R. physician: "I would not transfer patient in a coma unless I was riding along. The patient could go into respiratory arrest, could have a cardiac arrest, or could breathe in contents of the stomach."

5. *Patient:* A 51-year-old man with head injury, source unknown.

Emergency room action: Blood tests performed. Drugs given to counter possible drug overdose. Intravenous fluids given. Back, chest, spine, and skull X-rays. Patient held one hour and 40 minutes, transferred eight miles to LA–USC.

Consultants: Patient was given two liters of fluids, which implies he was in shock. Medication notes imply he was unconscious. But nothing was done to determine if his condition was due to hemorrhaging. Little or nothing done to assess head injury.

E.R. physician: Patient should not have been transferred. He was given 2000 ccs of fluids in under two hours "and that means that they worried he was in shock. This was a sick patient."

[Ed. Note: The remaining cases in the article have been omitted.]

COUNTY'S TRANSFER PROGRAM BLEEDS TAXPAYERS THROUGH OVERPAYMENTS

Los Angeles County's unique program aimed at ensuring distinguished emergency medical care to the poor has become an administrative and financing calamity with waste reaching into the millions, a continuing investigation by the *Independent, Press-Telegram* has discovered.

The size and cost of the taxpayer-supported program—the Emergency Aid Program—has grown beyond all expectations since its fledgling days in 1947, and several officials close to the program acknowledge that it now operates without adequate planning or controls.

Those who speak officially for the program deny that EAP is beset with problems.

However, a three-month investigation by the *I,P-T* found case after case of waste and abuse within the program.

The primary aim of the private hospitals participating in the program is to make money on tests and then ship critically and seriously ill or injured patients off to county-operated hospitals, says one physician, who is regarded as an authority in trauma and emergency medicine and has firsthand knowledge of EAP.

In the last two fiscal years, private hospitals have collected more than $4 million from the county through the program.

Judging from reviews of confidential medical and financial records, the amount of waste of taxpayer dollars may be as high as 50 percent of the county's reimbursement to the hospitals, the medical experts say.

"The whole name of the game is to get the patient to another place, to make some money on the tests, and then transfer the patient so you don't have to take care of him," says a physician who until recently worked at the Los Angeles County–USC Medical Center, the largest of the county-operated hospitals, which receives thousands of patients who are shunted there by the private hospitals yearly.

The waste occurs because of the way private hospitals manage to use the program and because the Department of Health Services operates the system based more on faith that it is working properly rather than on adequate safeguards.

The result has been the rendering of useless and unnecessary tests and X-rays on patients by private hospitals and widespread duplication of services after those patients are transferred to county facilities.

"Despite all the money that is spent, it just does not do patients much good," says a noted physician who has witnessed the program firsthand for years. "Money makes all the rules. And medical care is impeded."

During its investigation, the *I,P-T* obtained financial records of 100 patients who were treated under and paid for by the county's EAP. Those documents were examined by physicians who are recognized as experts in emergency medicine and hospital administration.

Among the findings were:

• Many hospitals frequently take laboratory tests that require several hours, sometimes as many as 12, to complete. Yet they transfer patients to county-operated hospitals before the test results are ready, requiring the county to duplicate them.

• Hospitals sometimes take tests and perform other services for patients that medical experts believe are "unnecessary" and "inappropriate."

• Many tests—for which the county pays—have to be repeated because private hospitals routinely fail to send complete medical records when they transfer EAP patients to county-operated hospitals.

• Some hospitals "overtreat" patients at the county's expense in attempts to reduce the risks of malpractice suits against them.

Also, the *I,P-T* found that despite previously known weaknesses in the program, the county health establishment has taken no formal steps to correct them.

And although the county has overpaid private hospitals by millions of dollars, the Department of Health Services still lacks a comprehensive and formal system of monitoring and controlling costs.

Since the program began—when Los Angeles County had only half of its current 7.1 million people, and the deserts and coastal areas remained substantially undeveloped—the emergency program has ballooned into a massive and, many people contend, unmanageable plan.

"One can't demonstrate that a system exists, because the word denotes certain sensitivity, interaction, feedback, and internal evaluation," says a physician who has worked closely with EAP for several years. "There is very little of that."

And a highly placed official within the county's Department of Health Services admits, "One of the problems is that you can't find a single person in the department who has a feel or understanding of the whole program."

The county has contracts with 21 ambulance companies and 73 private hospitals that span the nation's most populated county. Of those, about half have joined the program since 1967.

The county's rate of reimbursement—which is tied to the state's Medi-Cal fee schedule—averages about 80 percent of the hospitals' normal charges, according to health officers.

Many hospital administrators, bolstered by their powerful professional arm, the Hospital Council of Southern California, contend private medical facilities are losing money because of the level of reimbursement.

But the Emergency Aid Program has evolved into big business— "megabucks," as one physician, who asked not be named, put it.

The point is underscored by the hospitals' mounting opposition to a recent county proposal to cut EAP funding.

In 1978 there were 1,525,999 emergency room "visits" at the 73 hospitals participating in EAP, according to figures obtained from the Department of Health Services. Of those, 126,269, or 8.27 percent, were EAP referrals, although only about 26,000 patients a year are ultimately determined to be indigent, and their medical bills are covered by Los Angeles County.

In fiscal 1977-78 the county reimbursed those hospitals $7,674,464, according to the county health department records. Last fiscal year, the hospitals collected $4,770,611 from the county for participating in the EAP program.

The county expects to spend about the same this fiscal year, according to officials.

But much of that money is being wasted, according to detailed examinations of records for 100 EAP patients by medical experts who are close to the program.

In the 100 cases examined, the hospitals billed the county for $24,993 for treating EAP patients before transferring them. They were ultimately paid $13,060 after the bills were adjusted downward to reflect the state-established Medi-Cal rates.

"Virtually all" of that money was spent unnecessarily, says one noted emergency physician, who see EAP patients almost daily.

At least half of the services the patients received in the emergency rooms were either not required or had to be duplicated later on by the county, says the physician, who asked not to be named.

One of the most common practices of the hospitals, the *I,P-T* found, is taking X-rays of the skull in suspected head injury cases—a practice that for years has generally been regarded as "virtually useless."

Of 27 known or suspected head injury cases, the hospitals took skull X-rays in 26, according to records obtained by the *I,P-T*.

And in one drug overdose and two seizure cases, the hospitals also took skull X-rays, those records show.

The county paid a total of $947 for the X-rays in those cases, official county documents show.

"Skull X-rays are rarely needed," one of the nation's foremost neurosurgeons, who asked not to be named, says. "Because people with fractures of the skull are treated in the same way as people who don't have fracture of the skull. The only thing that indicates treatment-is what has happened to the brain, and you assess the brain based on the neurological examination—patient's responsiveness [and] reflexes. . . .

"X-rays of skulls do not give you that. If a patient has a depressed fracture of the skull, you diagnose not with an X-ray but by looking at the wound."

And the emergency room director at one of the large private hospitals acknowledges that it has been recognized at least since 1972 that skull X-rays are not needed.

Dr. Marshall Morgan of Santa Monica Hospital says those X-rays are ordered "less and less, because they are never useful."

"There have been several studies," Morgan says, ". . . which indicate that skull film is not a very useful diagnostic tool.

"Even if the findings of a fractured skull were useful, which they usually are not, a lot of people are having skull X-rays done when there is no reasonable chance that they have a skull fracture. . . . You had a situation where people were getting skull X-rays when any idiot could have told you they don't have a broken skull. . . .

"The skull X-ray will not tell you anything about whether the brain is damaged. It will not tell you if there is a blood clot inside pushing on the brain. It will not tell you any of that stuff. If the patient has a depressed skull fracture where the fracture might be pushing on the brain, you can tell that by feeling it with a finger. Essentially, it is not a very useful test."

But of the 27 known or suspected head injury cases examined by the *I,P-T*, five were patients treated at Morgan's Santa Monica Hospital. And in every case the hospital charged—and collected from the county—for skull X-rays.

Morgan defends the practice by saying that historically it has been one way of avoiding malpractice suits: "One of the reasons given for that is that . . . [although] I don't know what it [skull X-ray] is going to tell me, you have to do it because if anything happens to the patient subsequently and you haven't done everything you could do, you're going to be in trouble."

The practice of taking unnecessary tests is not limited to skull X-rays, however. In case after case the *I,P-T* found hospitals performing tests that medical experts acknowledge were not appropriate.

"Hospitals frequently overtreat patients," an official of one of the nation's largest medical insurance companies said. "Sometimes they do it because they are afraid of malpractice. But they also do it—give unnecessary tests and X-rays—to help make more money."

And Los Angeles County is doing the same.

"Without any question, much of what goes on in pit-stop medicine is the acquisition of non-useful data that cannot be used by anyone anywhere else," says a noted physician at the UCLA Medical Center who has firsthand knowledge of the EAP program.

According to emergency medical experts consulted by the *I,P-T*, the number of laboratory tests and X-rays necessary can be substantially reduced if the private hospitals are going to transfer an emergency patient.

They pointed out, for example, that emergency rooms do not have to take blood counts, urinalyses, X-rays, and other tests on a routine basis—particularly if the hospitals are going to refuse to admit the patients or decline to send medical records.

In its review of 100 patient financial records, however, the *I,P-T* found that routine urinalyses were performed 29 times, routine blood counts were taken 32 times, twice hospitals typed and crossed blood without giving the patients blood transfusions, and eight times cultures—tests for infectious microorganisms—were taken.

Also, the *I,P-T* discovered that in those 100 cases the private hospitals took 143 X-rays in addition to the skull X-rays. For those the county paid the hospitals $2,227, according to official documents.

Hospitals frequently take lab tests that require several hours before the results are ready—and in the meantime they transfer the patients.

Two County–USC Medical Center physicians who are in charge of the Medical Alert Center, Gail W. Anderson and Gerald C. Crary, acknowledge that many lab tests take long periods of time to get results.

The responsibilities of Crary and Anderson include overseeing the transfer of EAP patients from private hospitals to county facilities.

In drug overdose cases, for example, it is common for a variety of tests to be performed by the private hospitals, according to records obtained by the *I,P-T.*

"You cannot base your decision on what to do on the basis of laboratory results," says Anderson. "Most of those are six hours away—long-term turnaround time."

Department of Health Services officials say they are not aware of hospitals performing unnecessary tests or that duplication of services is a major problem.

But the department lacks a systematic procedure of reviewing what it is paying for.

And a ranking official of the department, who asked not to be named, puts it more bluntly:

"I don't think there is any way we can monitor the costs. We're pretty far removed—even with Anderson and Crary, and these are the guys closest to it."

Among the problems plaguing the Emergency Aid Program, thus sharply increasing the costs to taxpayers, is the routine practice of hospitals of not sending medical records when they transfer patients to county-operated facilities—requiring the county to duplicate the X-rays and laboratory tests.

The hospitals are supposed to send charts and other complete medical records whenever they transfer a patient, according to Department of Health Services officials.

But in the 100 cases examined by the *I,P-T*, only twice did a hospital, Cedars–Sinai Medical Center, attempt to meet that obligation.

Yet when questioned, emergency room physicians and hospital administrators maintain they never transfer a patient without sending the medical records.

"There's no use in doing it all over," says Steven Hirsch, assistant administrator of Marina Mercy Hospital.

But according to confidential medical records and interviews with dozens of physicians close to the EAP program, seldom are complete patient records and charts sent with the transferred patient.

It means that the county not only pays for services performed at the hospital where the patient is first taken, but then must pick up the costs again when those very same services are duplicated at one of the county hospitals.

Example: In November 1978, a 97-year-old woman, Maria Sanchez, was taken to St. Mary Medical Center–Bauer Hospital in Long Beach, suffering from lower-lobe pneumonia, hypnoxia, and dehydration. She received a battery of X-rays, lab tests, and other services. The bill, in just under five hours, had risen to $540. Then she was transferred to the county-operated Harbor–UCLA Medical Center.

"The chest X-ray is OK," says a medical expert who reviewed the case for the *I,P-T*. "But the lab fees, including routine electrolyte, calcium, acythone, and cultures, are not indicated if the patient is to be transferred. Routine blood count and urinalysis should be done if the patient is to be admitted. But the patient was transferred, so the tests were inappropriate."

Example: Thirty-four-year-old Donald Edwards was rushed to Studebaker Community Hospital after taking an overdose of drugs. In the emergency room several lab tests were taken, his heart was monitored, and he received fluids and had his stomach pumped.

Then, 95 minutes later, and after Edwards' medical bill had reached $265, he was transferred to Martin Luther King Hospital for further treatment.

"If the patient is transferred, they [lab tests] would be duplicated," says one authority on emergency medicine who reviewed the records. "They were unnecessary, even for getting a base line [at the private hospital]. Because if they are in another hospital for an hour or two, the county hospital would have to establish its own base lines."

In those two cases, the county was billed a total of $805 and eventually paid the hospitals $350 based upon the Medi-Cal fee schedule.

Not only is the practice of not sending medical records a financial waste, but physicians acknowledge it can endanger patients by delay-ing definitive medical treatment.

"Any amount of [medical] data on the patient should be sent . . . or there's no point in having it done," says Anderson, director of County–USC Medical Center's Department of Emergency Medicine.

Crary, the associate director of that department, says, "The bigger your data base, the better your [medical] position."

Anderson estimates that in fewer than half the cases are medical records sent with transferred patients.

Crary says he believes that perhaps up to 51 percent of the time records are sent with patients.

But several physicians at county-operated hospitals say medical records seldom accompany patients who are transferred by the private hospitals.

And the practice is costing Los Angeles County taxpayers hundreds of thousands of dollars annually.

COUNTY MAY HAVE WINKED AT EAP'S OVERPAYMENTS IN TREATMENT OF POOR

Back in 1947, Los Angeles County unveiled what officials then proudly boasted was the nation's first program to guarantee quality emergency care for the poor.

Through the Emergency Aid Program, those officials promised no one in the county would ever again be denied necessary medical treatment simply because he lacked money.

What emerged, however, was not a systematic medical program but a financial scheme.

"The EAP plan itself is more financial," says Dr. Jerry Hughes, director of Long Beach Community Hospital's emergency department. "It is not an organized system of patient care. It is not a plan of action on how to respond to injury accidents, and so forth.

"I don't know if there are any clinical criteria or medical care criteria in the EAP program."

Now, 33 years later, the Emergency Aid Program has evolved into a multi-million-dollar system that ensures neither good medical care nor controls on the taxpayer's money, an investigation by the *Independent, Press-Telegram* has found.

Instead, the waste of tax dollars has reached into the millions, and the county is left operating a program that few like but even fewer seem willing to change.

There is still loose control over the EAP despite a $5 million sting in the form of overpayments by the county.

Under the two-phase Emergency Aid Program, ambulance companies agree to transport any victim in the county to the nearest emergency room. And the hospitals promise to provide whatever medical treatment the patient requires—at least until he is stabilized—regardless of his ability to pay.

Los Angeles County guarantees to pay the medical costs of indigent patients served through the program.

There currently are 73 private hospitals and 21 ambulance firms that have signed formal contracts with the county to participate in the emergency-care network.

In the last two fiscal years, according to official documents, the program has cost the county's Department of Health Services more than $17.5 million.

Los Angeles County officials, in and out of the health department, now are beginning to worry out loud about the amount of money needed to finance the Emergency Aid Program.

But a substantial part of those increasing costs could have been avoided.

The *I,P-T* has learned that the county:

• Spends hundreds of thousands of dollars annually for unnecessary and duplicated services and lacks a serious system to analyze the bills submitted by the private hospitals.

• Pays more than $1 million a year to have indigent patients transferred by ambulance from private hospitals to the four county-operated facilities but it has never conducted a formal study to determine how many of those patients were transferred when it was medically unsafe or if there is a more economical way of handling transfers.

• Does not enforce requirements that hospitals send complete medical records when they transfer patients, which adds substantially to the program's costs by requiring duplication of services.

Officials of the Department of Health Services say they are not aware of significant and widespread medical or administrative problems within the massive Emergency Aid Program which would warrant comprehensive and continuous monitoring.

But a few months ago there was the first public indication that the program lacked adequate controls.

While the Emergency Aid Program began to drastically increase in size and costs in the mid-1960s, the county's health establishment was overpaying private hospitals participating in the plan by millions of dollars.

The practice—which several sources say was an informal "under-standing" between the hospitals and the Department of Health Services—went unchecked until late last year, when another branch of the county bureaucracy discovered it.

The overpayments range from a high of $493,669 to California Hospital in downtown Los Angeles to a low of $595 to Avalon Municipal Hospital, according to official documents.

But the practice perhaps best illustrates the lack of direction the county has exerted over its own creation—the Emergency Aid Program, which several medical experts and county officials acknowledge has grown with only scant control.

The official total of overpayments to the hospitals, which the county puts at $5,311,750—a staggering 24.9 percent of its total reimbursement of $21,330,826 to them from July 1975 to March 21, 1979—is a conservative figure, officials say.

The statute of limitations prohibits the county from trying to collect for overpayments made before July 1, 1975, but several sources, who asked not to be named, say the Department of Health Services practice of overpaying the hospitals probably dates back 13 years.

Then, in 1967, the county renegotiated its EAP contracts and tied its hospital reimbursement schedule to state-established Medi-Cal fees, which average, officials say, about 80 percent of a hospital's normal charge.

Despite the contract changes, the health department continued to pay hospitals at full rates because it did not revise downward the bills submitted by the private hospitals.

The county has not attempted to determine the full amount of the overpayments, but officials privately acknowledge the figure would be millions above the $5.3 million already identified.

The county counsel's office has filed suit against the hospitals to recapture the money. The hospitals have joined together to fight being forced to repay the funds.

Several hospital officials and persons with close connections with both the county and private medical establishments told the *I,P-T* it was known all along by many—and certainly by the Department of Health Services—that the overpayments were being made.

The rationale for the practice, according to those sources, was that the county lacked the personnel to adjust by hand the thousands of bills submitted by the hospitals for treating the poor through the EAP.

"They [health department officials] knew and may even have brought it to the attention of the hospitals," says one official close to the EAP program and the hospitals. "... I think that without speaking between the two parties, that the contract was abridged—that it was abridged with the ongoing knowledge at least of the county. ... There was an implied modification in the contractual terms."

Top county health officials, who were not associated with the department at the time the overpayments were made, cautiously guard against saying their predecessors may have knowingly allowed those payments to have been made, although they acknowledge that could be the key to the case.

The department's director, Robert W. White, was not available for interviews, but his chief deputy, Richard Gates, says:

"The only way I can answer that is, I have been here two years [and] the director has been here two years, approximately. When this matter first came to our attention ... we acted quickly to stop the practice.

"I don't know, and I don't think the director knows, what went on before. I think that's going to end up being the essence of the lawsuit— or one of the key points."

Even now, however, the county's accounting system for the Emergency Aid Program remains virtually unchanged, and it has failed to aggressively correct obvious weaknesses in the system which have added substantially to the county's costs.

For example, the Department of Health Services still adjusts by hand each bill for treating indigent patients submitted by the private hospitals.

A full listing of all medical treatment and services given each patient must be submitted. Depending on the extent of the injury or illness and how long the hospital kept the patient, the bill may be three pages long, with as many as 40 items for which the hospital is charging the county.

Each item—which by law the hospitals must submit at full rate— must be hand-checked and adjusted downward so that it accurately reflects the state-established Medi-Cal fee schedule.

Each year the hospitals bill the county for between 24,000 and 26,000 indigent patients treated under the Emergency Aid Program. In 100 cases reviewed by the *I,P-T*, there were an average of 12 separate billing items for every patient.

That means that between 288,000 and 312,000 individual items must be hand-checked. Not only is it a tedious and time-consuming job, but it allows for greater error than a computerized system would, officials acknowledge.

Moreover, many medical experts have told the *I,P-T* that many of the services patients receive in the emergency rooms of private hospitals are unnecessary and that there is considerable duplications of services—all of which increases the cost to the county.

Those experts, who reviewed 100 EAP financial records obtained by the *I,P-T*, estimated that perhaps as much as half of the county's payments to the hospitals represent "waste."

However, the Department of Health Services lacks any system to formally analyze the charges and services of the private hospitals.

More importantly, the department also lacks the will to establish such a monitoring plan.

"We review each bill as it comes in," says Chief Deputy Gates. "... They are reviewed as to the appropriateness of the amount, and in most cases it's adjusted downward to reflect what Medi-Cal would have paid for that service."

Deputy Director Douglas Steele acknowledges, however, "There's not a full-blown utilization review—the correct treatment for the injury that was determined to be the diagnosis."

Furthermore, those reviewing and adjusting the bills, Steele says, are a "non-medical staff. It's a clerical bill-processing kind of staff." Gates says a continuous monitoring system would be too costly to the county: "It would represent an added administrative cost to make those kinds of reviews."

He also notes that the Department of Health Services has not felt there was "enough of a problem there to justify that administrative expense."

But the department's lack of control doesn't stop there, the *I,P-T* has learned.

For example, the county has paid $3,150,100 in the last two fiscal years to ambulance companies to transport injured or ill victims to the emergency rooms.

It has paid an additional $2,089,729 to those same companies for them to transfer patients from the private hospitals to the county-operated facilities.

A review of official documents by the *I,P-T* indicates that there is little official control over that program.

Under a special contract—officially entitled "Overflow Contracts" with the ambulance companies, the county will pay those firms to ship patients from private hospitals to the county's facilities when the county is unable to provide its own transportation.

When ambulance companies are called to transfer more than one patient, they charge full rate for the first patient but only $19.31 for the others.

But the *I,P-T* found hundreds of cases where ambulance companies were called by a hospital to make repeated runs—each time to pick up a single patient.

And the county ends up paying full rates for each run.

Last Dec. 13, for example, Schaefer's Ambulance Service had to dispatch ambulances three times to Hollywood Presbyterian Hospital—each time to haul one patient to County–USC Medical Center.

In each case, the ambulance company was paid $42.16 by the county.

Last Dec. 11, the McCormick Ambulance Service made separate runs to Daniel Freeman Hospital to pick up one patient at a time and transfer them to County–USC Medical Center.

The county had to pay McCormick its regular fee of $53.46 for each trip.

And on Dec. 27, for example, Schaefer had to make four separate trips to Queen of Angels Hospital to transfer seven patients to County–USC Medical Center. The company collected its regular fee of $39.90 four times and charged the lower rate for three of the patients.

Yet officials of two of the county's largest ambulance companies—Schaefer's and Goodhew—acknowledge that their vehicles are capable of carrying four patients at a time.

WEALTH IS NO GUARANTEE IT WON'T HAPPEN TO YOU

Although the Emergency Aid Program (EAP) is largely designed to service the county's poor, the well-insured and the affluent are no strangers to EAP—or the vicissitudes of the transfer system it sustains.

"We had a woman come in here on an emergency because she had fallen and broken a bone," recalls Dr. Jerry Hughes, director of the emergency room at Long Beach Community Hospital.

"The next morning, I came in and she was gone. I asked about her and was told that she had been transferred to UCLA–Harbor. And when I asked the clerk from the office here why, she said 'Well, the woman had no money.'

"'Are you kidding?' I asked her. 'Look at this address [on the woman's emergency room admission record].'

"I mean, this woman lived in one of the wealthiest areas of Long Beach and probably owns half the town.

"And when I talked to her doctor, he couldn't believe it either. That woman, he told me, could buy and sell your hospital.

"It happens all the time. You hear of someone coming into an emergency room and being transferred out because they had no money.

And then it turns out it was someone with a grandfather who could have come in and paid cash or someone who had $150,000 in the bank just down the street."

BUDGET CUTS MAY FORCE COUNTY'S POOR TO FEND FOR THEMSELVES

It has been nearly 3½ decades since Los Angeles County officials first declared that the poor were entitled to the same quality medical treatment that other, more affluent residents of the sprawling county received.

And although that commitment—through what became the Emergency Aid Program—has undergone change over the years, the county has steadfastly refused to embrace a double standard of medical care for the poor.

Until now.

In a dramatic shift in position that came swiftly and with virtually no public pre-warning, the county has given notice that no longer will *everyone* be treated the same.

Concerned with budget costs, coupled with taxpayer-imposed budget limits, Los Angeles County is pushing a plan to slash the Emergency Aid Program—leaving in doubt the medical safety of thousands of the county's poor.

The proposal to cut EAP funding from $4.7 million to $2.3 million for the fiscal year that began July 1 has the backing of Department of Health Services officials, who for years have run the EAP program, but now agree that it is someone else's obligation—namely the private hospitals—to see that the county's poor receive proper medical care.

The result for patients—mainly the poor, Chicano, and black—could be even greater risk than they face now with the program that too often has not looked out for their welfare.

However, the brunt of the cuts is likely to fall heaviest on illegal aliens—the "undocumented," as officials prefer to call them—who will be carelessly shunted by the county which is gambling that *someone else* will care for them.

Until now, the illegal aliens have been covered by EAP because of the county's longstanding decision that anyone in need of emergency treatment should receive it.

The Board of Supervisors has given preliminary approval to the cut.

Strangely, the plan is advancing with virtually no discussion by

THE *LONG BEACH INDEPENDENT, PRESS-TELEGRAM* 153

county officers and despite evidence that the risk to EAP patients could be great.

"I don't think we know what it means yet," says Baxter Ward, chairman of the Board of Supervisors, who supports the cut.

Supervisor Peter F. Schabarum, an opponent of the slash, puts it more bluntly: "Regrettably, it was a subject of almost zero discussion. It is probably the most unthoughtful budget conclusion that has come out of the Board of Supervisors in my eight years here."

And a spokesman for Chief Administrative Officer Harry Hufford, who asked not to be identified, said, "Discussions will be initiated with each hospital and with the Hospital Council [of Southern California] to determine the impact of the proposed cutbacks."

The director of the county's Department of Health Services, Robert White, says he suspects the policy change will have negligible impact on providing medical services to the poor. But White's optimism, he acknowledges, is based largely on the *assumption* that private emergency rooms will not turn away indigents and illegal aliens.

"I expect them [private hospitals] to provide care or take down their emergency sign—one or the other," White says. ". . . [The] health care of the undocumented is a community problem—it is not a county problem."

But the new position of the county bureaucracy is not a comforting signal to the county's poor.

Those patients inevitably will receive poorer care and will be "dumped" quicker by private hospitals because of the county's switch, several physicians and hospital administrators admit.

Hospital officials see the job of ensuring prompt and adequate treatment to the poor as at least a joint responsibility with the county. And they acknowledge privately that hospitals will be less inclined to spend time with those patients if the county withdraws its financial backing.

But the county's top brass, including the supervisors and health department officials who are responsible for aiding indigent patients, have given notice that there is a new game in town—which some critics have dubbed "medical roulette."

And even if the Board of Supervisors relents under the pressure of the powerful hospital lobby and continues in full the Emergency Aid Program, it seems unlikely that county officials will be any more interested in making the system work properly than they have in the past.

And some medical experts fear the county may demonstrate even *less* will to clean up the emergency care program.

County officials point to increases in the size and cost of the Emergency Aid Program for their decision to place stiff restrictions on the program.

White says it's simply a matter of "priorities."

He adds that "this is not a program change I would have proposed in the absence of Proposition 13," the voter-imposed initiative that cut property taxes in California. But White acknowledges "one can make the case that the EAP program has been underwriting private hospitals' bad debts for years."

The Department of Health Services, says its chief deputy, Richard Gates, is "$30 million in the hole" and the EAP program—just one of many projects operated by the department—is costing $3 million a year more than anticipated.

Yet, an investigation by the *Independent, Press-Telegram* has found that both the size and cost of the countywide program could have been substantially reduced by the Department of Health Services.

In the last fiscal year, the hospitals collected $4.7 million and the ambulance companies $1.7 million from the county for participating in the program. The county expects to spend about the same this budget year.

But under its latest plan, the hospital budget for the Emergency Aid Program would be reduced by $2.4 million, a move that could cause many private hospitals to bail out of the program, according to the Hospital Council of Southern California and several spokesmen for private hospitals.

The county also proposes to limit the program only to those who are not eligible for state financed Medi-Cal coverage, and to restrict EAP support to "lawful residents" of Los Angeles County—a major policy shift that is aimed directly at illegal aliens from Mexico.

Both limitations, in the opinion of several medical experts, would substantially reduce the number of poor people who could count on the county's Emergency Aid Program for medical services.

Even worse, they could close the door to any medical treatment for some.

Many hospitals, backed vigorously by the Hospital Council, are opposing the planned cutback, insisting it will cause financial troubles for some of the private hospitals and admitting it could jeopardize medical care for the county's poor.

The hospitals are expected to resist the county's attempt to make their emergency rooms the place for screening out illegal aliens.

"That places a monumental administrative burden [on the hospitals], as well as one that is philosophically obnoxious to the medical profession," says Anthony J. Abbate, vice president of the Hospital Council of Southern California.

The irony in the fight over the future and scope of the Emergency Aid Program is unmistakable.

And it points to the fundamental weaknesses within the program and underscores that seldom has the care of indigent patients been paramount.

First, the program has always been keyed to finances.

Los Angeles county officials, who have allowed the EAP program just to evolve—lacking serious planning or controls—are willing to virtually wash their hands of much of the program now that fiscal troubles confront them.

Moreover, everyone—the county, private hospitals, and the federal and state governments—is trying to duck responsibility for *financing* medical care for the thousands of illegal aliens who cross into the Southland annually.

"It's the State of California and the federal government who have essentially allowed this problem to occur," says Abbate. "They've ignored the needs of these people."

The result is that *medicine* often is lost in the battle over who will provide the dollars and cents.

And the private hospitals, which for years have complained about the county's rate of reimbursement and still bemoan how much trouble the emergency care plan is to them, now are fighting to save the program because they sense the loss of county money.

Second, the medical community—which has righteously denied that the poor frequently receive inferior treatment under the Emergency Aid Program, despite evidence to the contrary—suddenly is concerned with the welfare of the indigent.

Abbate, for example, predicts that non-county residents, particularly illegal aliens, may stop seeking medical care: "We're liable to see some bad situations become serious. . . . We're concerned with contagious diseases [spreading].

"There are a large number of people, our neighbors, many of whom are working and paying taxes, who are not recognized [as lawful residents]. . . . The government has looked the other way.

"I am not sure where they are supposed to go for care."

White counters that the county should not "render services to patients who are not the county's responsibility."

Abbate says the private hospitals will probably just transfer those patients to county-operated hospitals, which, he claims, "will defeat the whole point [of the county's position change]" because taxpayers will end up paying for their treatment anyway.

Despite the expressed concern for the welfare of the poor by the medical community, the prevailing attitude of the private hospitals toward treating indigent patients seems summed up by Dr. Jerry Hughes, director of the emergency department at Long Beach Community Hospital, and who has an unusually sharp and candid tongue:

"The hospitals don't need any EAP patient. They don't need it. . . . As far as the EAP plan, my administrator here asked me some time ago, 'What if we refused to sign this EAP contract?' I said, 'What if we don't?'

"There is not a hospital I know [of] that would really suffer. Well, there might be a few that are heavily indigent. But take a common, typical hospital—a hospital that is basically supported by revenue from, as I usually say, clean, intelligent, communicative taxpayers, employed citizens with insurance. That is how they are usually supported. You take someone who is an unemployed John Doe and whisk him down the street to another hospital and let him spend some time in their ICU [intensive-care unit] at a cost of $1,000 a day, and most hospitals really don't care.

"If those same hospitals, physicians and ambulances and so forth [are] in a large group with consumers and with minorities and Medi-Cal [officials] . . . and [you] ask them, 'Will you accept a certain number of patients every year and eat that dough [bad debts]?' they'll say, 'Oh, absolutely, no problem at all.'

"Now, when the accountant talks to them and he has got a sharp pencil and he's paid to make sure the hospitals can pay the bills, he says get these patients somewhere else. . . . As far as would a hospital administrator dare stand up in front of a civic group and say, 'We don't want [indigent] patients, we don't want the reimbursement from the county—we would rather have Connecticut General and Prudential insurance patients?' Yeah that's the answer. [But] that is what they cannot say."

However, county officials, who for years have boasted of their commitment to the medical well-being of the poor, now claim it isn't, after all, the county's responsibility to underwrite a program that assists private hospitals in caring for the injured and ill.

That job, they insist, rests with the private hospitals.

"The underlying theory is that the [private] hospitals who are receiving emergency patients have a legal obligation to provide necessary care under state law," says Richard Gates, chief deputy of the Department of Health Services. "That's primarily what the [EAP] program is paying for.

"If something comes along that might otherwise have been a bad debt [for the private hospitals], it's not a bad debt because the county picks it up under the EAP. Maybe it's a hard way of looking at it. But one way of looking at it is we are simply subsidizing or underwriting what would normally be a bad debt under other circumstances. And we have found that many other large counties don't do that—L.A. is somewhat unique in that respect."

Gates says the Department of Health Services supports "in full" the proposal to substantially reduce the Emergency Aid Program.

The private medical community sees it differently, and makes warnings of serious problems if the county carries through with its plan.

An assistant administrator of St. Mary Medical Center–Bauer Hospital says if the county pulls out of the program it is likely to result in the unsafe transfer of poor patients from private to county hospitals on a broad scale.

"A dumping syndrome could be started," he says.

It is a theme repeated by the Hospital Council, the professional arm of the county's private hospitals and which often works hand-in-hand with the county's Department of Health Services.

"I don't really know," Gates says of the suspected dumping syndrome. "I am inclined to think there wouldn't be a great difference. Right now they [private hospitals] are basically covered for the care in the emergency room and they're [patients] stabilized and in most cases they're transferred now. So I don't see any major increase in transfers."

Moreover, the Department of Health Services doesn't believe the cutbacks will have other damaging effects.

White, for example, acknowledges "I have some concerns," but quickly adds there will be "no significant change. That's my assessment."

But a spokesman for the county's chief administrative officer admitted the impact of the cutbacks is not known, and said discussions will have to be initiated with each hospital "to see if it wants to continue in the program."

The spokesman, who asked not to be named, said, however, "We do not anticipate that the level of services will be drastically cut . . . since the hospitals are legally required to provide these services anyway."

But the Hospital Council also forecasts economic problems for some of the largest private hospitals, which, it says, "are devoting a major portion of their resources to caring for the elderly and the poor."

The financial loss to those hospitals, the Hospital Council says, would amount to $1.28 million. The hardest hit, according to the council, would be California Hospital in Los Angeles' inner city, which would lose $285,000.

County officials, however, say that in the case of California Hospital— and a handful of other institutions that treat an unusually large number of indigents in their emergency rooms—they will make necessary "accommodations" to ensure against excessively deep cuts.

However, when pressed, these officials admit that they have not thought out the scope of these so-called accommodations.

4

THE *SALT LAKE CITY DESERET NEWS*

Gordon Eliot White was scratching around for a story during the summer of 1977. The *Salt Lake City Deseret News*'s one-man bureau in Washington did not often get the luxury of dull days. He usually had to scramble to keep up with breaking events. White began to ponder an idea that had been nagging at the back of his mind for a while.

Back in the spring, White had covered the story of former Army Sgt. Paul Cooper, 44, who had appealed to the Veterans Administration for disability payments. Cooper, who was in a Salt Lake City hospital, blamed radiation he had been exposed to in 1957 as an Army witness to a nuclear bomb test in Nevada for the leukemia he now suffered. After a nationally publicized debate, the Army agreed with Cooper, marking the first time the government had conceded liability for health damages supposedly caused by the atmospheric testing that had gone on all through the 1950s and early 1960s.

One reason Cooper won was some statistical evidence that indicated fallout may have caused a higher-than-usual incidence of cancers among the soldiers ordered to witness the tests. White began to wonder. What about the citizens in nearby Utah whose homes and cars and livestock had been coated over and over again with radioactive powder from those tests? Could that have made them ill too?

"It seemed like a interesting question," White recalled. The problem was where to look.

"As a generalist, you have a ridiculous number of trivial items in your head that occasionally come together to make a story," White said. He also had 20 years of experience at finding facts in the maze of Washington bureaucracy.

"I found a little guy in the depths of NCI [National Cancer Institute] who had a whole computer full of figures. Eventually, he was able to pull out some rates by county [in Utah] for leukemia," White recalled.

White also asked some contacts at the Defense Nuclear Agency (DNA) in the Pentagon to check where the fallout had concentrated as it moved east from Nevada. "They dug out charts, a chart for every test. Some of [the charts] had been made public in congressional hearings in the late '50s, and some of them are still classified. They got me most of them, and some overlays showing a composite of a number of tests."

Meanwhile, White picked up the cancer statistics at NCI. Rates were noticeably high in five southern Utah counties, and nearly twice the national average in a sixth.

When he put the cancer figures together with the charts of the downwind fallout patterns from the Nevada tests, he saw that the heaviest concentrations of fallout had consistently dropped over those five counties that now showed a higher than normal rate of leukemia.

"It seemed to me that indicated something," said White, a quiet man given to understatement. Actually, the finding was startling. Its significance gave him pause.

"I didn't trust myself as a statistician," White admitted. Besides, he always had been skeptical about the hazards of fallout and other low-level radiation. White himself had witnessed an atmospheric bomb test in 1958 when he became the Washington correspondent for the *Deseret News*.

"Then I came back here [to Washington] and was given the treatment by the AEC [Atomic Energy Commission] that nothing can go wrong and that there was no radiation danger from the tests. It was just harmless," White recalled.

He had believed the AEC. In 1962, the Army was doing underground tests, and White covered the story when the researchers at the University of Utah and the Utah public health department claimed that radioactive iodine had infiltrated Utah's milk supply at levels exceeding the AEC guidelines. The Kennedy White House had dismissed the scare as "a lot of baloney," as White remembered. After that, White and almost all of the news media considered the milk scare a closed subject. (It was not until 1979 that White himself reopened it.)

Over the years, White wrote stories about the peaceful use of the atom and the safety of nuclear energy and generally came to regard those who cried about low-level radiation as alarmists whose views were without solid basis in science. Then came Sgt. Paul Cooper and his claims.

White's editors had been interested in Cooper's story, but White had not been able to come up with much more than just routine coverage. At least it had been routine until those slow summer days when White started to look at the civilian population's cancer statistics.

He was not sure what to do with what he had found. If he released the story as he had it, he would be strongly implying that the Army's tests had caused leukemia among the residents of southern Utah.

"I tried to get some of the Public Health Service people to look at the figures and to corroborate what I thought," White said. Eventually, officials at the Centers for Disease Control in Atlanta did look at what he had and told him they thought it was more than mere coincidence.

"That's the point at which I decided there was a story there," he said. He sent it off to Salt Lake City with a cover letter to the city editor suggesting he check out the story with local scientists.

The story by Mary Lubben and Joe Bauman that appeared as a sidebar to White's August 12, 1977, story was not done to "check out" White, according to William Smart, editor and general manager, but to support his story with local reaction.

Startling as they were, the August 12 stories by White, Lubben, and Bauman did not excite a political storm. A few congressmen, including David D. Marriott, R-Utah, called for further studies. But the *Deseret News*'s revelations stood on their own for a long while. White had no follow-up.

The following winter, in February 1978, the House subcommittee on health and environment began hearings on the effect of low-level radiation. Several scientists disputed one another's studies. Testimony about the 1957 Smokey test in Nevada and the soldier-witnesses who had leukemia were the focus of most reporters covering the story. The hearings were dramatically punctuated when Sgt. Paul Cooper died, succumbing to the leukemia he blamed on Smokey.

White went looking among the experts who testified at the hearings to show them what he had published the preceding August. "Was there anything to it? Did they agree with my thesis or not?" he remembered asking them. "I think with one exception, people felt supportive of it." Still, he began to wonder, was that the end of the story?

It remained dormant for many months. Then in the fall of 1978, word began to leak out that a University of Utah researcher secretly had set out to disprove White's 1977 story. Instead, the scientist was getting data that supported White. As the leak became public, events began to happen quickly.

Citizens in southern Utah organized a Committee of Survivors and began pursuing the possibility of government compensation for illnesses and damages they claimed had been caused by atomic tests. *Deseret News* reporters began interviewing citizens who felt they had claims. Utah's Representative Marriott urged the government to begin an intensive study of a possible link between nuclear testing in Nevada in the 1950s and "the unusually high leukemia rate" in southern Utah. On October 5, 1978, congressmen from Utah, Nevada, and Arizona signed a letter to President Carter calling for a study of the highest priority to "ascertain the risks and hazards associated with the Nevada tests."

That October and November, well over a year after White's first story, he got two big breaks which opened a second phase of his investigation and kept his typewriter humming for months. The first came when someone, he can no longer remember who, tipped him that federally financed studies of leukemia in the Utah fallout areas had been made in the 1960s but subsequently played down if not suppressed.

White called the Centers for Disease Control in Atlanta on the tip. The scientists there acted as if they had been expecting his call, White said. He got the sense that the scientific community was already abuzz.

"It was right on the top of their minds. It wasn't something they had to dig in the files for," White said. Officials at CDC identified some of the studies, filled him in on some background, and sent him the original text of some reports. On November 13, 1978, White published the first results of what he found.

The studies had not been classified. "They just had never been published," White said. His story got national play.

Utah Gov. Scott Matheson went to Washington and received a promise from Health, Education, and Welfare Secretary Joseph Califano that the government would finance a speedy review of the possible link between atomic tests and cancer. Then on November 28, President Carter announced on a visit to Salt Lake City that the government would reopen the earlier investigations. Carter's decision was sparked, at least in part, by White's November 13 story.

As the *Deseret News* reported in December, the government was spending nearly $15 million to identify and test military and Defense Department civilian personnel who participated in atomic weapons tests in the South Pacific and Nevada between 1945 and 1962. Yet virtually no money had been budgeted to study the effects of these tests on civilians outside the test-site boundaries. Within a couple of weeks of White's article, Califano announced a new federal probe into the fallout-cancer link through the Centers for Disease Control.

Governor Matheson set up a special committee to oversee Utah's effort to investigate the fallout question, and he ordered a wholesale housecleaning of the state files. The state, as it turned out, had been sent copies of the earlier studies but did not know it had them. "The state people had filed them, filed 'cancer' under 'C,' and that was about it, " White said.

Joe Costanza, the *Deseret News* reporter assigned to the story in Salt Lake, got word that Dr. Edward S. Weiss of the U.S. Public Health Service in Utah had done a leukemia study of considerable significance in 1965. Costanza and White began trying to get in touch with Weiss.

Along the way, they found out that the *News* was not the only paper on the story. The *Washington Post* had filed a Freedom of Information Act (FOIA) request for massive amounts of material on the cancer-fallout connection in Utah. Just as White was about to close in on the Weiss story, the key documents were about to fall into the hands of the *Post*.

"I was trying to get hold of Weiss on the phone, and I couldn't get him," White said. He flew out to Utah on a Friday. "The *Post* and I were fighting over minutes." Costanza finally reached Weiss. The *News* had the story, but not in time for the Saturday deadline. The *News* had no Sunday edition. Both the *Post* and the *News* carried the Weiss story in Monday's paper, but the *News* came out in the afternoon. Its local competition, the *Salt Lake City Tribune*, picked up the story on the morning *Washington Post* wire and ran it Monday morning.

"So we got beat on the Weiss story, much to my chagrin," White recalled.

"Weiss had concluded that there was an unexplained excess of leukemia cases in the fallout area. He made it quite clear," White said. While Weiss's results might not have been medically conclusive, their long-delayed exposure was politically explosive.

The day after the Weiss story ran, the *Deseret News* carried a story about whether the scientist's findings had been suppressed by the state. There seemed to be little evidence that the state had done anything more than simply ignore what Weiss had found. The federal government, on the other hand, may have been more culpable.

Members of a Washington ad hoc committee, consisting mostly of Public Health Service employees investigating the cancer-fallout connection, began to leak documents and information to White. Some of these sources were also on an HEW task force headed by Peter Libassi, HEW general counsel, which had begun a study of the health effects of low-level radiation before the Utah stories had broken.

"They [the sources] would call me every once in a while and say, 'You're really getting at this thing. There's something in this pile of papers that might be helpful.' Some of it was. Some of it wasn't," White said. The leaked material led to the January 29 and 30 (1979) stories of AEC cover-ups of studies by Weiss and other scientists on leukemia and thyroid nodules among southern Utah residents.

White eventually was able to piece together a new angle on the old story about iodine in the milk that he had covered in Washington in 1962. Back then, Dr. Robert C. Pendleton of the University of Utah had discovered that one of the underground tests in Nevada had dropped radioactive iodine into Utah's milk supply. Pendleton "made a great flap over it," White recalled. "He got the state health people involved. They discovered that there was more radioactivity in the milk than met AEC guidelines."

The scare got national publicity, but the White House insisted there was no danger and, as a result, the controversy soon faded. President Kennedy, nettled by the disclosures, ordered that any information about radioactivity or atomic tests be cleared by the White House before being released.

So, in 1965, Weiss's leukemia studies were "passed up to the White House and never came out," according to White. The AEC was afraid of the consequences if they were released. President Johnson, invoking Kennedy's 1962 edict, made sure Weiss's work got limited exposure. It had not actually been suppressed, White pointed out. "They were published in the scientific literature, but had never been made public to newspapers," he said. Weiss, who saw his job as collecting data and writing reports, didn't care what anyone did with the information, White said, so he never objected.

Pendleton's milk studies may have been a different story. "Pendleton told me that his research had been cut by the Department of Energy because he was getting too close to the truth. It was a good story, if you look at it uncritically. But Pendleton didn't turn out to be quite as solid as I would have liked," White said. He was sorry later the story (January 27, 1979) had been given such large display.

Pendleton claimed the government had cut off his funds before he could process his data. He had raw figures but no funds for the computer time necessary to run them. "It eventually turned out that the University [of Utah] offered him the computer time to process it. . . . Essentially, it was put up or shut up" for Pendleton, "and he decided not to do it."

All these stories—of Weiss, Pendleton, and the cover-ups—had been triggered by the first tipster who steered White in the fall of 1978 toward the unpublished, federally financed studies from the 1960s. The other big break that came White's way in November 1978 was handed to him by Stewart Udall, former Secretary of the Interior during the Kennedy administration. Udall, now a lawyer representing the alleged victims of the nuclear testing in Nevada, was about to file the first 100 claims for $100 million against the government on December 21.

"A mistake of great magnitude has been made," Udall told the *Deseret*

News. "I see a moral responsibility the government will have to face as things come out that will shock a lot of people."

"I've known Udall for a long time, and he's a very emotional person," White said. "He got emotionally involved in this whole thing, as well as professionally. He said: 'Isn't there anymore that can be done? Do you have any more information? Can you write any more stories?'" White told him he was trying but that he did not exactly know where to go. "I'd tapped my sources without a great deal of success," he told Udall. The Atomic Energy Commision was then being incorported into the new Department of Energy, and things were a mess. Offices and files were being moved; phones were disconnected. White was having trouble getting in touch with sources.

So, Udall used his connections. He had someone inside the AEC leak to White a recently declassified National Security Council (NSC) paper on how the site for the first nuclear test in Nevada had been picked. "It had been highly classified," White said. "Anything that dealt with atomic energy was classified to the highest degree." On December 8, 1978, White published "Nevada A-Site Picked in a Hurry."

"Under the pressure of the Korean War and the Chinese Communists coming in. ... the military intelligence people panicked," White explained. "They were seeing the Chinese coming all the way down into Korea, the Russians attacking Europe, and World War III breaking out," he said. "I found it fascinating—the way Truman made the decision [to test the new weapon], and how little deliberation there was. It was a month from the time the recommendation gets to him until [he approved it]. Nothing happens around here in a month."

As a student of World War II and its aftermath, White was able to supply much of the information for this story. "I had a good deal of background, just general knowledge of that period, and I'd been out to the Trinity site," White said. Trinity was the spot in the New Mexico desert where the first atomic test was made in 1945, just weeks before the bombs were dropped on Hiroshima and Nagasaki.

White worried about making use of the NSC document, wondering if Udall might be using him as a pawn to help him win his legal case. In the end, White felt the story was justified.

"This was a solid story. There wasn't any doubt in my mind that I was being given valid material. ... I thought a bit, even so, about the source of it. ... A lot of sources have axes to grind. That's standard procedure. But you worry about it, you know," White said.

There comes a point in any major investigative work when a reporter "has got to become obsessed with it for a couple of months," White said, "as I assume some police become obsessed with catching a criminal." The reporter has virtually nothing else on his mind, because so many things begin to fall together. For White, the point at which this story became an obsession occurred when he obtained this NSC paper.

It was not just this story that grabbed him. The NSC document consisted of four or five pages on legal-sized paper with references and a bibliography referring to other documents, most of them still classified. White was surprised, but pleased. "I suppose you might say that they should have obliterated all references to other material, but they didn't," he said.

With the name of a document cited and a number under which it was filed, White had the beginning of a paper chase. With specific references, "you can go and say: 'I want THIS piece of paper,' and they can't say it doesn't exist," he said. He did not get everything he wanted. Some of the cited materials were still classified. And he did not always get a document from the first person he asked.

"The NSC itself was very difficult to deal with," White recalled. "But a lot of that stuff is spread around in enough places that you can find copies of it." The Atomic Energy Commission, for example, might be willing to declassify the same document that the NSC would not.

White used the Freedom of Information Act (FOIA) to pry some of the documents loose, but more often just the threat of invoking it proved effective. "It was much simpler to declassify a document and give it to me under the table, so to speak, than to have the whole panoply of FOIA," White said.

The most important document listed in the original NSC paper was the minutes of a symposium of scientists at Los Alamos in 1950, where they assessed the health impact of the planned bomb tests. Today, White explained, such an assessment "would be considered the environmental impact statement and everything else." But all the "20 tons of paper that today would be prepared on that kind of decision was all done in one day. . . . They sat around a table and talked about what it would mean," White said. But none of them considered what long-range effects nuclear explosions in Nevada might have on the local population and its livestock.

White came across this document in an odd way. He had long before put in requests for it at the AEC headquarters in Germantown, Md., but he was told it was highly classified. Then one day in early 1979, he was in the Forrestal Building, where part of the Department of Energy had been moved. "Things were a mess. The floor was covered with heaps of papers and boxes," White recalled. He was sitting on the floor in the midst of all the material, looking at some "not very interesting papers." Someone, whom he did not recognize, came along, bent over him, and mumbled, "There will be an envelope in your name at the main desk [at AEC headquarters] in Germantown tomorrow." White rushed the next day to get it, and found the document he had been after for months.

"The people at Germantown gave me this in a plain brown envelope. They would never be held responsible for giving it to me, but they got me off their backs," White said. "Now I don't know whether that was merely for convenience or whether somebody thought this needed to be out. That was serendipitous, I guess, getting somebody who was willing to downgrade it. I never knew the motives for that."

The next day, February 3, 1979, the *Deseret News* printed White's story, "Experts Never Weighed Long-range Fallout Risks."

White was astounded by what he found in these documents. The top scientists discussing the health effects of setting off a nuclear explosion in Nevada understood almost nothing of the hazards involved. "It finally struck me that they were talking about caution and making sure that nobody got more than 50 roentgens. . . . Fifty roentgens is just a ridiculous dose, far beyond any guidelines now. . . . There were people who later turned up who had symptoms—reddening of the skin, headaches, hair falling out, and so on—that are found at the level of 50 roentgens."

No one ever measured fallout doses that high at the Nevada tests, White pointed out, but the monitoring was spotty. AEC monitors probably were not well designed yet, White suspected. And, he explained, because the monitoring for the earlier shots in the late 1940s in the South Pacific had also been bad, the scientists had no reason to expect hot spots of fallout. As White explained in other stories, the early techniques for measuring radioactivity in milk were not adequate to find radiation in the food chain. During the tests, samples of milk were heated before they were tested. Since radioactive iodine is volatile, it vaporized and went undetected. Although White contended that most of the AEC's monitoring problems were due to insufficient knowledge, he also suspected that officials managed to overlook what they did not want to see.

Since the fall of 1978, White and others had been hearing rumors about a study being conducted by Dr. Joseph L. Lyon, coordinator of the Utah cancer registry. Lyon reportedly set out to disprove White's August 1977 story but instead was finding that he was right.

As Lyon later recounted, when he read White's first story on the fallout-cancer link he was sure the *Deseret News* was "nutty" and promptly set out to prove it.

On December 12, 1978, Lyon came to Washington to brief a group from the Senate, the Departments of Energy and Health, Education, and Welfare, and others interested in his results, which Lyon himself called "explosive." Also in the audience: Gordon Eliot White.

"I was allowed in, " White recalled. Guards at the door knew he was a reporter. No one else asked. "I have a certain rule of thumb about my own behavior, about where I go and what I do, as far as misrepresenting myself. If I can walk in, I walk in. I don't tell them I'm the janitor, but I won't always tell them I'm a reporter."

White taped Lyon's presentation. "And it was beautiful from my point of view. He corroborated everything that I had written in '77. He told some anecdotes about how he hadn't believed it, and then he discovered evidence that supported it," White said.

Afterward, White went up to talk to Lyon. "He just went through the ceiling" when he found out a reporter had been in the room, White recalled. Although Lyon had not finished writing the results of his study, he had a commitment to publish it from the *New England Journal of Medicine*, the most prestigious publication for a medical researcher. But if the study comes out somewhere else first, the *Journal* will not publish it. That, Lyon argued to White, would have diminished the credibility of his information in the eyes of the scientific community. White would be doing a great disservice to the people of Utah if he published what he heard that day, Lyon argued. Then Lyon called the *Deseret News* to argue his case. White was just as happy to let the decision be bumped upstairs.

The *News* decided to sit on Lyon's story for awhile. "That was a tough decision," recalled editor William Smart. "We spent a lot of time on it."

The paper did not want to jeopardize Lyon's publication with the *Journal.* On the other hand, Smart and his colleagues knew that other newspapers were on to the story. They were afraid of getting scooped.

In the end, they agreed to hold the story until the *Journal* was ready to publish if Lyon would give them the story exclusively with more detail and background. The paper carried a "teaser" story on December 20, quoting Lyon's prediction that his findings would cause a "major furor." Finally, the *News* ran the story on February 13, one week before the *New England Journal of Medicine* came out, but after the *Journal* had been set in type and Lyon's article could not be pulled.

"The publishing of Lyon's findings is probably the single strongest story as far as substantiating that there was harm [from the fallout]," White said. After the publication, Congress opened hearings and more and more events took shape beyond what White and his newspaper were publishing.

The *News* was copyrighting White's key stories, so when other news media picked them up, they said, "In a copyrighted story in the *Salt Lake City Deseret News. . . ."* Everyone who cared about the issue knew that White was the reporter breaking trail.

He put long hours into tracking down documents that had been buried under top secret classification for 25 years. He pried many loose, but he also spent hours in searches that ended without any treasure. He pored over records at the former AEC (now DOE) libraries in Los Alamos and Germantown.

"I went to Germantown looking for a few specific things that I had designations on. That's a classified library," White said. "Their procedure is to let a reporter come in and look at the material, and then he has to clear his notes—or clear anything he takes out. . . . The theory was they were supposed to have somebody take me by the hand and escort me and get me what I wanted. Eventually, they got tired of that."

After many hours, his escort got bored hovering over him and went out for coffee, leaving White in front of the microfilm file. "So I started digging. . . . The way the stuff is filed is not very well organized, not properly indexed," White said. He found a rotating index file and began spinning it, skimming the titles, looking for anything he might make use of. It was there he found the basis for a two-part series on monitoring and milk testing that appeared on March 20 and 21, 1979.

The rest of the information for that series came from a mass of material released under the FOIA that March. The *Deseret News*, the *Washington Post*, the *Washington Star*, and the Associated Press and United Press International had made broad, general FOIA requests for all material concerning the fallout from the Nevada atomic tests of 1951-63 and their possible health effects. Each got about 35,000 pages.

At first the reporters were told they had to go through their copies at the Hubert Humphrey Building where the materials were being distributed. The wire services sent two or three reporters; the *Star* sent its medical editor. "We all plowed away through this huge pile of papers that generated a number of national stories," White said. "It was a big job."

After a couple of hours, the reporters were told they could take the materials home. White remembered loading the papers in a grocery cart and taking them to his car.

White was way ahead of his competitors because he had already seen so much of the material. He found most of it served only to confirm things he had already learned.

Meanwhile, back in February, Utah Governor Matheson's order to his staff to search through all the stored records for materials concerning fallout produced more fruit. Some 400 pages of documents, particularly reports from the Public Health Service that had been filed with the state, showed the government had ample evidence that ranchers who had claimed their sheep had been harmed or killed by fallout from the Nevada tests may have been right.

Deseret News reporter Joe Bauman had found a rancher in Cedar City who claimed to have lost up to 1,200 sheep when fallout showered them more than 25 years ago. Bauman went to federal district court in Denver where this and other ranchers' claims against the government for livestock losses had been heard. Bauman found some old transcripts, but he discovered that much of the testimony had never been transcribed.

"Bauman spent a lot of effort on that," White recalled. "It seemed obvious to both of us that fraud had been committed on the court" by the Atomic Energy Commission, White explained.

"So we were very disappointed when the transcripts weren't in usable form. It was going to cost several thousand dollars to transcribe them. The paper didn't really want to do it," he said.

Eventually, Rep. Bob Eckhardt, D-Texas, chairman of the House Oversight and Investigating Subcommittee, which held hearings on the Utah fallout case in 1979, ordered the transcription. New evidence emerged.

Before the ranchers' case had come to court in 1955, the AEC had conducted studies on the effects of feeding radioactive iodine to pregnant ewes. In the study, the ewes and their offspring suffered the same harm the ranchers and veterinarians had described in the Utah sheep after the 1953 tests. Nevertheless, the AEC blamed the symptoms on "a combination of factors, including malnutrition, poor management, and adverse weather conditions. The animals probably ate poisonous plants due to poor range conditions, extreme drought on the range, and low temperatures."

The government denied that any sheep examined showed any evidence of exposure to abnormal radioactivity.

The *Deseret News* tracked down Dr. R. E. Thompsett, who had worked for a veterinary hospital under AEC contract in Los Alamos and who had examined the damaged animals in 1953. Thompsett had told the AEC he believed the sheep were killed by "fissionable material." (See March 8, 1979, story.) Dr. Thompsett and other scientists had reported in court that the sheep suffered from lesions identical to those found on cattle near the first nuclear explosion at Trinity in 1945 and that their thyroids had elevated levels of radioactivity.

Bauman found a former Public Health Service veterinarian, Dr. Arthur Wolff, who also had helped investigate the southern Utah sheep deaths in 1953. Wolff had worked with another PHS vet to autopsy a couple of animals and to take radiation measurements.

"I was able to determine, yes, there was a relatively high level of radiation in the Iodine-131 in the thyroid and some radiation on the wool of these sheep," Wolff told the *News*.

The AEC's expert witnesses in the case "no doubt knew that what they told the court was written so as in some instances to be technically correct, and in other instances it was clearly just not true, clearly a lie," White found. But the witnesses were cunning. When the complete testimony became public through the Eckhardt hearings, the whole story came to light. "For example, [the AEC witnesses] said that sheep fed this level of radioactivity did not produce lambs that died shortly after birth," White said. "That was true—the lambs were dead at birth. There were several instances of that kind of thing."

Federal District Judge A. Sherman Christensen had ruled in 1955 that the ranchers had failed to prove their contentions. He admitted he was dismissing the case reluctantly. After the revelations in the *Deseret News*, the ranchers or their heirs refiled in federal court and ironically were assigned again to Judge Christensen. In the fall of 1982, the judge found the government guilty of fraud upon the court, the first such conviction in U.S. history. It paved the way for the ranchers to reopen their claims against the government. Christensen heard the case in the fall of 1983 and ruled in favor of the shepherds. The 10th District Court of Appeals in Denver reversed the decision, then heard an argument by the plaintiffs that the appeal brief filed on their behalf was inadequate. Over the objections of the government, the Circuit Court has accepted the shepherd appeal for a rehearing and a resubmitted brief.

In late February 1979, Representative Eckhardt announced that his Subcommittee on Oversight and Investigations would hold hearings in the spring on the apparent fallout-cancer connection. The panel operated as an investigative arm of its parent Commerce Committee. Eckhardt wanted to examine agency responsibility, overlapping and possibly conflicting department interests, access to information, government liability and credibility, and radiation dose rates in the area.

In early March, the Interagency Task Force on Ionizing Radiation issued an 800-page draft report. It said that the fallout-cancer link in Utah might be impossible to prove beyond doubt and that, in the absence of such proof, the government would have no obligation to provide compensation. The task force, headed by Peter Libassi, HEW general counsel, had been empaneled to report on low-level radiation before White's stories had raised a controversy about cancers in Utah.

Scientists reviewing Libassi's report had mixed reactions ranging from caution to calling it "trash."

In April 1979, the Three Mile Island nuclear power plant near Harrisburg, Pa., suffered an accident that resulted in radiation leakage. The chairman of the Nuclear Regulatory Commission asked officials to evacuate children and pregnant women when the radioactivity level approached five millirem per hour.

White reported that if federal officials had been as concerned about radiation during the Nevada tests, they would have ordered more than 20 partial evacuations of civilians in Utah, Nevada, and Arizona. White reported:

After the Smokey test on Aug. 31, 1957, fallout patterns taken by the Atomic Energy Commission showed a five millirem per hour "hot spot" as far as Rock Springs, Wyo., about 410 miles from detonation.

Although monitoring reports for some of the Nevada tests are still unavailable, Public Health Service data on the 1953 series show that five shots dropped fallout in off site areas with readings as high as 1,000 millirem per hour.

The current federal radiation guidelines recommend a general civilian exposure of no more than 1,500 millirem per year.

White noted other tests with fallout heavier than that at Three Mile Island as late as 1970 when only underground tests were being conducted. He also pointed out that fallout of solid particles from the Nevada tests was much more deadly than gas from Three Mile Island, which is more readily dissipated into the atmosphere.

In mid-April, a joint committee of Congress, co-chaired by Sens. Edward Kennedy, D-Mass., and Orrin Hatch, R-Utah, and Representative Eckhardt from the House, along with Utah House and Senate members, opened hearings in Salt Lake City on the fallout-cancer link. Kennedy read into the record previously secret minutes of a 1955 Atomic Energy Commission meeting in which the commissioners determined that health concerns should not stand in the way of further atomic blasts. White had been trying unsuccessfully to pry this document out of its classified status.

One of the first witnesses was Libassi, who had just completed the 800-page task force report on low-level radiation. He said the AEC suppressed evidence of the possible dangers connected with fallout from the Nevada tests "because the American people could not be trusted," according to the *Deseret News* report.

Don Fredrickson, director of the National Institutes of Health, testified that the AEC had issued press releases making it appear that the Public Health Service concurred with its opinion that radiation was not responsible for the Utah sheep deaths. The AEC's public statements failed to reflect the serious concerns the PHS expressed.

Much of the testimony reiterated information White had been reporting in his newspaper over the past five months. Several politicians at the hearing commended White for his investigation and several clippings of *Deseret News* stories were placed into the record. The hearings concluded that the government's responsibility for harm done had been proven to a moral certainty. The House Judiciary Committee, the Senate Judiciary Committee, and the House Oversight and Investigations Subcommittee all began consideration in the summer of 1979 of legislation to compensate the fallout victims and their families.

In July 1979, President Carter ordered a task force to examine how victims of atomic test radiation could be compensated. The panel promised to report by October 1, but it did not do so until February 1980. Although the report was kept classified, an insider leaked it to White. He taped over all markings that might implicate his source, photocopied the document, and threw away the original. The FBI tried unsuccessfully to track down White's source.

The report, White found, concluded that harm had been done, but it "did not come up with a mechanism for compensation of the victims."

"The government's test program caused fallout, and fallout emitted radiation which increased the risk of illness in the entire population exposed," the report stated. "This exposure in all probability caused a small number of cases of death or disease for which the government should accept responsibility."

The task force dismissed litigation as a cumbersome and inadequate means of settling claims. Negligence and wrongdoing would have to be established, the report pointed out, and litigation could set a precedent that would hurt the government in other cases involving toxic substances.

The legislation that had been introduced by then into the House and Senate was too broad because it established eligibility by geographic location rather than actual radiation exposure, the panel concluded, and because it failed to "address the amount of damages or place any limitation on the amount to damages."

The task force recommended an administrative remedy as "a 'middle ground' between litigation and blanket compensation. Such an approach would provide a remedy similar to that available to former [armed] service members and federal civilian employees who allege radiation-related injuries." The task force left it up to the President and the Congress to set out the specifics of such a remedy.

The Carter White House, caught up in its upcoming battle for the

Democratic nomination, largely ignored the report. As of this writing, the Reagan administration has not acted to promote any remedy for the Utah fallout victims. The bills introduced in the House by Rep. Gunn McKay, D-Utah, died under opposition from the left and right. In the Senate, bills by Sens. Kennedy and Hatch remain on the back burner at this time.

White contended his theory about the fallout-cancer link had been confirmed three times: by Dr. Joseph Lyon's study, by the conclusions of the Kennedy-Eckhardt hearings, and by the Carter Task Force.

Then in May 1984 came new support. Federal District Judge Bruce S. Jenkins ruled that the bomb blasts were responsible for at least nine cases of cancer in Nevada and southern Utah. The ruling marked the first time the courts found the tests responsible for causing cancer in humans and the first time the federal government was found negligent for allowing citizens to be exposed to the fallout. The judge awarded $2.66 million to the survivors and their families. The government has indicated it intends to appeal.

Working on this story alone and 2,500 miles from his newspaper caused problems for White.

"There was no organization the way you would get in *All the President's Men* at the *Washington Post* on the Watergate story," White said. Back in Salt Lake City, editor William Smart, city editor Lou Bate, and associate city editor DeAnn Evans edited White's work closely and watched for any holes in the story. Nevertheless, White alone knew and covered the Washington developments.

He was working 18 hours a day on nothing but this story for most of the period from October 1978 through April 1979. Another disadvantage was that few of his sources in Washington saw what White published in Salt Lake City. But as his big stories broke and the wire services picked them up and distributed them across the nation people began to realize that White was leading the pack. Sources began to come to him.

As he got information, he wrote it up; stories came "episodically" in the paper. Because there was competition from other papers and politicians were publicly expressing interest and taking stands on the fallout-cancer link, White could not afford the luxury of investigating his topic for months and then gathering everything into a neat and comprehensive series. He admits readers may have had trouble wading through the sporadic and complicated reporting.

White's story was not one a reporter new to Washington might have tackled. From the start when he put together information from such disparate sources as the National Cancer Institute and the Defense Nuclear Agency, White knew where to go and whom to tap. He found that the Public Health Service people often bent over backwards to be helpful, and the agencies in the Pentagon were honest, while the Department of Energy (and the former AEC) personnel "hated my guts."

"As far as compensating the people who are either victims or heirs of victims, that may never happen," White conceded. "I really think that it should. I'm really biased on that score. . . . With all my experience in Washington, I'd say it's an iffy proposition." Should a reporter be so concerned about the results of the story? "I kind of think he shouldn't be," White admitted. But he also contended that he was professional enough to keep his feelings from interfering with his reporting.

White is not an emotional man, and his writing reflects his cool approach. He did not want to focus on the victims, for example. "I distrust emotional writing that poses a question that is not properly answered. A lot of people died of cancer, which is really a tragedy any way you look at it, but to tie this to fallout without having some logical reason made me very uncomfortable."

But, White was deeply moved by the human dimension of the story. As he was about to go to press with the results of Dr. Lyon's study, "it suddenly hit me," White recalled. This was no longer just another story about political charges or bureaucratic mismanagement. " But now we were getting into a story that would really hit people's lives," he said. As with so many other investigative reporters who say they were stunned by a similar realization at some point in their work, White said to himself, "My God, it better be correct."

And this reaction, White points out, is what marks the difference between a reporter and a crusader. The reporter wants only to get the story right.

"Generally, If I have all the facts, " White said, "I don't think I have to hit the reader over the head with the fact that this is bad. The reader draws the moral conclusion, not me."

Gordon Eliot White and the *Deseret, News* won a number of awards for these stories from the National Press Club, the Scripps-Howard Foundation, Sigma Delta Chi, Investigative Reporters and Editors, and the White House Correspondents' Association/Standing Committee of Correspondents.

August 12, 1977

DEATHS HIGH IN UTAH FALLOUT AREA

By Gordon Eliot White
Deseret News Washington correspondent
Copyright 1977 *Deseret News*

WASHINGTON—A farmer working in a field in southern Utah may have the seeds of cancer in his veins as a result of radioactive fallout which drifted across the region many years ago.

He is one of thousands of rural residents in five Utah counties who lived downwind from atomic testing carried out in Nevada during the 1950s and who may be reaping a long-delayed harvest from that exposure.

A nearly-forgotten U.S. cancer study completed in 1970 and unearthed by the *Deseret News* shows that leukemia deaths over a 20-year period were nearly twice the state and national average in one county and significantly higher than average in the others.

The survey by the National Cancer Institute, part of a nationwide county-by-county examination of deaths between 1950-1969, indicated that leukemia deaths of males in Iron, Washington, Garfield, San Juan, and Kane counties were at least 143 percent of the state average.

Questions about Utahns exposed to fallout arose after several former U.S. soldiers who watched a nuclear blast, code-named "Smokey," during military maneuvers in 1957, came down recently with leukemia and blamed it on that long-ago test.

A move is afoot to track down all 2,232 soldiers and civilians who watched the Smokey test to find out if a higher than normal rate of leukemia has turned up among them—a finding that could have significance for Utahns.

The *Deseret News* questioned scientists, doctors, and statisticians in an effort to find out how Utahns might have been affected by fallout from repeated tests in the 1950s, and discovered the previously un-publicized 1970 National Cancer Institute survey.

That survey showed that the Utah leukemia death rate per 100,000 white males averaged 8.17, or less than the U.S. average of 8.81. But in Iron County, in the fallout path, the death rate for males was 15.7.

The death rate for white females in Iron County was 9.3, compared to a statewide average of 5.49 and a national figure of 5.74.

Iron County, according to figures from the National Oceanic and Atmospheric Administration (NOAA), probably received the heaviest fallout from the Nevada testing in the 1950s.

Winds from southern Nevada would carry debris from the nuclear test site across Cedar City. Dust from the blast would be lifted high in the air and drift back to earth as the cloud moved northeast over parts of Utah.

According to this hypothesis, the nearby Nevada area would tend to be cleaner than some Utah areas downwind. Nye County, Nev., where the tests were carried out, showed a leukemia death rate of 9.4 per 100,000, compared to the state average of 8.45.

Across the Utah line, Washington County showed a white male mortality rate of 10.8 and a female rate of 9.5. In Garfield County the rate for men and women was 12.4 and 9.9 respectively and in San Juan County they were 10.4 and 3.1. In Kane County, 9.0 males per 100,000 population died and no report was available on females.

Medical experts in Washington, D.C., suggested that as high as the rates were, they may not reflect the whole story because patients with acute leukemia were likely to go to major metropolitan centers, such as Salt Lake City, for treatment.

If they died there, their deaths would not be certified to their home counties. For example, Sgt. Paul Cooper, who blames his leukemia on the 1957 Smokey test, is an Idahoan, but is being treated at the Veterans Administration Hospital in Salt Lake City.

Comparing the southern Utah rate with Cache County, which has similar population and geography, but lies outside the fallout area, showed a leukemia rate of 7.7 for males, about six percent below the state average.

No comparable study has been done since the survey ended in 1969 and the proposed examination of those at the Smokey test will give a more recent picture of cancer rates among those who were exposed to radiation.

Dr. Glen Caldwell of the Public Health Service Communicable Disease Center in Atlanta, Ga., told the *Deseret News* this week he is going to try to find everyone who was at the Smokey test in 1957.

He expects to trace more than 2,000 persons, or nearly 90 percent, and to prove, if possible, whether being at the test significantly increased the chances of developing leukemia.

If that higher leukemia rate is found it will come as a surprise to most medical scientists, who have discounted the hazard because of the low level of radiation from the test.

Although there was discussion 10 years ago of possible thyroid cancer caused by fallout in southern Utah, the results of studies were inconclusive and federal funds eventually were exhausted.

Although some thyroid nodules were found in children in southern Utah, they eventually were attributed to a benign hereditary factor in several closely related communities.

Dr. Caldwell said that among the approximately 500 participants in the Smokey test he has traced so far, he has found two certain, one probable, and one suspect leukemia case. Statistically there should be 1.5 cases in a sample of 2,232 persons of that age.

Using probability theory, he said zero to four cases would be in the ordinary range for that size sample. Finding a fifth would be ambiguous and six or more would be significant.

If two or more leukemia victims show up among the remaining 1,732 participants from the Smokey test, the Public Health Service is likely to conclude that they were exposed to radiation which contributed to their developing the disease.

The exact process by which radioactive fallout might produce leukemia is not clear, Dr. Caldwell said. While Strontium-90 and similar calcium-like isotopes tend to concentrate in the bones where the blood is produced, there has been no prior experience that low exposure produces cancers.

Iodine-131 is picked up by cows and transmitted by their milk, to concentrate in the thyroid, where in heavy doses, it is a proven carcinogen. But there is "no evidence of a similar event causing leukemia," Dr. Caldwell said.

He postulated that radioactive iron particles might be concentrated in red blood cells, but he admitted that he does not have any proof of that idea.

The Smokey test was fired atop a 700-foot tall steel tower to prevent the fireball from picking up dust which would become radioactive. The tower was vaporized into iron molecules. Did some of them fall to earth at ground zero to contaminate the troops who marched through the area?

There were dozens of tower-mounted atomic tests in those years that could have generated iron fallout particles. Right now no one knows what happened, or if indeed anything happened to those who lived downwind.

In the Pacific tests, islanders developed radiation diseases far earlier, but they received larger doses. More recently, those exposed to lower level radiation have begun to fall ill.

In Japan, radiation illness peaked nine years after Hiroshima and Nagasaki, but this might be because there was less iron in the bomb bursts over the two cities.

There have been few studies of low-dose radiation on large populations over long periods. If Dr. Caldwell is successful, the Smokey study will be definitive.

He is searching Army, VA, and Social Security records, death records of U.S. hospitals, and Army graves registration data to find as many of the Smokey people as can be traced 20 years later. It is a slow and difficult task.

A failure to find all of the cancer-caused deaths among the participants would skew the results in a negative direction. Privacy legislation prevents medical experts going directly to people traced through Social Security numbers.

Anyone who was at Smokey should contact Dr. Caldwell at the Communicable Disease Center in Atlanta and give the Public Health Service an outline of his medical history. All such data will be helpful to the scientific study.

August 12, 1977

NEW CANCER STUDY REQUESTED

By Mary Lubben and Joe Bauman
Deseret News staff writers
Copyright 1977 *Deseret News*

Several of Utah's cancer experts today called for an exhaustive study to see if atomic tests in Nevada caused cancer in Utah.

The experts were commenting on a seven-year-old report, with disturbing implications, that was unearthed by the *Deseret News* and is published for the first time today on this page.

"Yes, there is a risk. The risk is small, but it's real," said Dr. Charles R. Smart, a cancer specialist at LDS Hospital and a member of the American Cancer Society's national board.

"I don't think, though, that we want to cause a mass hysteria." Radiation dissipated soon after the tests. Intensive exposure lasted about 50 days.

Dr. Robert C. Pendleton, with the University of Utah Department of Radiological Health, has studied the fallout patterns, or "tracks," of 55 atomic tests, as radiation from the blasts swept from Nevada into Utah. The tests were conducted between 1947 and 1969.

He said some very intense concentrations of radiation fell on small portions of Utah from time to time during the tests.

"Leukemia apparently can be caused by radiation, all right. It can be found in the offspring of the exposed victim," Dr. Pendleton said.

"Radiobiologically, the effect is spread over a long period of time. It is a delayed effect. I would think that we would have to get the exposed people and the young ones, tabulate who they are and where, and then check it against their health records.

"We would need to follow those, get those children who were exposed here, then track them out to their locations."

He called for a new study concentrating on the leukemia rate in the tracks of the many radiation clouds that floated over Utah, instead of comparing death rates on a county-by-county basis.

Countywide data could be misleading because if there is a real danger, all the deaths from leukemia in a county could be happening in a small area that was hit hard by radiation. But the county average could disguise the problem in an overall figure.

"If we were going to have a maximum epidemic—maybe we did but we didn't see it—it would have resulted from the exposures in 1962 and 1950," Dr. Pendleton said.

Those atomic tracks crossed northern Utah and Washington County, respectively.

Dr. Pendleton said of the proposed new study, "I think it is something that is needed from the very fundamental aspects of public health and radioactive fallout."

It should be possible to reconstruct the fallout clouds' paths across Utah in the 55 tests, he said. "We can obtain trajectories of virtually all tests that were shot. On the basis of the kind of shot, we can get a judgment as to the kind of fallout."

Some of the tracks were in narrow strips 100 to 150 miles wide.

Before 1962, most of the fallout tracks were quite tight, with very intense radiation going across southern Utah, he said. Later, the paths changed and the small town of Garrison, Millard County, and western Utah as well as eastern Nevada towns were in the paths. Also hit by radiation were some eastern Utah areas, he said.

In the later tests, there was some heavy fallout in Salt Lake City, Ogden, and Provo. In fact, he said, northern Utah actually received more fallout than southern Utah, although it was more dispersed rather than in intense bands.

"If we go on the quantity of material in the soil, Cache Valley was the most heavily hit, and the fallout in high mountains was greater than anything in valleys," he said.

But some of the most intense radiation was across Washington County, close to St. George. Also hard hit was the region of Cedar City and Beaver County. Some of these shots were in 1958 and 1959, Dr. Pendleton said.

Some experts say there is no reason to believe any leukemia cases have occurred among Utah's civilian population because of the test.

Dr. Marvin L. Rallison, a pediatrician and endocrinologist who did studies of thyroid abnormalities in southern Utah, said thyroid problems are usually expected to show up before leukemia, in cases of radiation-caused disorders. He said in Marshall Islanders, exposed to heavy fallout from atomic tests, numerous thyroid abnormalities were found, but no leukemia.

The study in southern Utah revealed "a lot of thyroid abnormalities," he said. But this could be the result of environmental and heredity factors, the study indicated.

Dr. Rallison said just as many cases of abnormal, nonmalignant thyroid conditions were found among children who later came into the area as among children who lived there during the atomic testing.

Another explanation for the higher rate of leukemia in the five southern Utah counties may be that a virus is suspected of causing it in some cases.

This could make it cluster in certain areas of the world, even in countries that have never had atomic testing.

If leukemia does occur in clusters, there could be parts of the state where none of the disease virus has ever spread and other regions where there are clusters of leukemia victims.

The statewide leukemia death rate is an average of all areas, both places where there are clusters of leukemia and where there aren't.

The areas where leukemia does occur will have a much higher leukemia death-rate than the state average, and the other areas will have a much lower death rate than the average.

At any rate, because so few people live in southern Utah, and because leukemia is a rare disease, just one or two more cases over a 20-year stretch could make a small county seem to be having a major epidemic, compared with the state average, said Dr. Smart.

That single death was enough to put the statistical rate of leukemia deaths up to about one and a half times the normal rate for women in Utah, Dr. Smart said.

"It points out the problem of a small population. One case can make it look like an epidemic." Dr. Smart said.

November 13, 1978

LEUKEMIA REPORTS NEVER PUBLISHED

By Gordon Eliot White

WASHINGTON—Reports made by the U.S. Public Health Service in 1967 showed there were unexplained "clusters" of leukemia in southern Utah, but the reports were never published.

The *Deseret News* has obtained reports made to Utah health officials by the National Communicable Disease Center in Atlanta. They are marked "For official use only. Not for Publication."

They show that leukemia cases found in Parowan, Paragonah, and Monticello far exceed the number that would have been expected to occur naturally.

Parowan and Paragonah, in Iron County, were in the path of nuclear test fallout in the 1950s and 1960s. Monticello is well out of the fallout area, but it has been a uranium mining and milling center. The reports did not determine a cause for the cancers, despite intense investigation.

Apparently neither the Public Health Service nor the State Health Department followed up on the reports.

Dr. Glyn G. Caldwell, of the leukemia branch of the Centers for Disease Control in Atlanta, said he wasn't in the job during that period, but to the best of his knowledge, nothing was done.

Utah was participating in a leukemia case reporting program and when the unusual clusters showed up on reports in 1967, more intensive studies were done with team members from some federal agencies participating. The reports obtained by the *Deseret News* were the results of these studies.

Dr. Lyman J. Olsen, director, State Division of Health, said the study was before his time at the health department and he could not comment on it.

He said some studies have been done from time to time since then. Some have shown evidence of a high number of cases in a single year, but he said when spread out over a number of years, the figures have not been significant.

Dr. Robert C. Pendleton, director of the University of Utah's Department of Radiological Health, said he was aware of the study, but he was "rather ignored" and knows nothing of what the results were.

Pendleton has been calling for intensive studies on the effects of radiation for years.

"It is quite probable that the people of this area, having been exposed to extra radiation risk, would show a higher incidence of radiation-induced problems than others, but exactly what that would be can't be determined until the studies I have been calling for are done."

Dr. Lynn Lyon of the Department of Family and Community Medicine at the U. of Utah, has done an extensive statistical study, but his information will not be available until published in a medical journal.

A wider study of children in southwestern Utah between 1965 and 1971, carried out by the Public Health Service, looked for thyroid nodules that might have been caused by fallout. The PHS concluded, however, that there was no significant difference between groups that had been exposed to fallout and those which had not.

Dr. Glyn G. Caldwell, of the leukemia branch of the Centers for Disease Control in Atlanta, suggested last week that the thyroid nodule study might have been looking for the wrong disease. Caldwell noted, however, that the effects of low doses of radiation, over relatively long periods, are still not well understood and added that the incubation period for various forms of cancer is about 10 years—a delay that adds greatly to uncertainty in determining the cause of a particular case of the disease.

In Parowan and Paragonah, four cases of leukemia were diagnosed between 1956 and 1967, a rate of 18.5 per 100,000 of population, 2.6 times the expected rate of 7.1 per 100,000. In San Juan County, in the period 1956-65, six cases were found, five of them among children under 19, 11.7 times the rate for that age group in the entire United States.

The *Deseret News* reported last winter, after comparing fallout patterns and cancer incidence statistics, that the overall leukemia rate in southwestern Utah was twice the national average. Health officials since then have been examining death records in an attempt to find whether there is a leukemia "epidemic" in the state or whether the cases are a statistical accident.

If there is an excess number of such cancers, health agencies will have to try to determine the cause, and the link, if any, to nuclear weapons fallout or uranium mining.

December 8, 1978

NEVADA A-SITE PICKED IN A HURRY

By Gordon Eliot White
Copyright 1978 *Deseret News*

WASHINGTON—Just declassified information obtained this week by the *Deseret News* indicates that in 1950 the United States rushed into selection of the Las Vegas–Tonopah bombing and gunnery range in Nevada as an atomic test site despite questions about possible radiological contamination up to 125 miles downwind.

Under pressure of the Chinese entry into the Korean War, President Harry S. Truman approved use of the Nevada site just 34 days after the National Security Council directed the Atomic Energy Commission to make a selection study and recommendations. Truman signed the order on Dec. 18, 1950, even before a Corps of Engineers survey of the

Nevada site was complete and without specific examination of radiological safety factors.

In its public announcement of the selection, however, the Truman
administration glossed over safety questions the secret documents
made clear were still unanswered.

Over the next 12 years, at least 26 test explosions resulted in meas-
urable radioactive fallout in southwestern Utah. In the same area, raw
figures from the National Cancer Institute have shown double or triple
the expected incidence of types of cancer that have been associated
with radiation exposure.

The newly uncovered documents include minutes of AEC meetings
in late 1950, and National Security Council memoranda that until this
week have remained top secret. Reading them, it is clear that the
Truman government felt that World War III was a looming threat that
overruled the unknown factors of safety. In fact, the papers make clear,
top U.S. officials were preparing for the possible denial by enemy action
of the two existing U.S. test sites, one in the Pacific and the other in the
Aleutian Islands off Alaska.

To set the scene, in the fall of 1950 the United Nations command
under Gen. Douglas MacArthur was sweeping the North Korean Communists back toward the Yalu River border with China. MacArthur told
his troops they would be "home by Christmas."

Peking radio had threatened Chinese intervention, but few believed
they would enter a war already lost. On Oct. 16, the first Chinese units
crossed the Yalu, but they were not positively identified by U.N. intelligence until 10 days later. Within another week, the Chinese trickle
became a flood. By Nov. 7, the Chinese were attacking the First Marine
Division in overwhelming numbers at the Chosin Reservoir.

The joint chiefs, Truman later wrote, thought that possibility would
mean Soviet entry and World War III, with fighting extending to every
point of contact between East and West.

On Nov. 14, citing the possible denial by an enemy of U.S. access to
atomic test areas at Eniwetok and Amchitka, the NSC ordered that a
secure test site within U.S. continental boundaries be found.

In less than a month, on Dec. 12, the AEC sent its recommendation
to the president, who signed it six days later. The first detonation was
set off in Nevada on Jan. 27, 1951. Although AEC officials noted that
safety of the civilian population was important, that consideration was
judged only "adequate" at the Nevada site, while other factors were
found to be "good" or "excellent." The only safety study cited in the
NSC papers was a safety conference report made Aug. 1, 1950, before
the Nevada site was considered.

The end of 1950 was a dark time. President Truman, with access to secret intelligence reports, probably saw more peril in the situation than most Americans outside the top level of government realized.

By Dec. 3, Korean commander General Douglas MacArthur cabled the Joint Chiefs of Staff that he was faced with "the entire Chinese nation in an undeclared war" in which "steady attrition leading to final destruction" of his United Nations command "can reasonably be contemplated." Secret reports reached Truman indicating that if the U.S. bombed Chinese bases in Manchuria, the Soviet air force would strike back in force.

"We had reached a point," Truman said later, "where grave decisions had to be made."

One of those decisions was to set up, as rapidly as possible, a location where atomic weapons could be tested.

In choosing the Nevada site, the AEC considered and rejected four others, including Dugway Proving Grounds, Utah; the Alamogordo–White Sands guided missile range in New Mexico; the Fallon–Eureka area in Nevada; and the Pamlico Sound–Camp LeJeune area in North Carolina.

Safety was considered, chiefly as a function of population density.

"A comparison of total populations in a base area site plus a 90-degree fallout sector to a radius of 125 miles downwind from site, shows the Las Vegas site as involving the fewest people," the AEC reported on Dec. 12. Dugway was eliminated because, being upwind from Salt Lake City, it would threaten the largest population of those locations under study.

"There seems to be no doubt among experts," the study noted, "that a continental site can be used safely for atomic testing of shots of relatively low-order yields."

"Not only must high safety factors be established in fact, but the acceptance of these factors by the general public must be insured by judicious handling of the public information program," the recommendation added.

Questions of radiological contamination "may be answered satisfactorily as test knowledge increases through experiments . . . but they are not satisfactorily answered at present," the AEC noted in its secret report to the NSC.

In the public announcement by the AEC, made on Jan. 11, 1951, the commission sought to allay public fears, saying "radiological safety and security conditions incident to the type of tests to be undertaken have been carefully reviewed by authorities in the fields involved. . . ."

Between January 1951 and June 1953, 31 weapons and experimental devices were fired at Frenchman's Flats and Yucca Flats, Nev. In that period, the highest yield was 100 kilotons, or twice the "probable" safe limit anticipated in 1950. Tests were resumed in 1955 and 1958, with several series of explosions until the nuclear test ban treaty was signed in 1962.

That debris, which later falls out as the cloud drifts with the wind, was judged more hazardous than expected by the AEC, particularly during the 1953 tests, and subsequent shots were fired.

MacArthur was relieved by Truman in April, for advocating an attack on China, and his successor, Gen. Matthew B. Ridgeway, forced the Chinese and North Koreans into a stalemate that ended in a military truce which remains in effect today.

December 20, 1978

SCIENTIST SEES "MAJOR FUROR" IN CANCER STUDY

By Gordon Eliot White

WASHINGTON—The University of Utah scientist who did a still-unpublished study of the possible link between atomic fallout and leukemia in Utah says his findings will probably cause a "major furor" in scientific circles when printed in the *New England Journal of Medicine* this winter.

Dr. Joseph L. Lyon, co-director of the Cancer Registry at the university, declined to make public specific findings of his study before they are scrutinized by his scientific peers. But Dr. Richard D. Lee, dean of the University of Utah College of Medicine, has said that "preliminary indications of our study show a cause for concern and strongly suggest that the question should be studied in greater detail."

Lyon said the question of the effect of low-level radiation exposure from fallout is a "terribly emotional one" for some people who were in responsible government positions during the period of the tests. He predicted that a major scientific investigation would be required to follow up his study, which Lee called "preliminary."

Lyon said that, until his study is published, the "only solid evidence" of a fallout-leukemia link is a *Deseret News* story published in August 1977.

That story reported that in certain Utah counties in the path of the test fallout, leukemia cases had occurred at rates nearly twice the national average.

. . . .

"I was negative myself on the Deseret News story," he said. "Then I thought, we ought to get to the bottom of this thing, and now that our data is in, I think we are beginning to see a change; people are beginning to realize that there is something going on here."

January 8, 1979

'65 STUDY CITED HIGH CANCER RATE

By Joe Costanzo
Deseret News staff writer

A 14-year-old federal leukemia study shows that two southern Utah counties experienced a greater than expected leukemia death rate between 1950 and 1964.

The study, which has just been rediscovered by University of Utah researchers, was conducted by Dr. Edward Weiss, formerly an epidemiologist with the Bureau of Radiological Health of the U.S. Public Health Service.

Weiss, in a telephone interview with the *Deseret News*, said his research showed 28 leukemia deaths in Iron and Washington counties in the 1950-64 period.

"Compared with national figures, we expected to find 20 deaths," Weiss said. "We attempted to make an appropriate comparison, but we didn't have the refined data we have today."

The Weiss report, dated Sept. 14, 1965, stunned federal officials and researchers who have had a revived interest in the effects of open-air nuclear tests in Nevada ever since the *Deseret News* disclosed last year that the tests may be linked to higher than average cancer rates in Utah.

The discovery of the Weiss study prompted HEW Secretary Joseph A. Califano to order a search of federal health files for any other studies on the effects of fallout on health in Utah.

Weiss said his statistics were developed through a search of all death certificates filed in Utah after 1950. He was looking for all leukemia deaths from Iron and Washington counties, which received the most fallout from the Nevada tests.

He said one of the most significant items in his study was the fact that there were six deaths in 1959, five of them children.

"The hypothesis at that time was that radiation was a great risk at the fetal stage," Weiss said. "In 1953, there was one of the biggest and dirtiest tests, and we wanted to see if humans in the fetal stage developed cancers by the time they were five or six."

Despite the figures, Weiss said, "We did not believe the leukemia had anything to do with the fallout, so we invited the Communicable Disease Center to pay some attention to that part of the country."

The center was to explore the possibility of family relationships and their links to leukemia, Weiss said. The results of that study were inconclusive, he added.

Weiss, who now lives in Maryland, said he has thought about the research over the years "and as I reconstruct it, I became more interested in the possibility of thyroid injury than leukemia."

He said a thyroid study was conducted immediately following his own report in 1965.

The thyroid study was filed with the Bureau of Radiological Health in 1971 by Dr. Marvin L. Rallison, who is now an associate professor of pediatrics at the University of Utah Medical Center.

January 9, 1979

STATE DIDN'T COVER UP, EX-HEALTH OFFICIAL SAYS

By Gordon Eliot White

Was there a cover-up of reports that indicated a possible link between A-test fallout and excessive leukemia deaths in southern Utah?

Not at the state level, according to Dr. G. D. Carlyle Thompson, director of the Utah State Health Department at the time of a report by Dr. Edward S. Weiss, of the U.S. Public Health Service.

"I don't know what the federal officials did with the Weiss study, or if it was ever published," Thompson, who is now retired, told the *Deseret News* Monday, "but it was one of the things that led to the establishment of the Utah Cancer Registry."

The registry, a confidential listing of all cancer cases in the state as reported by doctors, gives scientists a way to keep track of cancer cases, including, presumably, early warning, and information of possible cures.

As a result of the Weiss study and other reports of possibly excess cancer cases in fallout areas of the state, thyroid studies were done in 1967. Using control groups of children not exposed to fallout, federal scientists concluded that they could not find a link between the atomic testing and cancer.

No such study was done on leukemia victims, Thompson said, because the numbers were smaller and statistically more difficult to deal with, and because the easier thyroid investigation dealt with the cancer cause question.

Federal officials were reportedly "horrified" at the Weiss study, uncovered by accident at the state level last week after being misfiled. The *Deseret News* and the *Washington Post*, which obtained the study over the weekend, published portions of it Monday. Stewart L. Udall, attorney for more than 130 cancer victims in southern Utah, said he suspected that there was a cover-up of unfavorable cancer evidence at both the federal and state levels.

Cover-up or not, the Weiss study was not mentioned in subsequent federal investigations of leukemia clusters in Utah, and it apparently was not known to scientists now investigating persistent reports that leukemia has followed the fallout paths from atomic testing in the period 1951-62.

Thompson said that aside from the inconclusive thyroid study, and the cancer registry, nothing was done to follow up Weiss because his department estimated it would cost $1 million to do a full investigation, and "there was no chance we'd get that kind of money" from either federal or state sources.

"The chance of providing anything was very small," Thompson added.

Thompson said that he spoke about the Utah fallout problem to several conferences of health officials and generated considerable reaction each time, but that there was never any long-term reaction and as far as he knew, no action at the federal level.

. . . .

January 27, 1979

U.S. HUSHED FALLOUT STUDY IN '60s, U. SCIENTIST SAYS

By Gordon Eliot White
Copyright 1979 *Deseret News*

WASHINGTON—A University of Utah scientist who made fallout studies for the U.S. Public Health Service and the Atomic Energy Commission told the *Deseret News* late Friday that federal officials forced him to quit some of his work in the 1960s because he was turning up radiation levels that were "too high."

Dr. Robert C. Pendleton, head of the university's Radiological Health Department, said he was pressured and coerced into abandoning work that contradicted government statements about the safety of the Nevada atomic tests.

He told the *Deseret News* that "very heavy repressive action" was threatened if he did not stop his "inappropriate" attacks on the nuclear test program. He said funds for the University of Utah Radiobiology Laboratory were put in jeopardy, and that he ceased some of his efforts because he could not justify continuing them in the face of a real threat to the jobs of 120 of his colleagues.

Pendleton said he and his group made three large reports and 16 or 17 smaller ones for the AEC on the radon daughter project. These were submitted to the government, although nothing was published in the scientific literature.

Much of Pendleton's work was done under Public Health Service grants, but AEC funds for a study of radon gas daughter products, or byproducts, in the atmosphere were cut off before the results could be published, he said. According to documents which the *Deseret News* has seen in government files, commission officials told Pendleton they were dropping his work because he had failed to publish reports in scientific journals as his group's contract required.

Pendleton said Friday that he got into a heated argument with one of the government scientists over his work and went to the AEC office in Las Vegas, Nev. to plead for money to finish the project, but he was turned down.

The Atomic Energy Commission was replaced with the Energy Research and Development Administration on Jan. 19, 1975, and ERDA became part of the federal Department of Energy last year.

As an example of fallout levels, Pendleton said his researchers found occasional post-test radiation levels of 20,000 picocuries per cubic meter of air in Ogden. He estimated there were levels of 200,000 picocuries per cubic meter in St. George from the July 6, 1962, Sedan test.

It is difficult to translate air levels to radiation doses, but present population guidelines allow 170 millirem per year. Some scientists have estimated that an actual intake of 50 picocuries per day would give an annual radiation dose of 100 millirem.

Analysis of one of Pendleton's studies of fallout doses in Utah remains incomplete because funds for required computer time were denied, the Utah scientist said. Gov. Scott M. Matheson asked Sen. Jake Garn, R-Utah, in December for help in getting $18,000 to finance the work, and that request has apparently gone unanswered so far.

Pendleton said "a million dollars worth of research" on fallout levels and population doses was going to waste for lack of money to compile his figures. Later he said the work had not cost that much to gather, but it would be "of great value to the new studies that we are talking about now." The figures, he said, would help provide approximate dose estimates at locations in the fallout path.

Lack of precise dosimetry was cited by Dr. Joseph L. Lyon of the

University of Utah as a problem in compiling his still-unpublished study of the suspected link between fallout and childhood leukemias.

Work on a Health-Service-funded study of fallout was "arbitrarily chopped off," Pendleton said, then reinstated after certain health officials sided with him, but the analysis money was never made available.

"I was told I couldn't expect further support," he said.

A federal health aide, asked about Pendleton's charges, said it is possible that the cutoff came because Pendleton's research failed to meet scientific standards required by his grant or contract.

The University of Utah scientist said in an off-the-record Salt Lake City interview two weeks ago that he had been "pressured to say nothing" about his findings on several occasions. Pendleton went on the record with the *Deseret News* on Friday, after the *News* learned independently of the cancellation of the radon daughter or byproduct work.

(Daughter products are products of radioactive decay. Radon is a gas found in uranium mines and tailings dumps, as well as deriving from certain fallout substances.)

In the original interview, Pendleton said he believed there was no cover-up of fallout data at the state level, but he said there had been a "whole series of federal problems, including out and out repressive action" against himself and his colleagues.

"I know where it came from and who it is," he said, but he has refused to name the officials who he said coerced him to remain silent.

"There was a rather phenomenal reluctance to do anything to protect our people," he said. "We were bucking a hugh military-industrial complex which believed the weapons tests were for the benefit of the country."

"I have taken my lumps," he said, "but a scientist is remiss if he does not try to bring these things to public attention."

Pendleton said he believes Matheson has moved wisely to set up a group to follow through on the currently-planned fallout studies.

If Dr. Joseph Lyon, U. of U. assistant professor of community medicine, can get the funds to do that job, "It will be objective and of high quality," Pendleton said.

One AEC project he opposed, Pendleton said, was a plan to set off a large number of underground atomic explosions in Sublett County, Wyo.

In August 1967, Pendleton warned the *Deseret News* that planned "Project Schooner" explosions in Idaho "would make guinea pigs out of thousands of people" who lived downwind along the fallout track.

Richard Hamburger, of the AEC's office in charge of peaceful uses of atomic energy, said then that the Schooner blast would cause "no dangerous radiation to populated areas."

Throughout the 1960s, the AEC repeatedly told the public, the press, and political leaders that there was no danger from the Nevada tests.

January 29, 1979

AEC PUT LID ON LEUKEMIA STUDY

By Gordon Eliot White
Copyright 1979 *Deseret News*

WASHINGTON—The White House and the Atomic Energy Commission apparently blocked the release in 1965 of a report of suspicious "excess" leukemia deaths in Utah, documents obtained by the *Deseret News* indicate.

Dr. Edward S. Weiss studied leukemia cases occurring in southwestern Utah between 1950 and 1964. He completed his work in the late summer of 1965 and reported finding more cases of the disease than would normally be expected in the population investigated.

The Public Health Service, which funded Weiss' work, recommended that his findings be released. But the AEC and at least one White House aide objected, and the results were never published.

Portions of Weiss' study were found in Utah by the *Deseret News* early in January, and his findings were reported Jan. 6 by the *Deseret News* and the *Washington Post.*

The White House role in controlling data released by scientists monitoring the fallout and its health consequences in Utah, Nevada, and Arizona was confirmed last week by Dr. John C. Villforth, director of the Bureau of Radiological Health.

Villforth told the *Deseret News* that during the atmospheric testing, the White House insisted upon clearing all of his agency's releases before publication. Documents obtained under the Freedom of Information Law confirm that by 1965 clearance by the White House and the AEC of Public Health Service data on fallout was customarily required.

PHS documents indicate that on Sept. 1, 1965, Dr. Peter Bing, of President Lyndon B. Johnson's Science Advisor's Office, called Dr. Donald R. Chadwick, then chief of the PHS Division of Radiological Health, and asked him, "What would be the federal government's liability for any clinical effects possibly due to radiation, which might be discovered" in a proposed follow-up to Weiss' work.

"After considerable discussion," a Sept. 2 memo related, Chadwick agreed to meet the next day with Bing; Dr. Charles Dunham, chief of the PHS Division of Biology and Medicine; Assistant Surgeon General Allen M. Pond; three lawyers from the Department of Health, Education, and Welfare; Gordon Dunning, sei ʌi scientist of the AEC division of Operational Safety; Assistant General Manager Dwight Ink of the AEC.

According to the PHS memo, "Dunning attacked the scientific validity of the leukemia paper, and the choice of Safford, Ariz., rather than another Utah community, as the control population" for a planned study of thyroid cancer.

Ink said the AEC "wanted to suggest certain changes in the release [on leukemia], and were quite concerned about the present version of the report."

Ink, for the AEC, commented that the number of subjects involved in the PHS studies "is so exceedingly small ... that results can be statistically suspect even before obtaining them."

He objected to a statement in the study that the relatively high concentration of fallout debris in the air in southwestern Utah constituted evidence of high external radiation exposure, a connection, he said, that "has not been established."

Ink objected as well to methods of estimating thyroid radiation doses to St. George children and claimed that levels of Strontium-90 in foodstuffs in the Nevada-Utah environs "are among the lowest in the country."

Prodded by the AEC, one of Weiss' PHS colleagues wrote after the meeting, "A few minor changes might be made in the report that would be consistent with the AEC view and would not degrade the results. I'm sure Ed Weiss would not object to those."

The report prepared by Weiss for the Public Health Service examined leukemia deaths in Washington and Iron counties between 1950 and 1964. As reported in the *Deseret News* Jan. 8, Weiss found 28 cases of leukemia, of which seven had their onset in 1959-60. Weiss reported no causal factor other than the coincidence that the victims had all lived for extended periods in the fallout area.

The AEC said of the Weiss report in an internal memo, "We have a number of problems with it, and serious reservations ... that the proposed follow-up studies will produce unequivocal data."

In fact, a Public Health Service reviewing officer described the Weiss study as "very mild" in tone and commented that the report did not point out "the high numbers of [leukemia] cases that were found" in the time period six to eight years after the peak 1953 fallout, which coincides closely with the latent period of leukemia.

Weiss did not note, the PHS memo continued, "the coincidence that in these particular counties [where the higher number of leukemia cases were seen to occur], which were in the path of the fallout, many of the residents drink fresh, unpasteurized milk."

Weiss used the word "cluster" to describe the cases he found, the PHS comment continued, and did not state his chief finding, that excessive leukemia was "clearly demonstrated."

The version finally submitted said in its conclusions, beyond the fact of extended residence in the area, "there is no evidence to associate these cases with fallout exposure, other environmental contaminants, or familiar disabilities."

A review of PHS files indicates that no press release was issued on the Weiss report, nor was it published in scientific literature. HEW did put out releases on Sept. 16 and Oct. 28, 1965, announcing studies of dental, eye, and thyroid characteristics of 2,000 Washington County school children, without mention of the Weiss work except to note that an examination of leukemia deaths had been started in Utah in 1959.

Weiss told the *Deseret News* that there was no publication of his study and that only manuscript copies were sent to the Centers for Disease Control in Atlanta and the Utah Division of Public Health.

Weiss left Washington immediately after his report was submitted to the PHS to carry out a thyroid study in St. George, which was the second of three studies of possible medical results of fallout. He said he spent the next three years in the state on that assignment.

"There was no pressure on me," he said, "to suppress the report. I guess they felt it was inconclusive. Since it was made available to the health officials in Salt Lake City and Atlanta, I cannot support any assertion it was hidden."

. . . .

January 30, 1979

**'65 NODULE REPORT RELEASED ONLY
AFTER A FIGHT**

By Gordon Eliot White

WASHINGTON—The Public Health Service had to fight all the way to the White House in 1965 to make public its study of thyroid nodules in St. George, Utah, documents obtained by the *Deseret News* Monday indicate.

The PHS, which lost a request in September 1965 to release data on a leukemia study in Utah, asked for a decision by President Lyndon B.

Johnson the following month on releasing news of the discovery of thyroid nodules in 70 St. George school children.

Internal government memos show that Secretary of Health, Education, and Welfare John W. Gardner wrote to the White House to urge release of the Utah thyroid data. The Gardner memo was addressed to Douglas Cater, special assistant to the president, after Dr. Donald R. Chadwick, chief of the PHS division of Radiological Health, had suggested "the President be informed so he can decide how this information can best be made public with due regard for its effect on national policies related to international relations, defense, and peaceful uses of nuclear energy."

The memos underline the extraordinary importance the Public Health Service placed on its data and the strength with which the Atomic Energy Commission opposed its publication.

Gardner wrote that the thyroid findings, still incomplete then, were "suggestive" of nodules of a kind that had been attributed to radiation effects from fallout.

Although the fact that thyroid studies were being made had been publicized in Utah, federal officials and the State Department of Public Health had kept the early findings secret, Gardner noted.

"Although this evidence still is not entirely clear," Gardner wrote, "I seriously doubt that it is wise to delay further some sort of public statement. The facts are already known to a fair number of people, and if they begin to receive circulation as rumors, the nature of the problem will be considerably magnified. In addition to the anxiety of the parents and the children, we have to consider the possible charge that we have been withholding from the parents and the public information that they have a right to know.

"Clearly," Gardner added, "this matter has such broad implications for public policy that the White House, and the AEC, and possibly the State Department, will wish to be aware of it and to comment on how it should be handled publicly."

In his memo to outgoing Surgeon General Luther L. Terry which mentioned several attempts to draw conclusions about health effects of fallout in Utah during the 1950s, including thyroid and leukemia studies, Chadwick wrote that "any real or apparent attempt to 'cover up' the results of these studies would result in great damage to the reputation of the federal government."

Despite such strong language from HEW, a press release on thyroid studies was drafted Oct. 22 and redrafted, finally appearing in a third version Oct. 28 with reference to the leukemia studies again deleted.

Where the first two drafts referred to "an examination of leukemia deaths occurring in Utah and Nevada since 1959," the final version mentioned only a "long-term investigation to determine whether a statistically meaningful relationship might exist between certain health defects which may occur naturally, and exposures to radiation."

The release did spell out in general a progress report on thyroid studies that Utah State Health Director G. D. C. Thompson had given at a regular meeting of the State Board of Health the day before, and which could not have been kept secret.

When the thyroid studies were completed, over the next two years, scientists found "inconclusive" indications of thyroid nodules in children in the fallout areas.

Apparently children in a control group in Graham County, Ariz., had almost as many nodules as did children in St. George. The nodules were not cancerous at the time.

Those studies have since been questioned by a number of scientists and work on them has been re-opened this year by the Bureau of Radiological Health. The bureau is attempting to determine from the Rocky Mountain Cancer Registry whether any of the individuals examined in 1965-67 have developed thyroid-related cancers in the last 14 years.

February 7, 1979

FALLOUT LEVELS UNDERSTATED,·DATA INDICATE

By Gordon Eliot White
Deseret News Washington Bureau
Copyright 1979 *Deseret News*

WASHINGTON—The nation's top atomic scientists advised in 1950 that nuclear testing could be done in Nevada, apparently giving no consideration to the possibility that weak radiation could, over many years, induce leukemia or other forms of cancer.

The information is contained in a report which has remained secret for more than 28 years. It was declassified this week by the Department of Energy at the request of the *Deseret News*.

The report contains notes summarizing a day-long meeting held at the Atomic Weapons Laboratory in Los Alamos, N.M., during which the world's most brilliant atomic physicists, Enrico Fermi, Edward Teller, and 22 other sophisticated scientists, spent all day on Aug. 1, 1950, examining radiological hazards that would be associated with a continental test site for atomic bombs.

Nowhere in the 32 pages of notes taken for the Atomic Energy Commission by Los Alamos physicist Dr. Frederick Reines is there mention of long-range human risk.

The notes summarizing the meeting were presented to the National Security Council in November 1950 to support the AEC's request to set up the Nevada Test Site.

An apparent increase in leukemia and cancer deaths in southern Utah in recent years has raised the possibility of a link with fallout that drifted over the area from nuclear tests in Nevada.

The discussion of maximum acceptable radiation dose took up only five paragraphs in the report, most of which was devoted to meteorology.

Scientists at the Bureau of Radiological Health told the *Deseret News* on Friday that radiation was known to be a carcinogen in 1950, but that it is now known to be hazardous at lower doses than were appreciated in the 1940s and 1950s.

Doses as low as 6.5 (a roentgen equivalent) have been shown to cause thyroid cancer in patients in Israel. The present radiation protection guide for the general population is less than 10 roentgens in the first 30 years of life or 17 annually. These units are not necessarily the same as roentgens, but may be roughly compared.

"There should have been some concern for delayed effects, even in 1950," one public health service radiobiologist told the *Deseret News*.

"Twenty-five roentgens is not a minor dose," the doctor said.

The discussions of the atomic scientists were based on the assumption that a person could receive a dose of 25 roentgens whole-body gamma radiation rapidly administered at one time, without suffering physical disability, Reines wrote in the summary.

Army radiologist Gen. James P. Cooney was quoted by Reines as saying, "This number could be taken as official and he felt Shields, Warren, and others in the radiobiology field would accept it.

"The dose from which unmistakable signs of biological effect can be observed, but from which it is reasonably certain that no permanent injury will result, is one in the neighborhood of 100 R," the notes say.

The scientists took as a working dose 6.5 roentgens, based on calculations that below 6.5 no eyrthema, or reddening of the skin, would be caused. Reines wrote in a footnote that in an Aug. 11, 1950, memo, Cooney cited a figure twice as large before eyrthema would be expected.

Participants in the 1950 meeting were a who's who of nuclear science. Fermi was a Nobel Prize winner, the man who directed construction of the world's first nuclear reactor under the stadium of the University of Chicago in 1942.

Teller, then assistant director of the Los Alamos Scientific Laboratory, became known later as the "father of the hydrogen bomb." Others included physicist John C. Clark, associate division leader at LASL, and physicist Alvin C. Graves, deputy scientific director of Pacific Proving Grounds Operations (Bikini).

Chemist Joseph W. Kennedy, leader of the LASL Division of Chemistry and Metallurgy, and co-discoverer of plutonium, took part, along with Cooney, a 24-year Army doctor who had done field and laboratory studies on radiological hazards following atomic detonations.

. . . .

February 7, 1979

FALLOUT LEVELS UNDERSTATED, DATA INDICATE

Copyright 1979 *Deseret News*
By Gordon Eliot White
Deseret News Washington Bureau

WASHINGTON—A previously secret report of atomic test fallout, just made available to the *Deseret News*, indicates that charts published by the Atomic Energy Commission have seriously understated the amount of radiation that Washington County communities received between 1951 and 1959.

A report of the Public Health Service off-site monitoring activities during the spring of 1953 shows that just four tests between March 17 and May 19 dropped nearly four times the radiation in the St. George area as the AEC has maintained that St. George received in the whole first eight years and four months of the test program.

The AEC chart for January 1951 through May 1959 was reproduced by the *Deseret News* Jan. 10, 1979. It shows estimated cumulative external gamma exposures of 2.5 roentgens for most of Washington County, with a small area of 5.0 roentgen dose.

The PHS chart covering March 17 through May 19, 1953, and marked "for official use only," shows a 9.0 roentgen exposure contour reaching as far east as Springdale, Washington County, and a 3.0 roentgen line reaching as far north as Pintura, Washington County, and as far east as Kanab, Kane County.

Cumulative figures for all 26 blasts that dropped fallout in Utah would necessarily show higher doses, government scientists told the *Deseret News*, although the 1953 shots were apparently the dirtiest of the entire program in terms of effect in the state.

One of the 1953 shots alone, code-named Harry, deposited enough radioactivity at Hurricane and St. George, 5.2 roentgens, to more than double the figure of 2.5 roentgens at those communities on the AEC 1951-59 chart.

Harry was a 32 kiloton explosion fired May 19, 1953. It also left 4.0 roentgen at Springdale and 3.0 roentgen at Kanab, Orderville, and Rockville. Other fallout-producing tests that spring were Annie on March 17, Nancy on March 24, and Simon on April 25.

The PHS figures now back up another government report, one made by Harold A. Knapp for the AEC itself in 1962, that took issue with the commission's public position that there were no hazards in the radio-active doses being received by Utahns downwind from the Nevada test site.

A Lawrence Radiation Laboratory report, previously reported by the *Deseret News,* also indicated relatively high radiation levels of 120 rads in St. George that exceeded AEC published figures.

Neither Knapp nor Arthur R. Tamplin and H. Leonard Fisher, who did the Lawrence study, appear to have had access to the PHS fallout figures. Tamplin and Fisher do not cite the document in their paper, and Knapp told the *Deseret News* he had not seen the PHS data. In his paper he cites the official AEC chart, prepared by a commission group headed by Dr. A. Van Shelton and reported by Gordon M. Dunning, range safety scientist at the Nevada site.

Sources here indicated that the PHS work was considered restricted information and was never published. A notation on page 68 of the work states that, since "the degree of biological hazard with such amounts of air contamination over short periods of time is, however, extremely difficult to evaluate, and in the absence of specific information indicating existence of hazard, the panel of experts advising the Atomic Energy Commission on these matters now recommends that air concentrations be measured for purpose of record only."

The question of the doses received by off-site civilians is important because the official figures are below levels that scientists accept as dangerous.

Examination of Japanese exposed to the Hiroshima and Nagasaki bombings and British patients treated with radiation for a spinal disease indicate that for a one rem exposure, one case of leukemia and six of other cancers will occur per year per million population. Since Iron and Washington counties together had a population of 26,000 in the 1970 census, the expected number of radiation-caused cancers even over the 20 years, or 1951-71, would be less than two and would be unmeasurable.

From Dunning's AEC data, Knapp estimated that 120,000 people within 200 miles of the Nevada test site were exposed to an average of

700 milliroentgens, and 10,000 people in the area immediately adjoining the site received between three and five roentgens. The PHS data indicates that Dunning's figures are seriously underestimated.

Based upon Dunning's published figures, Knapp estimated iodine 131 exposures to the thyroid as high as 60 to 240 times the external doses, because of the concentrated effect of the milk chain, where a cow eats contaminated foliage, converts it to milk, which is consumed and reconcentrated in the human thyroid.

Knapp was bitterly attacked within the AEC and his paper was threatened with suppression in 1962. It was finally published with changes that masked its findings.

Knapp told the *Deseret News* that the commission censored examples of his findings, including an estimate of I-131 dose ranging from 110 to 440 rads at St. George. Templin and Fisher estimated a range of 30 to 240 rads at St. George in their 1966 paper, and Charles Mays of the University of Utah gave a 68 rad figure in his 1963 testimony before the Joint Committee on Atomic Energy, all based on Dunning's roentgen figures. If Dunning's figures are revised upward, the rad exposure in southwestern Utah could be multiplied sharply.

The *Deseret News* reported Knapp's findings and his difficulties with the AEC eight years ago, but nothing was done to follow them up, apparently because no link to disease had been found and thyroid studies had been inconclusive in 1965–67.

At the same time that Knapp was making his estimates, following not only Dunning's figures but also his formula used in another context to estimate the effect of an atomic war, the AEC was telling the public:

"The data and their evaluations clearly indicate that nuclear weapons testing over a span of ten years has not resulted in radiation exposures approaching the Federal Radiation Council guides established for normal peacetime operations."

Federal Radiation Council guides for normal peacetime operations in 1962 indicated an annual thyroid dose of 0.5 rads to "a suitable sample of the population" and 1.5 rads to individuals.

Dunning pleaded, in an exchange of memos, that reaction from the press and the public might be adverse if the commission, in effect, admitted that it had permitted the Utah and Nevada population to be exposed to the I-131 levels high enough to put a ten-year's allowance of I-131 into a single quart of milk in some communities.

"We have spent years of hard, patient effort to establish good and calm relations with the public around NTS," Dunning wrote. "Such action as the author's has been harmful."

Knapp related that he attempted to get data from Dunning's office at NTS on shots other than the 1962 smallboy test, but was told that no data existed. Dunning, Knapp said, was the only one who had the reports from off-site radiological safety organizations. According to Knapp, Utah health officials at the time were forced to set up duplicate monitoring facilities because the AEC would not give the state its figures.

Applying his data to available information on preceding shots, Knapp estimated that there have been "at least several" shots in Nevada that produced off-site exposures as great as the 1957 Windscale accident in England that caused milk levels to reach 1,300,000 picocuries of I-131 per liter and led to a major health crisis there. He noted that at Windscale, .16 kiloton equivalent of I-131 was released, and that through 1962, more than 1,000 kiloton equivalent had been released in Nevada.

5

THE *CHARLOTTE OBSERVER*

"When you're up to your neck in alligators," the saying goes, "it's hard to remember that your initial objective was to drain the swamp."

At the *Charlotte* (N.C.) *Observer*, they know what that expression means. In the summer of 1979, the *Observer* decided to examine the controversy over byssinosis, commonly called "brown lung," a crippling respiratory ailment alleged to be prevalent among the textile millworkers in the Carolinas. "I was thinking, well, two of us [would] take about six weeks," recalls Howard Covington, the paper's "projects" reporter. "But I've always been very unrealistic about that. I spent six weeks just looking at OSHA [Occupational Safety and Health Administration] records."

By February 1980, when the story was ready for publication, it had enlisted the efforts of 17 *Observer* reporters, photographers, and editors, some of whom had done little else for the previous six months. They produced 88,000 words of copy (edited down to roughly half that length), 22 articles, eight editorials, and more than 40 photographs. The paper spread all of this before its readers over eight days. It was by far the most comprehensive report ever published on the subject in the news media, and it earned for the *Observer* a satchel of awards: the North Carolina Press Association's Public Service Award, the Roy W. Howard Public Service Award (from the Scripps-Howard Foundation), and the Robert F. Kennedy Award for reporting on the problems of the poor. Most significantly, the series beat out 88 other entries to win the Pulitzer Prize for Meritorious Public Service.

With two exceptions, all of the interviews for this chapter were conducted in Charlotte. We talked with Howard Covington in Greensboro, N.C., where he had become city editor of the *Daily News*, and we interviewed Bob Drogin in Philadelphia, where he was a reporter for the *Inquirer*.

Other information came from these sources:

Bob Hall, "The Brown Lung Controversy, " *Columbia Journalism Review*, March/April 1978, pp. 27–35.

Wayne A. Clark, "How 'The Charlotte Observer' Won the Pulitzer Prize," *Tar Heel*, August 1981, pp. 30–34.

As the newspapers cited in this book amply illustrate, the decision to undertake a major investigative series on a sensitive issue is not made in a vacuum. We should not be surprised to find that a newspaper honored for an achievement of the scope of "Brown Lung" has a rich tradition of such reporting. During the 1960s and '70s, the *Observer* produced careful studies of race relations, hunger, poverty, and migration of Southerners to the North. In 1979, the paper won national recognition yet again for a hard look at the link between the state's major crop, tobacco, and lung cancer.

Their ears ringing with compliments, *Observer* staffers began casting about for a suitable topic for their next project. From his base in Raleigh, Covington sent a memo to his editors in Charlotte suggesting a series on the textile industry, the South's largest industrial employer (435,000 of the nation's one million textile workers live in the Carolinas). Covington originally wanted to delve into all of the industry's problems, including foreign competition, outmoded plants, and union organizing. "We just didn't have the horses to do the whole thing on textiles," he says, "so I narrowed this thing down to a proposal on brown lung."

Covington's memo was considered at a meeting attended by all of the paper's department heads. By all accounts, a consensus quickly developed, in the words of the project coordinator, Laura King, "that we ought to do it full-scale. That surprised me. People kept coming up with other ideas I hadn't thought about—'how about this [angle]? how about that?' " The department heads met to consider the series because a commitment to tie up even several reporters and editors would mean reduced coverage in other areas and extra work by those not involved in the project. "Everyone's going to have to really be behind it or else there's going to be some hard feelings," she explained.

That decision to involve many people in the planning process turned out to be even more important than the participants in the meeting could have foreseen because of the eventual scope of the series. "It just sort of mushroomed," King said. "It got even bigger than we intended originally." Added Covington: "The thing sort of took on a life of its own. Once you got started on it there was no going back. ... I don't think any of us—at least I didn't realize how much time it was going to take. I worked on it steadily from the first of August to the first of February."

Covington's first step was to examine the records of the state Labor Department. In most states, he would have gone to the federal Occupational Safety and Health Administration (OSHA), but North Carolina was among a handful of states that set its own standards and conducted its own inspections; this was permissible under federal law as long as the state's standards were at least as stringent as the federal ones.

"I spent the first two or three weeks finding my way around" the state Labor Department's Raleigh offices, Covington recalls.

"The records are public but nobody'd been over there to ask for them before." The agency wouldn't let him poke through its factory-inspection files at will because they contained what is known as proprietary information—facts about the mills of potential value to competitors. Another problem was that there are about 400 to 450 plants in North Carolina that process cotton. He needed to know which ones had been found to violate the federal cotton-dust standards.

Directories he obtained from the state and federal Commerce Departments enabled him to produce a list of all the plants in North Carolina that process cotton. In doing this, he met an industrial hygienist with the state Labor Department. "After talking to him and getting to know him a little bit, it turned out that he had a list of all the plants the Labor Department had inspected for cotton dust. So I wheedled out of him a copy of this list and on it it had all of the plants they had inspected, when they had inspected them, the ones where they had found serious violations. Well, then I had a starting point. I went through every one that had a serious violation," about 60 in all, recording the details of the findings and the dispositions of the cases.

Was it sheer luck that enabled Covington to stumble upon this list? "I knew there was a list somewhere. It was just a matter of finding the person who had it and convincing him" to part with a copy.

Covington found the officials cooperative, "most of the time. They knew they couldn't tell me 'no'; they knew these were public records. I think they hoped that after awhile I'd get discouraged and quit. But after they realized I wasn't going to quit, that I was going to be there and I had plenty of time, they'd say, 'Well, it'll take three weeks,' and I'd say, 'OK, I'll be back in three weeks.' "

Covington believes the officials became increasingly cooperative as they watched him return to their offices every day and doggedly turn the pages of the inspection reports. "By the time I'd been up there for two or three weeks, [the official in charge] would come in and sit down and I'd say, 'Well look. I don't understand this. What's happening here?' and he'd take the case file and go over it and we'd talk about it. I don't know that he ever said it but I had a feeling after awhile that he became convinced we were serious."

Covington, in turn, developed some sympathy for the hard-pressed officials responsible for the inspections. "There are a lot of villains in the story, but there are also a lot of folks who are caught in the crack. The [state] Labor Department has a limited number of people. We gave them a hard time for failing to inspect all these plants. Well, it's their responsibility to do the inspections. ... [But] they can't if they don't have the people, [and] they can't get the people unless the legislature gives them the money. This guy had seven or eight inspectors to inspect 450 plants and each inspection could take as much as a week. At the same time, cotton dust is one of a dozen hazardous agents they're responsible for looking after. If there was a difference between some plant emitting some toxic chemical that can kill you within 24 hours and making an inspection for cotton dust, where would you go? You'd go to the one where there was some immediate danger."

The officials, he added, were also understandably reluctant to enforce the then-prevailing 1972 standard for allowable cotton-dust levels because it was under review and soon to be replaced.

By the end of September, as Covington finished working on the OSHA files and turned to the problem of workers' compensation, he began to realize that he would need help. He'd been discussing the project with another *Observer* reporter, Marion Ellis, but " the more we got into it the more it became apparent that we'd need more than two people. We had started out looking just in North Carolina, but that didn't make any sense. We've got a textile industry in South Carolina with the same problems, and we circulate [there]." Labor reporter Bob Dennis was dispatched to South Carolina after Covington briefed him on the difficulties he was likely to encounter trying to learn the results of mill inspections. Medical correspondent Bob Conn began looking into that sensitive angle. Bob Drogin used his contacts in the Brown Lung Association to probe that aspect. And Ellis conceived what Covington described as "really a brilliant stroke": to find an example of a family with several generations of mill workers. " We settled on the little town of China Grove, which is [near] where I grew up, and he found the Faggarts. It took him a couple of weeks just to find the folks, and then he spent another two, three weeks getting to know them and producing just that one page."[1]

---

[1]The Faggart story is not included in this book.

To find out what was happening to the compensation claims filed by mill workers who had contracted byssinosis, Covington had to deal with a state agency known as the Industrial Commission. It has "an incredible amount of power," he found, but its files were closed to the public. He turned to some young attorneys in Raleigh who worked in an office on the floor below his own. He knew they had worked on brown lung cases and he asked to see their files. After getting the approval of their clients, the lawyers agreed. Covington also got copies of some of the commission's decisions from the Brown Lung Association. Between these two sources, he had records of about 60 cases, perhaps a third of all of the brown lung cases heard by the commission. "What I was primarily looking for was some pattern with the commission," he explained. "[On] what basis were they making their decisions?"

One of Covington's most significant findings as he dug into the record was that the state began testing mill workers for respiratory problems in 1969 but agreed with the mills not to tell the workers what the testing was for. And workers who were found to have serious problems were not told about them. A memo from the state to Fieldcrest Mills in Eaton detailing the arrangement fell into Covington's hands—given to him, curiously, by the company doctor who had conducted the research.

"Never could figure that out," Covington said. "He just gave it to me. I went to him and was asking him about the research that was done in 1969. Why did you do it? How did you do it? What did you tell the people after you tested them? What happened to the people after you tested them? . . . At the time he gave me [the memo], I didn't know what it was. He said, 'Well, here's an agreement Fieldcrest Mills had with the state when we did the tests,' and I said, 'OK,' and I just stuffed it in my notebook." It was several weeks before Covington recognized what he had.

On another occasion, a hunch led Covington to an interesting irony. Poring over some old clips in Raleigh, he found a 1972 news release from the American Textile Manufacturers Institute. "It was the industry statement acknowledging that byssinosis existed and that the industry was committed to doing something about it," Covington said. Some weeks later, as the series was being written, Covington was reading the release and he wondered what inspection records showed about Graniteville Mills, the mill owned by ATMI's president, Robert Timmerman. "Well, it turned out that Graniteville Mills was one of the grossest violators in South Carolina," Covington recalled. "They had been really obstinate and fought the Labor Department tooth and nail every time they had been cited." So while the industry was publicly recognizing its responsibilities, its chief spokesman was fighting a persistent rear-guard action against even the mildest reform.

Findings such as these were not exactly lucky accidents; they were the products of meticulous research. Covington amassed so many documents that Ellis gave him a newspaper carrier's delivery bag to keep them in; it must have weighed 40 pounds by the end of the project, Covington estimated. Drogin interviewed more than 150 people. Behind all of this effort lay the realization that this was no ordinary story: the largest newspaper in the Carolinas was tackling the region's chief employer. "If you're going to take on this issue," Convington explained, "you don't want to screw up, because you realize that if you do screw up, you're going to look awful damn bad when it's over with. So you might as well go on and do it right. You don't want to make a grand play and then have to turn around the next week and say, 'Gee, folks, we really did kind of screw up a little bit.'"

Besides an overriding concern for accuracy, the *Observer* team was painfully aware that past coverage of brown lung had often lapsed into the sloppily sentimental. They recognized that an industry spokesman's parody of that coverage was uncomfortably on target. Interviewed by the *Columbia Journalism Review*, he said that brown lung features

seem to follow an almost predictable pattern. They lead off with a reader-grabber, sob-sister approach. A sort of, "Here's poor Nellie Gray, who used to be healthy and happy. Now she can hardly move. Every breath is a struggle. The reason? Nellie worked thirty years in a cotton textile mill. She has byssinosis, an incapacitating and often fatal disease contracted by breathing cotton dust." Well, that's great for readership, perhaps. And, of course, readership is what newspapers are all about. But it doesn't do much to advance the search for truth.

Covington called such stories "shlock. You can knock one of those out in a week. It became a real matter of pride not to copycat the stories that had been done before and to do something that would be respected by the workers and government as a fine piece of work." Rather than just another emotional appeal, the *Observer's* managing editor Mark Ethridge told *Tar Heel* magazine, "I made the determination that it would be investigative, not sociological. We went for the hard facts."

The series did not entirely eschew the human-interest approach, however. Few readers would be unaffected by the photographs of mill worker Landrum Clary and his 20 feet of plastic tubing. Or by the story of worker English Smith, whose employer discovered his byssinosis but withheld the information from him and resisted his compensation claims despite the diagnoses of four doctors. Or by the plight of another mill worker, John Moore, whose compensation claim was denied because he did not have the symptoms traditionally associated with byssinosis—symptoms now recognized by his doctors as unnecessary to diagnose the disease.

But the reporters insisted that these examples, heart-rending though they may be, were used to illustrate particular things that had happened to many workers. "We didn't go out to find the people and then go research the problem," Covington said. "We researched the problem and you find the people by doing that." Tracking them down wasn't always easy. In the case of Clary, the reporters read an early medical-journal study on byssinosis which noted that of 499 workers tested, 50 were found to be sick. "Marion [Ellis] and I set out to find one of these 50," Covington said. Ellis did it by knocking on doors of the small mill town where the tests were conducted in 1969, confident that someone in the closely knit community of workers had been tested or would know someone who was. It took two days to find Clary.

Although Ellis was able to confirm from Clary's employer that he had been tested, the company declined to release further information, so the account relied largely on Clary's own recollections.

If the stories of English Smith, John Moore, and Landrum Clary almost certainly touched most readers, the reporters were not unaffected, either. Drogin was determined that these individual stories not be submerged in the mass of data. He was particularly moved by Smith's travails: "Here was a man who had worked hard and had gotten screwed all along the line. He was a victim of duplicity by the mills, by the state, by the doctors." For his part, Covington felt "a crusader's zeal that you're doing something right and maybe something good will come out of it. You get wrapped up in the folks you're dealing with."

Covington recalls one victim in particular. "Because I went to see her and talk to her about her problems, she got active in the Brown Lung Association. And she is now recruiting other people and talking to her friends and getting them to take breathing tests and pay more attention to the conditions in the mill. I could see that developing as I was talking to her. When I first saw her, she was kind of bewildered about her case, and the more I talked to her about her life and things that had happened to her, the more it all started coming into place in her mind. ... And that's going on while you're working on the story and you could see the changes in the people you're dealing with." He found himself inspired by the courage of the victims to pursue the tangled story as doggedly as necessary.

Keenly aware of their sympathies, the reporters strove to keep them out of their stories. Although Covington felt the stirrings of "a crusader's zeal," Drogin insisted: "I don't think we were particularly crusading journalists. I think we bent over backwards and then some to make the stories as fair as we possibly could. But I think on a personal level if you asked any of us what we thought was happening, we thought these people were getting screwed."

That raised some ethical problems: does the reporter have any responsibility to help the workers? Covington said he felt like a "messenger of doom" in talking with a brown lung victim who had received a negligible settlement from her employer. "You go in and say, 'They really took you for a ride, lady.' And you almost feel a responsibility to help out but you can't do it. You're no lawyer. All you can say is, 'Well, I think you ought to see a lawyer. I can't tell you what to do.' That's not your job. . . . Sometimes you feel kind of callous . . . but if you try to get involved in carrying all their problems, you're getting in over your head. You can't cope with it."

In early December, the massive task of converting all of the research into a series of stories for publication began. It took six weeks.

"We worked a week on the first story," said Covington, who shifted his base temporarily from Raleigh to a Charlotte motel. "Then we ripped it up and started over. We yelled and screamed a little bit; it relieved the frustration."

Editor Rich Oppel, one of four editors who worked closely with the reporters in the final writing process, described it as "gang bang journalism. Everybody had a hand in it. There were some frayed nerves."

Bob Drogin said the work was complicated by the fact that "none of us are great writers, and so it took a long time to write because we all had different styles and we all had individual batches of information that meshed. . . . It was a crazy situation. Howard [Covington] would write his piece and then he would ship it to me and I would put the lead on it and it would go to Marion [Ellis] and he would add his piece. It was writing by committee, and at the end it was very frustrating to virtually everybody involved because it went in a series of concentric circles." He recalls the first story being bounced back and forth among three editors and the three reporters who had researched it. "There was never any end to the goddamn thing," Drogin said.

But all hands agreed that the magnitude of the story required this painstaking attention to detail and the participation of the reporters as well as the editors. "There was constant revision from both ends," project coordinator Laura King said. "That creates its own kind of tension. . . . Although it was tough on our psyches, it was the thing to do because so much was at stake. This was not a story about a school board meeting."

The reporters saw the need to have copy pass through the hands of editors who had not been closely involved in gathering the information and could look at it with a fresh perspective and a concern for the needs of the reader. Covington said he found the first story tough to write because "your impulse is to write everything." Keeping in mind an overview of all of the stories in the package, the editors wanted to make sure that overlapping was kept to a minimum and that the mass of material remain organized and coherent. "No way you could really put it together without someone like that," Covington said. "This would have been an absolute failure as a one-man project."

At the same time, the reporters worried that the editors may not have understood enough of the subtleties and complexities of brown lung. Concerned with reducing the mass of information to publishable size, the editors might change the meaning of a sentence in small but important ways. Covington recalls repeated efforts to explain to his editors that "settlement" and "award" were significantly different and could not be used interchangeably. "After it happens a couple of times, you beat them over the head and they finally understand the difference," he said.

Even the nature of brown lung itself continued to confuse some editors. "Some people who had been very close to the project still didn't understand that when you suffer from brown lung you don't literally have little particles of dust clogging up your windpipe," Covington said. "It's a chemical reaction, like bronchitis, that's causing your breathing problems. You're not filling up your lungs with cotton balls."

When the participants in the editing process could not resolve such problems, managing editor Mark Ethridge stepped in. "My role was to referee the fights," he explained. "That's a little flip, but that's basically my job."

The newspaper's attorney also checked the copy to guard against libeling an individual or corporation. If he spotted something potentially damaging, he would ask to see the reporter's evidence before approving it.

"There is a lot of agony" in the final stages of any project, Oppel said. "A reporter wants to report the story, write it, and then push it away. There is a point when you finish writing that you don't want to have another darn thing to do with it. Well, that is the point where work really starts for people like me. We go through this time after time: management, the metro editor, the lawyer, all asking the same questions. The reporters get short fuses. There are fights and wars and two people siding against two other people. I am convinced there is almost no way to avoid that kind of agony."

He tries to minimize the hard feelings generated by the process. "A good part of my job is just kind of brokering the peace, calling the reporters in here, going out to lunch with them, putting my arm around them, saying, 'Hell of a good job, this is terrible, you got to hang in there. It's all gonna be worth it when this stuff hits the paper even though it takes another month.'"

Meanwhile, those *Observer* staffers not involved in the project were feeling the strain of having to cover for their missing colleagues for several months. "I wouldn't say there was resentment," Drogin said. "There were people who said, 'When are you guys going to be finished? Give us a break.' There was a certain amount of pressure to finish the damn thing so we could get on to other stories."

Oppel decided to accompany the series with an editor's introduction that began: "This series may make you angry. . . . You may be angry with the *Charlotte Observer*." After summarizing some of the key findings, Oppel wrote:

We're publishing this series to inform. We're doing it because the people hurt by byssinosis . . . are the voiceless members of our family of Carolinians. . . . We hope this series will bring improvements. . . . We hope to help make the Carolinas a better place to live and work.

Oppel said the statement reflected the paper's concern that readers would resent the series as an attack on the source of many of their livelihoods. "We were prepared to believe that it was going to make a lot of people mad, and it did," Oppel said. "And I didn't want those people thinking that we were doing that without an awareness of that. And I'm a believer in explaining what a newspaper does."

Efforts to deflect criticism, especially from the textile industry, actually began before the series hit print. " My approach is to immediately try to vent the wound," Oppel explained. "When somebody calls and says that what you're doing is bad for my company, my industry, my state, and the readers, my inclination is to say, 'Well, come on in, let's have coffee and talk about it.' . . . There were a couple of occasions prior to the publication of the series when a textile executive would visit here and talk. I made a tour of the textile plant and we went to lunch, and that probably went some of the distance to deflecting the building pressure when you don't listen."

On the day the second installment of the series was published, a trade association of the textile industry met in Charlotte. "There was talk of coming down hard on the *Observer*," Oppel recalled. "But I led a small delegation of editors to sit in with them and hear the speeches, which were fairly mild. I think you've got to be a lightning rod for that and take it all and be prepared to change your thinking."

Although the series on brown lung and the earlier takeout on the cigarette-lung cancer link were widely seen as courageous examples of a newspaper tackling the largest employers in its region, the *Observer* editors and reporters we interviewed routinely denied that publishing the stories required any courage. "Hell, there isn't a tobacco plant within 50 miles of Charlotte, either a plant in the ground or a plant out of bricks," Covington said. "So it really wasn't a terribly gutsy thing to do." As for the brown lung series, "What kind of pressure can [the textile industry] bring to bear?" Oppel asked. "Advertisers can bring pressure, [but] textile industries are not big advertisers. . . . They can raise hell with the publisher but we have a strong publisher who has no problem with investigative and provocative journalism as long as we have the facts right and are fair with people."

Covington, who said he experienced no pressure from the industry while the series was being researched or after publication, noted that the industry consists of small, hotly competitive mills rather than a few powerful ones. "They can't agree; they're jealous of each other," Covington explained. "While they get together in associations, they don't necessarily come together as a group to say, 'We're going to agree to get the *Charlotte Observer* because they're doing this series.'"

Even if they did, it is questionable whether they could hurt a paper the size of the *Observer*, supported as it is by the power of the Knight-Ridder chain. "If you live in a one-industry town and they supply 95 percent of your advertising and your readership, there is a reason to fear that if you offend that industry greatly it may affect your balance sheet," notes editorial writer Ed Williams. "So it's easier for the *Observer* in some ways because we are a very big newspaper [with] a lot of sources of income."

Williams believes timidity also helps explain why stories such as brown lung appear so infrequently. "The reason [the series] looks so courageous to many newspapers is that most newspapers are just cowardly. Journalism in America is just woeful when it comes to any power to stand up against wealth or a political force. It's just appalling."

The brown lung series was not a new idea; indeed, it is a classic illustration of the thesis advanced by reporter Jonathan Neumann, co-author of "The Homicide Files" (Chapter I), that the best stories are the ones already widely known and therefore routinely overlooked. Ralph

Nader coined the term "brown lung" in 1971 and charged that the textile industry denied the existence of the disease and sought to block efforts to study it. A survey of media coverage of the problem by the *Columbia Journalism Review* in 1975 found it largely sporadic and superficial. The article complained that no major North Carolina daily had done "a major investigative series on the issue, probing, for example, the role the medical community played, or might have played, during the years the textile industry refused to recognize the existence of byssinosis."

Why not? The article speculated that some newspapers hesitate to challenge the powerful industry, the main advertiser and employer in many Southern towns. It's also a tough, unconventional story, one reporter noted: "Middle-class journalists who are used to dealing with middle-class officials won't get off their asses to make the difficult effort to find people on the other side. You've got to get out and talk with elderly, sick, working-class Southerners who may not even be aware that it's important to talk to the press. Too many reporters wind up being establishment stooges, not because they're uncaring people, but because they're middle class and don't want to struggle with speaking another language, with different people." Finally, another reporter cited in the article saw brown lung as no more than a tapped-out feature idea: "How many times can you write a story about some old guy who worked thirty years in the mill and can't breathe?"

Observer staffers we spoke to denied that coverage of brown lung prior to the series was as poor as the article charged, but others conceded that the series revealed little that was not previously known. "Much of what we have in the paper is substantiating things which we have seen at various times," said Ed Williams, the chief editorial writer, who wrote all of the editorials accompanying the series. "I don't think a reasonable person living in the Carolinas, interested in the problems of the area, could not know many of these things. So many of these things are just there. If you live the life a journalist lives, you come in contact with them." Said Covington: "It's like anything else that becomes part of your everyday life: it doesn't stand out until you start putting it all together. And then after you start accumulating some things you realize what a serious problem it is."

To Bob Drogin, "Implicit in this [series] just by the tremendous amount of work that went into this was just how much was out there and how little had been in the newspaper."

Laura King said journalists "go for the easiest story. Who are the crooks? Who can we put in jail? We don't look for the more insidious problems. ... [They are] tough to report. It's very time-consuming.

There aren't many newpapers that are going to spend as much time as we spent on this."

Covington also cited the economic factor: "This was a very expensive undertaking. And there's the tendency to do things as quickly and as cheaply as you can—there's always another paper to put out, folks."

All of the project participants we interviewed flatly denied that industry pressure or fear of retaliation from the industry accounted for any shortcomings in past coverage of the issue. Furthermore, despite the nationwide chorus of praise received by the *Observer* for standing up to the industry, the reporters and editors all insisted that they had anticipated no pressure from industry to soft-pedal or abandon the series and there was none, nor any retaliation afterwards.

Finally we need to pose the question that is always raised about an investigative project: what results did it achieve? The brown lung series produced several small changes rather than a single dramatic one: beefed-up mill-inspection staffs in North and South Carolina, record high compensation to brown lung victims, a decision to permit public inspection of the Industrial Commission files in both states. State officials praised the series and acknowledged its influence in shaping policy in the area.

But it remains true, in Covington's words, that "it would really be hard to [find] tangible results." Because of that, he doubted the series had much chance of winning the Pulitzer. "I just had a feeling that if it was really going to score, there would have to be mountains moved and real reactions from people. It wasn't like that."

But the absence of any dramatic change did not discourage the project's participants. Covington believes the series may have produced invisible improvements. "There are probably a lot more doctors in our coverage area who know about byssinosis and who may be thinking about it the next time one of their patients comes in with a serious lung problem," he said. "And [the doctor] recommends that the person get another job. So he leaves the mill, and because he doesn't have severe or chronic symptoms, it'll clear up and he'll live a normal, healthy life."

To Covington and his colleagues, that increased awareness is their most lasting achievement. "What you do in something like this is you just raise the visibility of it somehow." Adds Williams: "It is not my thought that 90 percent of the mill owners, after reading this, said, 'Oh my God, this is a bad situation and we have to do something immediately.' I don't think a newspaper has that direct cause-and-effect power.

But I do think it's impossible after this series and these editorials for a sensitive and responsible person to deny some responsibility for it. That is the beginning of change."

And the *Observer* staff found one final source of pride. "We didn't have to skim back on a single word in that whole series," Covington noted. "There weren't any mistakes."

February 3–10, 1980

BROWN LUNG: A CASE OF DEADLY NEGLECT

AS SOME IN INDUSTRY STALL, THE VICTIMS ARE LEFT BEHIND

This story was written by Observer staff writers Howard Covington, Bob Dennis, Bob Drogin and Marion A. Ellis.

Thirteen years after a government-sponsored study said workers were being crippled by cotton dust, many Carolinas cotton mill owners continue to discount its dangers, fight workers' compensation claims, delay cleaning the mills, and violate government regulations.

Experts estimate 18,000 Carolinians—who have spent their lives in some of the industry's dirtiest, lowest-paying jobs—are disabled by byssinosis, or brown lung, the disease caused by cotton dust.

Yet, companies have compensated only about 320 former workers in the Carolinas for the loss of their health, paying them an average of $13,000 each in North Carolina and $14,000 in South Carolina.

And six years after the government ordered companies to clean up, thousands of Carolinas textile workers—at least 10,000 in North Carolina alone—are exposed to cotton dust levels that can kill.

While failing to clean up, some mill owners also concealed from individual workers the evidence of cotton dust's dangers.

State health department and other records show some mill owners identified brown lung victims in their plants and kept the information secret.

Government officials have made it easy for textile companies to resist the regulations they dispute. In North Carolina, officials have failed to inspect most cotton textile plants; in South Carolina officials grant plants an almost unlimited number of extensions of cleanup orders.

Textile industry spokesmen reject complaints of foot-dragging and negligence. They note—correctly—that some responsible employers have spent millions of dollars cleaning up the work place and compensating those disabled by byssinosis.

Industry leaders say their efforts to cope with cotton dust have been hampered by ambiguous government regulations, uneven enforcement, inadequate technology, and what they say are legitimate doubts over the cause of the disease they're supposed to prevent.

But during this past decade of legal arguments, scientific debates, and industry lobbying, the workers have been left behind.

In most cases, they have little education, minimum job skills, and small savings after a lifetime at one of the nation's lowest average hourly manufacturing wages. Many get no pension. They're no match for the Carolinas' largest industry.

"Working in a cotton mill was all he knew how to do," said a 1978 state order awarding disabled former textile worker Willie Prevatt, 56, of Roseboro, $114 a week, plus medical expenses, for life. "If he could not work in a cotton mill, he would be unable to live."

A Case in Point

The case of English P. Smith and the Graniteville Co. illustrates the problems surrounding brown lung in the Carolinas textile industry: Some companies don't tell workers they have byssinosis, resist paying their medical bills or compensation, and don't clean the work place even after workers get sick.

Smith, a weave room worker who quit school in the seventh grade, worked 34 years at the Granite Mill in Graniteville, S.C. In March 1978, Smith, then 51, collapsed on the job and was sent home under oxygen. His doctor told him not to return. He is crippled today.

Dr. Russell Harley, a pathologist at the Medical University of South Carolina in Charleston, told Graniteville officials in July 1974 that Smith had byssinosis—more than two years before Smith learned he had the disease from his own doctor.

Only then, in late 1976, did the company do anything. Graniteville officials transferred Smith out of the dusty weave room to a machine shop in the dye factory. They also cut his salary for six days' work from $244 to $227.

Smith filed a claim for workers' compensation in the summer of 1978. Four doctors diagnosed byssinosis but the company refused to pay. Six months later, too sick to keep fighting and too broke to pay his mounting medical expenses, Smith settled with Graniteville for $20,000—half the maximum amount.

Graniteville chief executive Robert Timmerman said the company was "more than compassionate" with Smith. He said he doesn't believe weave room workers can contract byssinosis.

"I don't believe today that E. P. Smith ever had byssinosis," Timmerman said. Even with diagnoses from four doctors? "Even with 40 doctors," he replied.

Timmerman, 59, is a former president of the American Textile Manufacturers Institute (ATMI). Speaking for the institute in 1972, he said the industry was trying to control dust and was protecting workers while doctors searched for a cause of byssinosis.

But two years later, S.C. Labor Department inspectors found dust in Graniteville's Swint Plant exceeded legal limits by at least three times. Workers were not wearing federally required respirators—face masks designed to filter dust—which Timmerman had said the industry was requiring in 1972.

The inspectors cited Graniteville four more times, between 1974 and 1979, for violating dust levels at other plants, including the Granite mill where Smith worked.

In July 1978, inspectors found six serious violations of dust standards at the Granite mill, including one area where dust was six times the legal limit, and three nonserious violations because workers were not wearing respirators.

A fine of $560 was proposed, then dropped to $100 after the company protested. Timmerman said the company paid the fine, but labor department records don't show the fine was ever paid or the violations corrected.

Timmerman said the company had spent $2.2 million for equipment to reduce cotton dust in the Granite plant, but the equipment wasn't operating right and needed "fine tuning" during the inspection.

Timmerman said the company, which made nearly $6 million in profits before taxes last year, has about 3,000 people working in cotton dust at its eight mills. But he said the company doesn't require they wear respirators, even in areas where federal regulations require it.

"Our people put it on and our people almost had a revolt," Timmerman said. "Our people said, 'Mr. Timmerman, we can't breathe with these, they're trying to kill us.'"

A Major Carolinas Problem

Byssinosis is not the burden of the Carolinas alone. The textile industry employs about 122,000 people in Georgia, and 50,000 each in Alabama, Virginia, and Pennsylvania. But nearly half the nation's textile workers—391,500—work in the Carolinas, making almost half the nation's $40 billion worth of towels, sheets, hosiery, blankets, denim, and other woven goods.

In North Carolina about 250,000 people—one of every three factory workers—work in one of more than 1,300 textile plants. About 70,000 workers are exposed to cotton dust. In South Carolina, about 141,500 people work in 388 textile plants, or two of every five industrial workers. About 45,000 work in cotton dust. The rest of Carolinas textile mills and workers—about two-thirds—handle only synthetic and other noncotton fibers.

N.C. Board of Health Study

Early medical research confirmed that Carolinas millworkers had byssinossis, despite denials by industry spokesmen. But state and company officials didn't tell workers why they were being tested.

In 1967, N.C. State Board of Health doctors agreed to disguise the purpose of a byssinosis study in Fieldcrest Mills Inc.'s Eden plants in central North Carolina near the Virginia border.

"We will tell them that the doctors are interested in the relation of smoking, heart disease, asthma, allergies, and dustiness to breathing difficulties," state doctor Peter Schragg proposed in a Nov. 10, 1967, letter to Fieldcrest. "This is honest but still avoids mentioning terms such as byssinosis, compensation, or occupational disease."

State health doctors determined that 63 of Fieldcrest's 509 workers had brown lung. Fieldcrest didn't tell any of the 63 they had byssinosis until several years later because the study, the first in a privately owned American textile mill, was "very, very crude," says Ken Baggett, Fieldcrest's safety director.

Baggett said two of those said to have byssinosis in 1967 are today breathing better than doctors would normally predict.

Baggett said the company used the study to identify a problem, not solve it. He added that some of those with the worst problems were moved to jobs where they would not be exposed to cotton dust.

It wasn't until 1971—four years later—that Fieldcrest took a major step to protect all workers by giving breathing tests to employees.

Baggett said the company has paid out about $300,000 in 17 brown lung cases. Another 28 claims are pending, he said.

Two of 19 workers identified in the 1967 study with serious breathing problems received compensation. One was Culas Mangum.

Fieldcrest gave Mangum $12,500 in disability compensation in 1974, but Mangum, now 58, says he didn't know what the money was for.

He only knew he was sick. Fieldcrest had transferred him from his dusty job following tests in 1971 because of his breathing problems, but he had collapsed in the mill in 1974. He was sick and out of work when company officials called him in to sign a compensation agreement that told him—for the first time—that he had byssinosis.

"I had done come out and was drawing unemployment. I didn't know what I was signing," said Mangum.

Today, Mangum lives with his sister in Eden. The money is gone—used to pay Mangum's living and medical expenses—and his health is so bad he can't walk a block without stopping to rest, gasping for breath.

Company and state researchers in North Carolina tested workers in at least three studies but didn't always tell them their breathing problems were caused by cotton dust. Only in recent years have some of these workers discovered their condition and filed compensation claims.

The three studies—Fieldcrest's, followed in 1968 at A. M. Smyre Manufacturing Co. Inc. in Lowell and in 1970 at seven Burlington Industries Inc. plants—prompted the N.C. State Board of Health to alert N.C. doctors and companies in 1971 that byssinosis was found in as many as 25 percent of workers in high-dust areas.

"Nobody Told Me"

That same year, the N.C. General Assembly included byssinosis victims under workers' compensation—designed to compensate people injured on the job. S.C. brown lung victims were covered by a 1949 law.

Millworkers generally remained ignorant of their rights under the law. They continued to accept cotton dust, noise, and other hazards as part of the job.

Elizabeth Clark, 64, of Salisbury, thought little of keeping her work clothes in a separate closet so they wouldn't rub lint onto her nicer dresses. She gave 35 years of her life to Cone Mills Co., but now feels she was mistreated.

She started working at night in 1944 at a Cone denim plant in Salisbury to supplement the family income. For years, she worked in the card room where dust levels are high, transferring loose strands of cotton from one machine to another.

"Of course, nobody told me I was endangering my health," Mrs. Clark now says.

By 1972, she noticed she had difficulty breathing when she went to work.

In September 1977, Cone medical director Dr. Charles Martin told her the tests the company had been giving her and other employees for the past five years showed her breathing problems getting worse.

He didn't mention brown lung, she says. A few weeks later, her daughter arranged for her to see a private lung specialist in Chapel Hill. He diagnosed byssinosis and reported it to the company.

Mrs. Clark says company officials told her not to worry about her future and gave her a job in a dust-free area. But on Jan. 10, 1979, Cone eliminated her job.

Mrs. Clark's doctor told the company in March she was totally disabled for work but Cone didn't tell the N.C. Industrial Commission she had byssinosis. N.C. law requires companies to report occupational diseases and injuries after the disabled employee misses one day of work. Her personal physician helped her file a claim with the commission in June. The case is not settled.

Today, Mrs. Clark has difficulty doing household tasks. She limits trips to her basement to one a day because climbing the short flight of stairs tires her.

Cone Vice President W. O. Leonard said Cone was unaware the law required it to file reports on sick employees. He said he isn't sure what the law means and still doesn't file the reports. The law, part of the workers' compensation act passed in 1929, carries no penalties.

He said the company has not turned its back on workers. He said the company prepared eight claims for workers considered totally disabled after company medical tests showed they were sick and an outside lung specialist diagnosed byssinosis. They didn't consider Mrs. Clark totally disabled. He said she was subject to recall if a job she could do came open.

"We recognize that there is a problem affecting some employees," said Leonard, who also is chairman of the N.C. Textile Manufacturers Association's Safety and Health Committee.

"We just feel like this thing has been blown out of proportion," Leonard said. He and others said the industry does not feel responsible for claims from workers who are sick because they smoked or workers they believe able to work.

Leonard said Cone had paid 29 of the 122 former workers who have filed claims with the N.C. Industrial Commission.

More than 900 workers have filed claims for brown lung compensation with the commission. The commission hears those cases in which companies deny liability or workers are not happy with company settlement offers. It must approve all settlements.

Eighty percent of North Carolina's brown lung cases are contested. Virtually all South Carolina's 200 cases have been contested—compared to less than 2 percent of other compensation cases filed in both states last year.

The commission decides whether a person is totally or partially disabled and how much compensation is due.

The potential liability for textile companies is enormous. Totally disabled workers can draw up to a $194 a week for life in North Carolina from their former employers or the company's insurers. S.C. workers can receive a maximum of $92,500.

18,000 Carolinas Workers

The late Dr. Arend Bouhuys, a Yale University medical researcher, estimated in 1979 that 30,000 current or former cotton textile workers were suffering from irreversible stages of byssinosis, including 18,000 in the Carolinas. Bouhuys based his estimates on more than a decade of research in South Carolina, North Carolina, Georgia, and Tennessee. He first identified byssinosis victims for the U.S. Public Health Service in 1967, calling them "respiratory cripples."

In 1977, industry witnesses testified at federal cotton dust hearings that only 2,500 workers had disabling byssinosis. Federal officials asked for the industry's backup data, but never got it.

The country's largest textile company, Burlington Industries Inc., and its former insurance carrier, Liberty Mutual, have paid more workers' compensation claims than any other company.

As of January, it had paid more than $2 million to 152 former workers—134 in North Carolina; 11 in South Carolina; 7 in Mississippi. The $1.9 million paid in North Carolina is more than half of all the money paid in the state's brown lung cases.

Burlington stands out because early studies conducted by the company and state doctors focused attention on byssinosis, said Dr. Harold Imbus, Burlington safety and health director. "It's made us a target and we've paid for it," Imbus said.

Burlington also was a standout within the industry. In 1969, the same year Burlington announced it was going to begin testing workers, ATMI executive Robert Armstrong was quoted as saying "this is a low-profit industry. We just can't afford such frills as medical examinations." Armstrong, now retired and living in Charlotte, denied he ever made the statement, claming he was misquoted by a reporter from the *Raleigh News and Observer.*

Workers Fear For Their Jobs

Retired workers have filed most of the Carolinas' claims. Active workers, even those diagnosed with breathing problems due to cotton dust, have not filed claims for fear of losing their jobs.

James Lee West, 59, of Mt. Holly, says Belmont Heritage Corp. fired him in August because he filed a byssinosis claim against Burlington Mills, his former employer for 21 years.

Steve McLean, Belmont personnel director, denies West's claim, He says the company—which hired West in 1975—fired him only after it was unable to find a job he could do and meet his medical restrictions.

"We tried to transfer him," says McLean, "but his doctor said he couldn't do the other job either. The doctors painted us in a corner so to speak."

Under the law, Belmont Heritage may have to pay West's compensation because that's where West last worked.

Some workers won't file because they fear companies will fire their relatives. In South Carolina, Columbia lawyer Bruce Dew said he recently interviewed more than 70 millworkers at a Brown Lung Association clinic in Aiken.

"I had a third tell me they had relatives working and they wouldn't file because they would be fired, or gotten rid of somehow." Dew said.

When they think they're going to have to pay a claim, companies will fight hard, then try to settle quietly and for as little money as possible.

Ollie Boykin filed for compensation in August 1976, two years after he quit his 23-year job in the card room at Pacific Mills, owned by M. Lowenstein and Sons, in Columbia. He had to use an oxygen machine at home.

The company refused to pay although two doctors, including one hired by the company, diagnosed lung disease due to cotton dust. The Industrial Commission held four hearing in the next two years but issued no decision. Boykin was eligible for up to $40,000 plus medical benefits.

On Feb. 15, 1978, Boykin, then 52, died at home in his sleep. The death certificate, signed by Dr. Robert Cochran of Elgin, S.C., lists the cause of death as heart failure and "chronic pulmonary disease [brown lung disease]."

Two days later, company lawyers told Boykin's lawyer, George Speedy, that they wanted an autopsy to see if Boykin had died from something other than byssinosis. The family refused, and Speedy settled for about $25,000, the state's largest brown lung settlement at the time.

Speedy said the company had been willing to pay more than they might normally "to keep this thing quiet."

Then there was the case of English Smith, the Graniteville worker who collapsed on the job. His company fought his claim, repeatedly denying he had byssinosis even though four doctors, two chosen by the company, had diagnosed the disease.

Smith began coughing and suffering from short breath, particularly on Mondays, in the early 1970s. Graniteville gave him breathing tests, then sent him to Dr. Russell Harley, a pathologist at the Medical University of South Carolina, in July 1974.

Harley diagnosed byssinosis and sent the report to the company. Harley says now he never told Smith about byssinosis, and Smith says the company didn't tell him either. Company chief Timmerman said he didn't have time to talk about the case last week.

By September 1976, Smith was in constant pain. His family physician, Dr. Richard Steadman, sent him to Dr. Richard Galphin Jr., a pulmonary specialist in Columbia. Galphin told Smith he had brown lung. Steadman agreed.

By May 1978, Smith was totally disabled, under heavy medication, and unable to sleep. Graniteville sent him to a fourth doctor. Dr. Alan Plummer of Emory University Clinic in Atlanta diagnosed byssinosis.

Company officials continued to deny that Smith had byssinosis. Lawyers on both sides shouted, cursed, and "almost came to blows" in hearings on the case, one state state official recalled.

But after they settled for $20,000 Graniteville's insurer, the American Mutual Insurance Co., asked for reimbursement from the S.C. Second Injury Fund, a state agency which administers a $2 million insurance fund to repay companies employing the handicapped.

Fund Director Douglas Crossman said American Mutual asked the fund to repay the $20,000 in July 1979 because Graniteville knew Smith had been diagnosed with asthma and byssinosis in July 1974 and September 1976. The company thus had employed a handicapped worker—Smith, handicapped by brown lung.

"Subsequent to both diagnoses," say insurance papers on the still-pending case, Smith "continued in employment of employer where he was allegedly exposed to substances which can cause byssinosis."

Smith got only $12,700 after he paid his lawyers and expenses. The settlement didn't cover his $1,000-a-year medical expenses since he left work. He has little money left.

"I don't feel good at all," Smith said recently, coughing and wheezing with each breath. "I'm so sore in my chest, I hurt all over, and I can't catch my breath. I can't sleep at night for my breath."

Smith, a burly man with thick glasses, talked in his living room in Monetta, S.C. A Graniteville award for 25 years of service, signed by Timmerman, hung on the wall. Smith said Graniteville, the only employer he ever had, didn't treat him fairly.

"You take a man who worked all his life and wants to work and you cripple him up," Smith said, beginning to cry. "What's he got left? I sit around and can't do nothing now. They took my decency away."

Despite Timmerman's 1972 announcement that the textile industry was trying to control dust and protect workers, Graniteville Co. was one of the first to contest the S.C Occupational Safety and Health Administration (OSHA), which like North Carolina's OSHA agency, administers the federal law. It challenged OSHA's citation of the company's Swint Plant in Graniteville for exceeding legal dust limits by eight times.

"We plan to contest the whole thing," the company's safety director Abbie Price told state OSHA officials, according to state records. In a recent interview, Timmerman said the industry is doing enough without federal standards.

"I think the American textile industry has been maligned," he said. "I think they've done a damn good job in cleaning up the mills. I think you've got to be reasonable, that's all I ask."

Inspection records at the OSHA offices in both states show many other companies resisted reducing cotton dust levels even after the industry recognized the dangers.

In South Carolina, 101 out of 128 mills checked since inspections began in 1974 have exceeded legal dust levels. Nearly 40 percent of the citations have been protested to the S.C. Labor Department, and four companies—Clinton Mills, Greenwood Mills, Hermitage Cotton Mills, and Milliken & Co.—have appealed the citations to state courts. By doing so, they can put off compliance for years, 5½ years, for example, in the Hermitage case. Hermitage still is not in compliance.

Since 1974, N.C. inspectors have cited 128 companies for violating dust limits out of 210 inspected. And the violations were big ones. A 1979 internal N.C. labor department study of 148 inspections showed three-fourths of the companies exceeded legal dust limits by an average of nearly three times.

To this day, companies have resisted government requirements that they clean up the mills.

Textile companies have known since 1969, when the federal government first set standards for government suppliers, that they'd have to clean their plants. Congress extended coverage to all plants in 1970 when it passed the Occupational Safety and Health Act.

Pending further research, federal OSHA officials adopted a temporary standard. Plants processing cotton were allowed to expose workers to no more than 1 milligram of dust and lint per cubic meter of air over an eight-hour period.

State OSHA officials began requiring mills to meet this standard in 1974. In a government study, textile engineers reported that same year that machinery was available that would allow companies to meet the standard in high-dust areas of cotton processing up to spinning.

Also in 1974, government researchers predicted that up to 30 percent of workers exposed at the 1 milligram level would develop byssinosis. They proposed a tougher standard.

Industry objections, voiced to OSHA, at the White House, and in court, have stalled tougher cotton dust regulations for nearly six years. The proposed regulations would allow mills only about half as much dust as the earlier standard and require them to test employees regularly to identify those reacting to the dust.

The ATMI plans to appeal the new regulations to the U.S. Supreme Court. If the court decides not to hear the case, the regulations become effective March 25. The industry will have four years to comply.

Most textile owners say they've done everything they can to clean up their mills and to do any more—to meet the new federal standard—is unreasonable.

"We've got several sound reasons for opposing [the new standard]," Burlington Industries executive Charles McLendon told N.C. textile executives in December. "It goes beyond what is necessary and it could put some of our companies out of business."

The industry says it will cost about $2.8 billion to meet the proposed standard. Technology is not available to clean up certain areas, officials contend, and a low-profit industry like textiles can't afford to comply with the regulations in the time allowed.

A 6 Percent Return

The U.S. Commerce Department estimates the 6,000 textile companies averaged an after-tax return on investment of about 6 percent in 1979, roughly half that of the auto industry.

State OSHA officials often have been lenient on mills because of the lack of a permanent standard.

Even after they are cited for violations, companies bargain informally and successfully with state officials for more time to clean up.

Cannon Mills Co. in Kannapolis is an example. In April 1975 N.C. OSHA inspectors found the company's Roberta Mill, between Charlotte and Concord, exceeded legal dust limits by more than three times. The company also wasn't obeying a law that required workers to wear respirators.

Reports and correspondence in the OSHA file in Raleigh show that Cannon knew as early as July 1973 that the plant exceeded the allowable limits but did nothing.

Then Labor Commissioner Billy Creel, elected on a 1972 campaign promise to "understand" unique problems of N.C. employers, revoked a proposed $650 fine after Cannon officials said they didn't understand OSHA cotton dust regulations.

Cannon operated that mill for three years without improving any equipment, then closed it in April 1978. All Cannon did as a result of the inspection was begin requiring masks.

Cannon officials told Creel they could not afford the $14 million that would be required to bring the plant into compliance. They said face masks had not been issued earlier because they misunderstood the regulations.

In 1977, Burlington Industries persuaded N.C. OSHA officials not to inspect its waste houses for three years. The waste houses, where workers rebale cotton lint and trash, are considered the dirtiest part of any mill. But during those years, OSHA inspectors were inspecting the waste houses of other companies.

Al Weaver, former director of N.C. OSHA, said the agency suspended the inspections after Burlington said it would require masks with hoses that brought clean air from outside the room. The company said it would work on a way to reduce dust levels to meet the standards.

Weaver said OSHA agreed to this because Burlington had acknowledged the problem and promised to work on it. He said inspectors were needed to check other areas of the mills where more people were exposed to high levels of dust.

The agreement expires this spring.

Burlington has spent $35 million on equipment to cut dust levels and still won't meet the proposed government standard in all areas, according to spokesman Dick Byrd. About 3,000 Burlington employees would be exposed to more dust than allowed under the proposed standard if it were in effect today, said the company's medical director, Harold Imbus.

Byrd and other company spokesmen say it is impossible to reduce dust levels to the proposed limits in certain areas, such as spinning rooms.

Springs Mills, with 1979 sales of more than $800 million, says it has spent more than $7 million companywide in the last five years to improve air quality and comfort. In 1980, the company says, it plans to spend $1.2 million more. Like Burlington, Springs Mills says it still won't be in full compliance with the new standard.

Cannon Mills has spent $16 million redesigning equipment to reduce dust levels and boost production, says Vice President William Adams.

Some of that equipment was considered the "best technology" available at the time, he said. "Unfortunately, that did not bring us into compliance," Adams said. It had to be removed.

Cone Mills has spent $30 million trying to meet the proposed standard but found that in some instances, entire plants may have to be rebuilt.

Other textile experts—including some of the industry's own—dispute how much it will cost the mills to clean up.

U.S. labor officials have said it will cost textile companies only about a fourth of the industry's $2.8 billion estimate.

N.C. State University textile economist Dr. Carl Dyer estimates that the new standards will cost the industry about $170 million a year, approximately one third of its net profits.

And John Lumsden of Raleigh, an industry consultant who formerly headed the N.C. Occupational Health Branch, discounts the industry's complaint that meeting OSHA standards will bankrupt companies.

"I don't know of anybody who has gone out of business solely because of the standards," Lumsden said.

Fieldcrest's Ken Baggett said he could not even estimate how much has been spent because new equipment increases production, offsetting some of the cost. Fieldcrest has spent $4.5 million at one towel plant in Fieldale, Va., "but we bought a Cadillac, not a Model T." He said dust levels in the plant would meet the proposed standards. No Fieldcrest employees will be exposed to dust levels over the proposed standard within two years, he said.

Lumsden and others say OSHA regulations may in fact make companies more competitive because of such changes.

That has been the experience of Riegel Textile Corp, a Greenville, S.C. based fabric and yarn manufacturer with 1979 sales of $360.7 million. Riegel employs more than 9,000 workers in 13 plants in South Carolina, California, Georgia, Missouri,and Virginia.

In July 1977, the S.C. OSHA cited Riegel's Ware Shoals plant for cotton dust violations in the waste house, the room where cotton bales are opened, and the card room, where machines straighten the fibers. The plant, in Greenwood County about 35 miles south of Greenville, employs about 700 people making unbleached cloth.

A month after the citation, the company notified OSHA it was going to spend $5 million for new card room equipment and an air filtration system. Two years later, inspectors found the plant in compliance.

"Nobody with common sense can argue that it isn't beneficial to clean up a work place," says Robert Coleman, Riegel board chairman. "But it's also money well spent regardless of whether we meet the OSHA standard or not. It provides a more attractive work place, and that allows us to attract workers more easily in a labor market that's getting increasingly tighter."

A LIVING DEATH: A WORKER WAITS FOR COMPANY'S HELP

By Howard Covington
and Marion A. Ellis
Observer Staff Writers

LOWELL—Landrum Clary, a 68 year-old former millworker, can't live these days without 20 feet of plastic tubing hooked to a liquid oxygen machine.

Clary suffers from chronic byssinosis, caused by breathing cotton dust in the mills for 38 years.

The last company he worked for, A. M. Smyre Manufacturing Co. Inc., discovered Clary's breathing problems in 1968, when it tested him and 440 other workers.

But for three years, until illness forced him to quit, the company kept Clary sweeping up cotton waste in the card room, one of the dustiest places in a mill.

Smyre, a yarn maker in Gaston County, has consistently denied the significance of brown lung, resisted paying Clary, and delayed cleaning up its mills despite government fines.

To this day, company President Rick Smyre says he doubts there is a difference between byssinosis and other lung diseases such as emphysema which aren't necessarily job-related.

Smyre, which employs 800 people at three plants, surveyed 441 workers Dec. 9, 1968, at the request of state health officials. Officials wanted to identify workers with byssinosis and probe the effects of job location, age, and smoking on the disease.

A team of six medical doctors and three specialists in occupational health, all employed by the state or Gaston County, found at least 25 workers had byssinosis. Company officials, who said they've lost the records, couldn't identify the 25.

But Clary believes he was one and recalls that test vividly.

"They asked us to blow in this little tube as a test," he said. The tube was part of a machine called a spirometer which measures lung capacity and breathing ability.

"They told us if you don't pass [the test], the company will get a letter," Clary continued. "Six or eight weeks went by and I was called out to the office. I was told I had a pretty bad respiratory problem. [Company officials] said, 'The doctors recommended that you get out.' They said they would get me something else, but they never did."

Rick Smyre and Dr. James Merchant, a state physician and leader of the research team, both say Merchant told the workers with serious problems they should seek medical help.

Clary's last job at Smyre—where he worked 17 years—was sweeping the card room floor and cleaning the machines that straightened cotton fibers for spinning.

He decided to leave in 1971 after he passed out three times.

"I just couldn't take it any more," he says. "My doctor said if you want to live you've got to get out of the mill."

Today clear plastic tubing connects Clary to his 84-pound, life-supporting machine, called a Liberator. He can move 20 feet in any direction. When he has to leave his house, he must carry a portable liquid oxygen set.

Clary, a slight man with sallow skin, says he can't stay off his oxygen system more than 30 minutes at a time. After that, "I can't take it. My chest starts to cave in."

"I'm a sick man," Clary says with a moan. "Sometimes I just don't care if I live or not."

Since Clary left Smyre, he and his wife, Ruby, have depended on his Social Security disability payments, now $322 a month, and her income from a job at the Belmont Heritage textile mill, where she makes $4 an hour.

Clary didn't realize Smyre might have to pay him workers' compensation until he went to a March 1978 breathing clinic run by the Carolina Brown Lung Association. He filed a compensation claim with the N.C. Industrial Commission June 12.

Clary figures he's eligible for a maximum of $18,000 plus medical benefits, based on the commission's scale. If the commission awards him compensation, the company has said it will appeal.

"He only worked here at scattered short times," says Smyre. "We feel any award should be prorated as to duration of employment."

Clary "quit voluntarily," Smyre adds.

Smyre Manufacturing has resisted state efforts to make it clean up.

Though the 1968 report showed it had a cotton dust problem, Smyre acknowledges the company didn't do anything immediately.

"We did nothing," he said, blaming financial problems and internal administrative errors.

When state inspectors started visiting the plants for the first time in the late 1970s, they found violations of the federal dust standard.

In January 1977, inspectors for the N.C. Occupational Safety and Health Administration (OSHA) found that Smyre's Plant 1 contained almost three times the amount of dust allowed by law. The company wasn't requiring workers to wear face masks, a minimum federal regulation.

OSHA gave the company a year to clean up.

In February 1978, OSHA inspectors returned to inspect Smyre at Plant 2, adjacent to Plant 1. They found dust levels there exceeded legal limits by more than seven times in one area, up to four times in another, and more than two in another.

The company was not requiring the use of face masks at Plant 2.

OSHA fined Smyre $600 and the inspector, Howard Bridges, noted: "Management has made little or no effort to reduce cotton dust levels and implement a respirator [face mask] program."

The two plants still are not in compliance, despite two extensions. The third plant makes synthetic material and isn't subject to cotton dust standards.

Rick Smyre says the company has spent $2 million on new machinery but probably won't meet the OSHA deadline of March for all sections of the mills.

He said Smyre will begin a $50,000 program this year to test workers' breathing—nearly 12 years after company doctors first documented Smyre workers' breathing problems.

Smyre still wonders if byssinosis is a serious problem.

"There are a limited number of physicians that have been trained to differentiate between emphysema and byssinosis," he said. "I'm just not convinced in my own mind of the ability to differentiate, although they say they can."

STATES LET VIOLATORS' CASES GATHER DUST

By Howard Covington
And Bob Dennis
Observer Staff Writers

On Jan. 5, 1976, N.C. state inspectors clipped an air filter to Willie Robinson's shirt collar to sample the air he breathed in the dusty No. 1 card room at J. P. Stevens & Co.'s Rosemary Plant in Roanoke Rapids.

Inspectors found more than triple the dust allowed by law. Yet officials fined Stevens, which had $1.8 billion in sales last year, only $600—$400 less than the maximum. They also gave the company a year to clean up.

When Stevens didn't meet the deadline, officials simply extended it—for three years.

Meanwhile, Robinson's breathing became so bad that he had to be moved to a less dusty job area.

Doctors say Robinson, 37, has byssinosis, a lung disease caused by breathing cotton dust which experts say has crippled 18,000 Carolinas textile workers.

Every day, health officials say, thousands of Carolinians—up to 10,000 in North Carolina alone—still work in cotton dust levels the federal government finds dangerous enough to cause serious injury, even death.

Foot-Dragging by Agencies

A key reason: foot-dragging by labor department officials in both states. These agencies have failed to force mills to obey federal regulations and to clean up.

The state labor departments have had six years to make textile plants comply with minimum dust levels established by the federal Occupational Safety and Health Administration (OSHA). That's a year longer than it takes some workers to develop byssinosis, according to British doctors.

Documents in state labor departments and interviews with OSHA and textile officials show:

• State hygienists have failed to inspect most cotton textile plants in the Carolinas. Officials have inspected about 170 of the 461 N.C. plants and 127 of South Carolina's 153 plants.

• N.C. officials have allowed companies that have violated OSHA standards an average of almost two years to clean up—twice the time the federal government says is necessary to do the job. Some companies have taken three years or longer.

• S.C. officials have given companies an average of 2½ years and allowed some to take more than three years.

• In both Carolinas, labor officials have never gone to court to try to close a plant, even when companies ignored cleanup orders.

• Generous officials sometimes give companies even more time to clean up than the companies request. Sometimes they approve plant cleanups without reinspection, based solely on the company's word.

• Officials routinely levy only modest fines, rarely imposing the $1,000 maximum. N.C. officials have never forced a company to pay an overdue fine.

• State officials don't inspect weaving and spinning rooms—where large numbers of people work—despite evidence workers in these areas develop brown lung.

Officials say they do the best job possible, given the limited number of inspectors, their responsibilities for other hazards such as asbestos and the uncertain status of the present dust standards.

New Standard Stalled

The federal government wants to toughen the existing standard of one milligram of dust per cubic meter of air to cut permissible levels about in half. But the proposal has been stalled in federal court since 1978, when the textile industry challenged the new standards as too tough.

Some officials say that because tougher new standards have been pending, they have not concentrated on enforcing current dust level requirements.

Meanwhile, medical research has shown that 30 percent of workers exposed even to the current permissible dust levels over a period of years would develop byssinosis.

The Stevens case in Roanoke Rapids shows the leniency of state officials.

Inspectors for the state OSHA, a division of the N.C. Labor Department, first arrived at Stevens' Rosemary Plant in January 1976. A worker there had complained to them about dusty conditions in late 1975.

Air in the card room where Willie Robinson worked—on machines which straighten cotton fibers for spinning—violated the federal dust standard. But it was relatively clean compared to other places in the 80-year-old mill. Dust levels in the opening room, where workers unpack 480-pound cotton bales, were more than 12 times the limit.

$600 Fine, "Good Faith" Credit

Despite the extent of the violations, inspector Lindsay Cook recommended a $600 fine, giving the company credit for no previous violations and "good faith." Stevens had a year to clean up.

When the company didn't make that deadline, OSHA director Al Weaver gave Stevens another year without reinspecting. The action was based on the company's brief, written progress reports that said workers were wearing respirators—face masks designed to filter cotton dust—and that the company was studying ways to control dust.

In June 1978, Stevens asked for three more months.

OSHA's Weaver obliged the company with twice that—six months.

This favor was earned, "in view of the company's demonstrated good faith reducing dust at its other plants," according to George Lennon, a state Justice Department attorney representing OSHA.

In February 1979, state OSHA hearing officer Alexander Denson of Raleigh criticized "the fact that the latest extension was more than requested by the employer."

Denson was hearing an appeal of the extension made by the Amal-

gamated Clothing and Textile Workers Union. ACTWU and OSHA settled their dispute before Denson ruled on the case, when OSHA agreed
not to grant further extensions without reinspecting.

File Closed—No Follow-Up

Rosemary Plant officials reported all areas were in compliance in
October 1979. OSHA closed the file without reinspecting, according to
OSHA enforcement director Ralph Dudley.

Dudley said last week he had "no idea" why there was no follow-up.

OSHA's attitude toward Stevens in North Carolina is not unusual,
according to a 1979 N.C. Labor Department internal examination of
148 cotton dust inspections since 1974.

The study showed OSHA had allowed mills an average of 20 months
to clean up. The same study said large companies such as Stevens,
Cone Mills Co., Burlington Industries Inc., and Cannon Mills Co. got
an average of two months more. Some plants inspected more than
three years ago still are not in compliance.

The review said 75 percent of the inspected plants exceeded legal
limits. Dust levels averaged two to three times higher than that allowed.

The department does not know the conditions in most mills, however. OSHA has inspected about 37 percent of the state's 461 cotton-
processing plants.

N.C. Labor Commissioner John Brooks, facing reelection this year,
says one reason his seven inspectors haven't gotten around to more
mills is that they're responsible for checking 10 other deadly job hazards. In 1978, N.C. OSHA conducted 421 health inspections, 73 for
cotton dust.

However, Brooks acknowledges he could have done more.

"Had I known in January 1977 [when he took office] that cotton dust
standards wouldn't be available for four or five years, we would have
gone ahead in a larger way for compliance with the temporary standard," he said.

S.C. officials also have had little success forcing mills to comply with
the standards, even though S.C. OSHA has inspected all but 25 of the
state's 153 cotton plants. Since inspections began six years ago, only 23
mills—15 percent—have met standards.

Sometimes, OSHA Backs Down

One reason for OSHA's failure is that about 40 percent of the S.C. mill
owners cited for violations have challenged the inspections and the
dust standard. And until 1978, the S.C. Labor Department didn't even

have its own lawyer to fight these challenges. Sometimes, OSHA backed down rather than continue a long fight.

William Pitts, president of Hermitage Cotton Mills in Camden, has kept OSHA at bay for more than five years with court challenges and appeals. Milliken & Co., the state's largest privately held textile firm, has taken OSHA citations against four of its plants to the S.C. Supreme Court.

Other S.C. companies have managed to maneuver around OSHA for years without going to court.

OSHA cited Springs Mills's Eureka plant in Chester in 1977 for "serious violations." Inspectors found dust levels 30 times too high in the picker room, where machines fluff the cotton, and nearly five times too high in the opening room. The S.C. labor department proposed a $700 penalty, $300 less than the maximum.

Springs challenged OSHA's methods for dust sampling and analysis, claiming they showed total dust and lint in the air, not just cotton dust regulated by the standard.

Citation Reduced

"If a citation is based on a faulty reading we're not going to roll over and play dead," said Springs senior vice president Dan Byrd.

Labor department officials defended sampling procedures, saying a total dust reading was reasonable. After 22 months, however, the officials reduced the citation to nonserious, threw out the penalty, and gave Springs until December 1979 to comply with the federal standard.

Springs officials say the company has spent $1.2 million at Eureka since the citation and that the mill is now in compliance. OSHA has closed the file without reinspecting.

S.C. inspectors give extensions averaging 2½ years, sometimes longer. Three years, two months and three extensions after OSHA cited Mt. Vernon Mills of Columbia for a serious cotton dust violation, a hygienist returned and found all areas in compliance except the waste house. In March 1979, the department gave Mt. Vernon another year to bring the waste house into compliance.

South Carolina has never tried to shut down a plant, Labor Commissioner Edgar McGowan said, because that would put people out of work. So the department usually extends the one-year deadlines to give the mills time to study the problem, change work practices, and order and install equipment.

McGowan says although he's stepped up enforcement since hiring a lawyer for the department in 1978, mills also have taken a harder line. Last year, mills protested about 90 percent of the cotton dust citations.

"Across the country there's been . . . a feeling [the Occupational Safety and Health Act] is a bad law so let's get rid of it," he said. "Industry says let's throw roadblocks in its way, so we're bucking a real strong headwind."

McGowan says complying with the OSHA law may be expensive but is worthwhile to protect workers' health and safety.

He says federal OSHA officials, who write all enforcement regulations, are partly responsible for state OSHA problems.

Since 1973, he said, "there have been four assistant secretaries, and every one had a different view of OSHA and what it should accomplish. With one, cotton dust was a minor thing. Noise was a big thing with another and carcinogens with still another.

"So we've had these different concepts applied to employers by different people at different times."

S.C. Gov. Dick Riley, McGowan's boss, defends the OSHA program.

"I've had complaints from working people that [McGowan] wasn't strict enough enforcing OSHA standards," Riley says, "while on the other hand I've had complaints from management that he's too tough."

N.C. Won't Close Plants

N.C. OSHA enforcement director Ralph Dudley said his department would not close a plant and put people out of work, even in a case like Bladenboro Cotton Mill Co.

Inspectors found the Bladenboro plant in southeastern North Carolina had done nothing to control hazardous dust levels about a year after they cited the company for violations in April 1976 and gave it a year to clean up.

Bladenboro vice president C. B. Hasbrouck had said in an October 1976 letter to OSHA that the company couldn't afford to make necessary changes.

After his year expired, he asked for an extension. OSHA officials initially denied his request. But in September 1977 they agreed to give the company more time on the condition it would apply for government-guaranteed loans and purchase new equipment with the money.

OSHA's latest extention, granted in December 1979, gives the company until April—four years after the first inspection—to clean up.

OSHA has not been back to reinspect since 1977 and Hasbrouck didn't return reporters' telephone calls.

Dudley said in a case like Bladenboro, OSHA would have a hard time proving that workers' health and safety were in "imminent danger." OSHA doesn't consider cotton dust immediately dangerous because workers develop byssinosis over time.

Dudley didn't know a single case in which OSHA tried to close a plant.

In at least one case, a textile company avoided OSHA penalties because OSHA officials misplaced the file.

In January 1977, N.C. inspectors cited Gurney Industries Inc. of Gastonia for dust levels six times higher than allowed. Some workers wore face masks but not the kind designed to filter cotton dust. Inspectors fined Gurney $700 and gave the company a year to clean up.

Five months later, an inspector found workers still didn't have proper face masks and levied an additional $500 fine. In September 1977, inspectors came back, found violations, and proposed an additional $1,000 fine.

By the end of 1979, more than 2½ years after the first citation, OSHA had only collected the $700 fine and had not reinspected.

When the *Observer* asked labor officials about the case, they referred reporters to George Lennon, the N.C. Justice Department attorney. Labor officials had asked Lennon to bring contempt proceedings against the company in October 1977. Lennon said he couldn't find the file or say what happened to the other $1,500 in fines. Gurney officials failed to return repeated phone calls.

Lennon later said that since the *Observer* inquired about the case, OSHA Director Don Wiseman has ordered reinspections of all old cases.

"Sometimes you wonder how much of it is a word game," said Bruce Gantner, a top industrial hygienist who left the labor department last year for a job with private industry in Texas.

Never the Maximum

Labor officials acknowledge penalties can be effective. "When you hit them in the pocketbook, you get their attention," Lennon said.

But N.C. OSHA has never levied the maximum $1,000 fine for a serious cotton dust violation, according to an *Observer* inspection of OSHA records.

Labor department spokeswoman Debbie Harmon says OSHA regulations allow for reductions based on the quality of the company's safety program and "how we have been dealing with them before."

The fines are usually modest. Since N.C. OSHA was created in 1973, it has levied an average fine of $52 for all violations, including cotton dust.

In South Carolina, the average penalty in 1979 was $53.

"OSHA was never passed to raise money," says Commissioner McGowan.

Neither state has ever taken a violator to court for not paying a fine.

S.C. officials levied $481,316 in fines in 1979 and collected $212,934, or 44 percent.

North Carolina has collected 68 percent of $1.2 million in fines since 1973. Lennon said the state had no attorney to force collections until last November, and is in the process of setting up a procedure to take scofflaws to court.

When OSHA inspectors in both states examine mills, they ignore weaving and spinning rooms, despite research by companies such as Burlington Industries and Cone Mills in the early 1970s that showed spinners and weavers get brown lung.

"I don't think we'd find high enough levels of dust in the weave room," says Burney Hook, South Carolina's chief industrial hygienist. "It's no longer raw cotton dust there."

N.C. officials say their "worst first" priority list usually excludes weavers and spinners.

Complaints about problems in the two state OSHA programs are not new.

In 1977, the Carolina Brown Lung Association, a disabled workers group, asked assistant U.S. Labor Secretary Eula Bingham to take over the S.C. program. The request came on the heels of a critical federal evaluation that noted the four-year-old OSHA department had never gone to court to enforce cotton dust regulations.

After McGowan hired a lawyer and stepped up prosecutions and inspections, federal officials said the state had improved its program and declined to take it over.

The most severe criticism of the N.C. program came in December 1975, when the N.C. Public Interest Research Group, a citizens' watchdog organization, published a report criticizing the program for not requiring textile mills to clean up, granting too many extensions, and not conducting training programs for workers.

Standard Is Outdated

The federal cotton dust standard is outdated, state and federal OSHA officials concede.

The federal government adopted the present dust levels in 1970, basing them on a 1966 limit recommended by government hygienists.

The standard was only temporary, pending further research on the effects of cotton dust on workers' health.

The National Institute of Occupational Safety and Health, the federal government's research agency, proposed tougher standards to OSHA in 1974. At the same time, federal researchers predicted 30 percent of the workers exposed to the one milligram level would develop byssinosis.

The proposed standard—which textile manufacturers say they will appeal to the U.S. Supreme Court—cuts the present dust level in half. Even at that level, OSHA witnesses predicted at hearings in 1977, about 12 percent of the workers may develop breathing problems.

The proposed standard also requires OSHA to use a more precise method of measuring cotton dust. It says mill owners should meet a prepared compliance schedule, regularly test workers for breathing problems, transfer those affected by cotton dust to other jobs, and train workers to do their jobs without creating excessive dust.

The industry argues the new OSHA dust levels are unreasonable and unnecessary. It says higher levels—about twice those proposed—regular medical testing, job transfers, and improved work practices are sufficient.

Unless the U.S. Supreme Court intervenes, new standards, postponed since September 1978, will go into effect March 25. OSHA will have to reinspect all mills.

OSHA officials will find enforcing the new standard as difficult as enforcing the current one.

Even if the departments got money for more inspectors, their beginning salaries—$12,000 to $14,000—can't compete with private industry, they say. Dan Baucom, chief of North Carolina's occupational health inspectors, says his office has suffered almost 100 percent turnover in the last 18 months.

North Carolina's Brooks said he isn't inclined to emphasize cotton dust inspections while waiting for the new standard. "I can't see spending time doing a wholesale job implementing a temporary standard," he said, "that when we get a permanent standard we have to go back and redo."

SOMETIMES DEATH IS VICTIM'S ONLY COMPENSATION

By Howard Covington, Bob Drogin, and Marion A. Ellis

Racked by painful coughing and too weak to climb stairs, Columbia cotton mill worker Spencer Wooten filed a claim for workers' compensation with the S.C. Industrial Commission in November 1975.

His doctor said he had byssinosis, or brown lung, a crippling lung disease caused by breathing cotton dust. When Wooten died at 67 on Dec. 4, 1978—more than three years later—his case still was tied up at the commission. He hadn't gotten a penny.

Lula Pendergraft, 64, from Selma in Eastern North Carolina, asked the N.C. Industrial Commission for help in 1973 after she said breathing problems forced her to retire from a Burlington Industries Inc. mill.

The commission sidetracked her case. Seven years late, it still hasn't ruled.

The two cases aren't unusual in the Carolinas. State industrial commissioners are charged with seeing that workers disabled on the job are quickly and fairly compensated. Yet, they have given little help to brown lung victims, many of whom are old, poor, and uneducated.

Today, a decade after N.C. health officials recognized brown lung as a major health hazard for cotton millworkers, the two commissions have approved only about 320 brown lung compensation claims—most of them in North Carolina—out of more than 1,100 filed. Commissioners acknowledge at least 10,000 other workers may be eligible for compensation.

Moreover:

Both industrial commissions have taken so long to decide brown lung claims that disabled workers have died without a ruling. One study found the N.C. commission takes an average of 26 months to decide a claim.

The commission sidetracked her case. Seven years later, it still hasn't ruled.

women who have worked decades in the mills get $13,000 in North Carolina and $14,000 in South Carolina—about two years' wages.

Both commissions have ignored state laws requiring textile companies to file reports on workers diagnosed with occupational diseases such as byssinosis. Even when the commissions get that information, they don't turn it over to the workers.

The N.C. Industrial Commission has violated its own rules by approving company-written agreements in which workers forfeit all future claims against the company, not just those connected with compensation benefits.

Both commissions keep all files confidential and don't publish their decisions. Unlike nearly all other state agencies, the N.C. commission is allowed to change rules in secret sessions without telling attorneys or workers whose cases may be affected.

The Carolinas legislatures set up industrial commissions in the 1930s, saying companies, not society, should pay disabled workers for lost wages and work-related sicknesses and injuries. South Carolina passed an occupational disease law in 1949. The N.C. General Assembly included byssinosis under workers' compensation in 1971. That same year state health officials issued a bulletin warning that cotton dust was endangering the lives of workers in Carolinas cotton mills.

Today, state officials estimate about one-third of the Carolinas' 391,500 textile workers are exposed to cotton dust.

Under compensation laws, workers can negotiate claims with a company and reach a private settlement. Or they may seek an award from the commission in cases involving disputed claims. In either instance, the commission must approve all payments and either party can appeal the commission's decisions to the courts.

Each year, the two commissions approve payments totaling more than $100 million to more than 300,000 injured workers.

Commissioners, who earn $44,275 a year in South Carolina and up to $35,820 in North Carolina, say this volume of cases and conflicting medical and legal opinions hinder their attempts to help brown lung victims. S.C. commissioners also blame the state's restrictive compensation laws.

"To say we are unfair and holding cases is totally ridiculous," said Harold Trask Jr., 33, chairman of the S.C. commission. "We're doing everything we can do within the limits of the law."

But the delays are often serious. Many N.C. workers wait more than two years before their cases are decided, according to a 1978 N.C. Insurance Department investigation of 221 byssinosis claims handled by Liberty Mutual Insurance Co. The report put part of the blame on the commission for not scheduling hearings promptly.

The N.C. commission has approved payments in 286 of 913 claims filed. Two hundred forty-nine cases still clog the docket; the rest have been withdrawn or dismissed or await initial hearings.

Gov. Jim Hunt last December appointed a commission to study these delays.

The S.C. commission has approved money in only about 40 of more than 200 brown lung claims filed. The figures are approximate because even the commission doesn't know how many byssinosis cases have been filed.

"It's about as easy to prevail with a claim at the industrial commission as to pass a camel through the eye of a needle," acknowledged S.C. Commissioner James Reid, 61, former chairman, who is critical of the compensation law.

In addition, Reid said, the commission approves brown lung payments that don't "cover legal expenses, medical expenses and [the worker's] own costs."

While brown lung settlements average $13,000 in North Carolina and $14,000 in South Carolina, a disabled worker loses far more in wages.

Preliminary findings in a U.S. Department of Labor study of 270 Carolinas workers who filed byssinosis claims show the average employee lost seven years of work—years in which he or she would have earned $56,000.

James "Shorty" Fisher of Stanley knows all too well about low commission-approved settlements.

Three doctors said Fisher was too sick to work, and one of them diagnosed brown lung. In 1974 the N.C. commission said he should get $600.

It was the lowest known award. Then there were legal fees—$150 to Gastonia lawyer James Atkins, who said he only took the case as a favor to the family.

Fisher ended up with $450—less than $11 a year for his 43 years in the mills.

"I didn't know anything about [the process]," said Fisher, who can't walk down his driveway without stopping to catch his breath. "I just took what they gave me."

Fisher believes the commission should have declared him totally disabled and given him the maximum $15,000. So far, he has been unable to get his case reopened. His lawyer, Fred Stann of Gastonia, says the chances are bleak since Fisher signed an agreement in 1974 not to purse legal action.

"Hell no, it's not enough," Stann said. "It's just real difficult to claim fraud or misrepresentation and that's about the only way his case can be reopened."

William Stephenson, now commission chairman, was on the commission that approved Fisher's claim. When told about the $600 settlement he said, "To me it sounds outrageous. It's highly unusual. I don't remember our approving one that low."

He said that state law prevented him from commenting specifically on Fisher's case. "I can't tell you why we decided on $600," Stephenson said. "I could not discuss it with anyone except with him. Obviously there was a reason for us to settle on that amount."

The N.C. commission awards compensation based on a worker's average weekly wage, degree of disability and education level and the job market. It can award up to $194 a week plus medical benefits for life.

South Carolina determines awards similarly. Only one S.C. resident, John Cobb of West Pelzer, is receiving the state's maximum compensation for byssinosis, according to Ben Bowen of Greenville, who handles more brown lung cases for workers than any other S.C. lawyer.

Kendall Manufacturing Co. agreed last summer to pay Cobb, 59, medical care plus $40,000 in 500 weekly payments. Cobb pays one-third of that money to Bowen, his lawyer.

The state since has raised the maximum to $185 a week, up to $92,500.

Some N.C. commission officials seem to resent awarding compensation to victims already receiving social security payments or modest pensions, although the law allows them to.

Mae Goodman of Salisbury was awarded $20,000 for byssinosis last December. But in granting the award, deputy commissioner Forrest Shuford II complained this was a misuse of workers' compensation benefits.

Shuford objected because Mrs. Goodman was "a retired person who is receiving social security and possibly other benefits."

Both commissions have ignored the law that says textile companies must report accidents, injuries, or occupational diseases like byssinosis.

For example, Cone Mills Co. doctors discovered in the early 1970s that 199 of 6,631 Cone workers tested had byssinosis. The company reported their findings in a medical journal but didn't tell the commission.

Cone spokesman W. O. Leonard said Cone doesn't believe the law requires such reports. Commission Chairman William Stephenson says it does, but the commission hasn't penalized companies that disobey. "Some have reported it and some haven't," he acknowledged.

The commission has the power to penalize companies that disobey its orders, but the law provides no specific penalty for failing to make the reports, Stephenson said.

The commissions could use these reports to alert the disabled workers, since companies don't always tell workers about their disabilities.

S.C. Commission Chairman Trask said he doesn't know of any company that has filed a report based on medical testing programs. Even if a company filed, Trask said, the commission has no policy to notify the afflicted worker.

"It's certainly something we should take a long hard look at," Trask added.

The N.C. commission isn't required to notify diseased workers either. And the workers can't count on the commission to do so.

"It's not our duty to tell the employee," says commission Chairman

Stephenson. "I don't think we have the capability, ability, or obligation to contact them one on one, or to seek one out."

In one recent example, J. P. Stevens & Co. Inc. reported to the N.C. commission that at least 22 Roanoke Rapids workers had breathing problems, according to company spokesman Paul Barrett.

But neither the company nor the commission told the afflicted workers they might be eligible for workers' compensation benefits, according to Clyde Bush, local representative of the Amalgamated Clothing and Textile Workers' Union. Workers first learned of the reports from the union during contract negotiations in September 1979.

Stevens also filed an undetermined number of reports in June 1979 on retired workers with breathing problems.

The retirees first learned of their breathing problems from Stevens's insurance company, Liberty Mutual, which sent adjusters to settle possible claims.

In South Carolina, the commission may fine companies $25 for not filing reports. But that doesn't always happen.

In November 1971, for example, Burlington Industries sent Hubert Waters, a picker in the Calhoun Falls mill, to a Greenville, S.C., doctor. The doctor diagnosed byssinosis, commission records show.

But Burlington didn't file a report on Waters until almost six years, in July 1977, a month after Waters retired.

S.C. Commissioner J. Dawson Addis, who approved a $7,000 settlement for Waters in February 1978, didn't fine the company for not filing an earlier byssinosis report. Addis, 56, said he didn't issue the fine because Waters wasn't totally disabled.

"They [Burlington] may have sent him to doctors, but if he was not disabled, he had no claim," Addis said. "They had no obligation. You might say they had a moral one, but they didn't have a legal one."

S.C. Commissioner Reid acknowledges the $25 fine for not filing is hardly a deterrent for big textile companies.

"You can see, if you have anything to hide, you go ahead and hide it," he said. "It defeats the legislature's intention in the proper delivery of justice."

When Waters, 69, signed his compensation agreement, he forfeited rights to any future legal claims against Burlington. He says a Burlington official told him, "Now when you sign, you can't sue us." Waters, unable to read or write, didn't have a lawyer and says, "I didn't ask no questions."

Waters's agreement was legal in South Carolina.

But N.C. commission rules forbid settlements in which workers sign away all future legal claims against a company. And commission chairman Stephenson said the commission goes over agreements "with a fine-tooth comb" to see that workers' rights are protected.

But that hasn't prevented the N.C. commission from approving at least four agreements violating the rule, the *Observer* investigation shows.

In one case documented by commission records, a woman was taken to the corporate offices of a major Piedmont textile firm and asked by a company vice president to sign a complicated legal agreement. The agreement settled a claim she hadn't filed but which company attorneys had prepared for her. The woman, who asked that her name not be used, now says she had no idea she was signing away future rights for $8,000.

Carlie Howard was another such worker.

After breathing cotton dust for 45 years in a Cannon Mills card room in Kannapolis, Howard was barely able to walk when he retired in 1975.

After Howard filed a claim with the commission, Cannon officials convinced him in July 1978 to settle for $25-a-week payments, up to $5,000, and give up future rights. He did not have a lawyer.

The law says Howard could have received $166 a week for life plus medical benefits if he were totally disabled.

Despite the improper agreement, the N.C. commission approved Howard's settlement.

When Howard died last June, commissioners also allowed Cannon to deduct 3 percent, or $148, from the $3,616 Cannon sent his widow. The reason, commissioners said, was that Cannon was paying off in a lump sum.

Stephenson says it was an "oversight" if the commission approved any such agreements.

In the woman's case, he conceded: "If you tell me the scales of justice are [fair] in that case, I'll say you're crazy."

If workers can prove that companies misrepresented agreements, workers can ask the commission to reopen their cases, he said.

Cannon officials say settlements provide workers with money they might not otherwise get and spare them legal fees.

Records which accurately reflect the commission's work are difficult, if not impossible, to obtain.

State laws allow both commissions to close their files to almost anyone they want. The *Observer* obtained case histories by contacting disabled workers and their attorneys.

The N.C. commission has denied attorneys access to what are normally public documents needed to prepare clients' cases.

In 1976, Robert Brown, then commission chairman, refused to give Greensboro attorney Henry Patterson copies of commission decisions in brown lung cases. Patterson said he was preparing an appeal and needed the decisions to determine legal precedent.

Stephenson said recently that the rule denying access to documents has been changed, though decisions still are not published or easily available for public inspection.

N.C. commissioners also write and rescind commission rules in private, one of three quasi-judicial state boards to do so. While these rules subsequently are filed with the state attorney general, Stephenson said the commission has some unwritten "in-house rules."

One such rule prohibits using tape recorders during commission hearings. Attorneys say they need the recordings because the commission takes months to provide the typed transcripts attorneys need to prepare workers' cases.

Stephenson dismissed these complaints as "laziness" and said lawyers should take better notes. He said the commission bans tape recorders because they make court reporters nervous.

In South Carolina, commissioners say the state compensation law has prevented them from awarding more byssinosis claims.

Until May 1978, for example, the law required workers to file claims within two years of when they knew, or should have known, they had byssinosis.

Commissioners thus decided many disabled workers were ineligible for compensation because they hadn't filed within two years of leaving the mills—even if byssinosis wasn't diagnosed until years later. The two-year time limit now starts at the time of diagnosis.

Another amendment, passed in May 1977, says workers must be exposed to cotton dust for at least seven years before being eligible for compensation—despite the fact some doctors say a worker can contract byssinosis in five years.

"I think it's [the seven-year amendment] probably unconstitutional," said S.C. Sen. Isadore Lourie, D-Richland, head of the legislature's workers' compensation committee and a lawyer for disabled workers. "It's a hell of a thing to say because I wrote that section. It was part of a compromise to get [the bill] passed."

Getting compensation was even more difficult when the law required a panel of three doctors to rule on any occupational disease claim.

Several doctors on the medical panel worked as consultants to textile companies. And the panel rarely if ever ruled in favor of brown lung victims, according to Commissioner Reid.

The legislature made the panel's recommendations nonbinding in May 1977, but they still apply to some cases filed before the law was changed.

Columbia attorney Douglas McKay Jr. wrote the 1949 occupational disease law which first covered brown lung. He is a former lawyer for the S.C. Textile Manufacturers Association, and heads the governor's advisory committee for the improvement of workers' compensation law, a post he has held since Gov. John West appointed him in 1975.

McKay believes many who file for brown lung compensation are "mental cripples . . . who just sit at home eating up that ol' comp money. They don't want to work."

N.C. commission Chairman Stephenson said N.C. law is adequate, but the commission needs the courts to help interpret the law.

Stephenson doesn't always appreciate the courts' guidance, however. He complained when state appeals courts eased filing requirements and increased compensation payments in 1979.

"Three recent cases in North Carolina lead us to believe that our appellate courts sometimes lack a complete understanding of what workers' compensation is," Stephenson told a national meeting of state legislators in Atlanta in December.

Industrial commissioners in both states say they are protecting workers as well as they can.

South Carolina has seven commissioners, three of whom are lawyers.

North Carolina has three commissioners, including one lawyer and nine deputies.

Brown lung cases take a disproportionate share of their time. N.C. textile companies contest byssinosis claims 80 percent of the time; S.C. companies contest virtually every case. Companies contest less than 2 percent of the 300,000 other claims in both states each year.

The situation may get worse before it gets better.

Commissioners in both Carolinas—where about 391,500 of the nation's 890,000 textile workers live—estimate at least 5,000 workers in each state are disabled by byssinosis but haven't filed.

Other estimates are higher. For instance, the Brown Lung Association, a group of retired textile workers, estimates byssinosis has disabled 13,000 workers in North Carolina and 10,000 in South Carolina.

Such numbers—and commissioners' explanations—mean little to Lula Pendergraft, who has lived on social security disability benefits for six years while her case languished in commission files.

After Mrs. Pendergraft filed her claim in 1973, the N.C. commission's former chief administrative officer, J. R. Mitchell, told her she probably wasn't eligible for compensation because her doctor had said she had emphysema, a lung disease often confused with byssinosis. But Mitchell said he'd have the N.C. Occupational Health Branch review her claim, as required by commission procedure.

He never did.

Mrs. Pendergraft heard nothing from the commission until August 1979, when her attorney, trying to file a second claim, found the original case still open. In November 1979, a lung specialist for the commission said Mrs. Pendergraft's lung disease is due partly to cotton dust. She still awaits a decision on her 6½-year-old claim.

Stephenson said state law prevents him from commenting on the case.

For some, the delays are even more tragic. Four of 37 workers who filed claims in Gaston and Lincoln counties since 1978 died waiting for commission rulings.

So did Spencer Wooten.

Wooten was a loom fixer at Pacific Mills in Columbia for 29 years. He filed his claim in November 1975, eight months after he quit because of constant coughing, wheezing, and severe chest pains.

The mill sent him to Dr. Robert Galphin Jr., a pulmonary specialist at Richland Memorial Hospital in Columbia. Galphin diagnosed permanent lung disease due to cotton dust. S.C. Industrial Commissioner Theodore Nelson held a hearing in May 1976. Nearly two years later Nelson ruled Wooten "obviously . . . is plagued by the classic symptoms of byssinosis" and awarded him $85.73 per week up to $40,000, the maximum award.

The company appealed, saying it hadn't completed its evidence, and the commission sent Nelson's ruling to the medical panel for review.

Still awaiting a final decision, Wooten died in December 1978.

Six months later, his wife, Mamie Wooten, 65, settled the case with Pacific Mills for $15,000. After paying the lawyer and her husband's medical expenses, she got a check for $9,739.25.

"My lawyer told me it might go into court for five or six years," Mrs. Wooten said softly. "I said, 'Oh Lord, I need it now, I don't want to wait like my husband until I'm dead.'"

TEXTILE INDUSTRY HAS CLOUT—AND KNOWS HOW TO USE IT

By Howard Covington and Bob Drogin
Observer Staff Writers

During the Great Depression, 62 N.C. counties and more than 150 cities and towns faced bankruptcy. Wall Street bankers demanded about $3 million in loans the state couldn't pay.

"We would like for you to renew the notes," Gov. O. Max Gardner pleaded in a meeting with New York bankers.

Then textile baron Charles Cannon spoke: "If you don't, our inclination is to withdraw all of our money from your banks."

Lose a customer like Cannon, head of Kannapolis-based Cannon Mills Co., one of the nation's largest textile companies? North Carolina's unblemished credit rating was saved.

Nearly 50 years later, the textile industry still wields political and economic clout on Wall Street, in the White House and Congress, and in state offices in Columbia and Raleigh.

That clout is important as the industry faces one of its greatest challenges—how to deal with federal regulations to reduce cotton dust in the mills.

About 115,000 Carolinas workers are exposed to cotton dust and experts say 18,000 active and retired workers already are disabled by byssinosis, a lung disease caused by cotton dust. The Carolinas have 391,500 textile workers, most of whom do not work with cotton.

The sheer number of workers is a key reason for the industry's clout.

One of every 20 American manufacturing workers is in textiles. In the Carolinas, one third of all manufacturing workers depend on looms and spinning frames for a living.

Largest Industry in Carolinas

No Carolinas industry employs more people, produces more goods, or is as involved in the daily lives of the people in this region. N.C. mill-workers make $11 billion in textile products each year, compared to the $1 billion N.C. farmers get for their top cash crop—tobacco.

The 1,800 Carolinas textile mills are concentrated in the Piedmont but operate in 82 of North Carolina's 100 counties, and 22 of South Carolina's 46 counties.

Mills in both states produced more than $17 billion in goods last year—including millions of towels, thousands of miles of sheets, more than half of America's panty hose and cotton cloth, and nearly all its yarn.

in Erwin, in Harnett County in Eastern North Carolina, a Burlington Industries Inc. plant produces more than a million yards of denim each week—enough denim to stretch 1 yard wide for 586 miles from Charlotte beyond Philadelphia. A single Cannon Mills weaver said he has made towels for 47,000 Hilton Hotel rooms.

Carolinas textile companies pay $4 billion in salaries and more than $50 million in state corporate income taxes.

Nine Carolinas textile companies are on *Fortune* magazine's most recent list of America's 500 largest industrial corporations—Burlington, of Greensboro, with sales of $2.4 billion; Blue Bell Inc., of Greensboro, $872 million; Akzona Inc., of Asheville, $868 million; Spring Mills Inc., of Fort Mill, S.C., $694 million; Cone Mills Corp., of Greensboro, $617 million; Cannon, $547 million; Dan River Inc., of Greenville, $530 million; Hanes Corp., of Winston-Salem, $471 million; and Fieldcrest Mills Inc., of Eden, $463 million.

Textiles use more electrical power than any other industry in the Carolinas, buying 17 percent of Duke Power Co.'s generating capacity. Duke, the region's largest power company, designed its two-state system to meet the needs of expanding cotton mills.

Though few mills have operated in Mecklenburg County, Charlotte owes much of its prosperous mercantile and banking business to the textile industry. Because the textile industry is nearby, Charlotte sells more industrial chemicals than all but five American cities.

Today, North Carolina is the nation's leader in the manufacture of textile machinery and equipment, producing 22 percent of all textile machinery.

The world's largest textile company, Burlington, is based in Greensboro. Company founder J. Spencer Love adopted the name from the town of Burlington, where local boosters offered him land and loans and helped him open his first mill in 1923.

The world's second largest textile firm, J.P. Stevens & Co., is based in New York City but has its manufacturing headquarters in Greenville, S. C., which local boosters call the "Textile Capital of the World." Stevens is Greenville's largest employer with about 9,000 employees.

It is little wonder that the industry is so much a part of our lives in the Carolinas.

The Carolinas textile industry began in 1813, when Michael Schenck and Absalom Warlick built a cotton mill near Lincolnton, about 25 miles northwest of Charlotte. Four years later, Rocky Mount Mills opened in Eastern North Carolina. It was heavily damaged by Union artillery in the Civil War but still runs today.

Mills sprang up after the turn of the century as companies—moving closer to Southern cotton fields—built plants along the Southern Railways main line. By the 1930s, the South surpassed New England in the number of spindles and looms in production.

Companies often built homes, hospitals, stores, roads, and schools for employees and their families. They provided the first steady paychecks for Carolinas workers moving from the farm to the factory. Companies sometimes built entire towns.

Erwin was built in 1903 around cotton mills owned by the James B. Duke family. When Burlington bought the Erwin Mills Co. in 1960, some Burlington officials didn't realize they had also bought the town of Erwin.

Burlington later sold all the store, houses, and other property to local residents. The city incorporated itself in 1967 and has about 3,000 residents today.

Kannapolis, North Carolina's 11th largest community, is the best-known example of a textile company town. Even the name Kannapolis is Greek for "city of looms."

James W. Cannon, who worked in a Concord general store, built two cotton mills on 600 acres of cotton fields in Cabarrus County north of Concord in 1907.

Cannon soon built homes, schools, parks, a huge YMCA, and a theater. The company gave land for churches and provided police and fire services and free electricity.

In 1937, James Cannon's son, Charles, hired a Chicago firm to redesign Kannapolis with colonial fronts and buildings similar to those in Williamsburg, Va.

Until he died in 1971, Charles Cannon's power was legendary.

"Mr. Cannon exercises about the same authority here that Prince Rainier does in Monaco," the *Wall Street Journal* said of "Mr. Charlie's town" in 1969.

The newspaper pointed out one difference: the 37,000 Kannapolis residents, who live in the state's largest unincorporated community, couldn't vote on local matters, as could the prince's subjects.

The company employs 16,000 of Cabarrus County's 19,000 textile workers, and company property accounts for about a fifth of the county's taxable property.

N.C. Democratic Rep. Dwight Quinn, first elected in 1952, is a Cannon vice president and has served more terms in the state House than any current member. Jim Dorton, a Cannon employee, is a Concord alderman. So is Robert Hayes, Charles Cannon's grandson.

The Cannon Foundation has put more than $16 million into Cabarrus Memorial Hospital in Concord and paid for the new Charles A. Cannon Memorial Library in Concord.

Last year, Cannon contributed $225,000 to the 41-member Kannapolis police department, built a 3-acre town park, and gave the Kannapolis school board 28.5 acres for a school.

The economic power, coupled with close involvement in Carolinians' daily lives, gives the textile industry its political clout—but there's debate about whether the clout is waning.

Charles Dunn, an administrative aide in the 1960s to Gov. Dan Moore and to former U.S. Rep. Horace Kornegay, D–N.C., and now spokesman for the N.C. Textile Manufacturers Association, thinks the textile industry doesn't have the power it once did.

"Most people think of the mills like they were 20 or 30 years ago," said Dunn, 45, director of the N.C. State Bureau of Investigation from 1969 to 1975, and editorial director of Capitol Broadcasting Co. in Raleigh from 1976 until 1978. "There have been changes."

Dunn noted that the tobacco industry, not textiles, won tax cuts from the legislature in 1977. He said textile executives probably pay more attention to Washington than Raleigh or Columbia.

Dunn said executives monitor international trade agreements and watch federal agencies that regulate company mergers, establish standards for water and air pollution, and set cotton dust standards.

And the industry has some powerful friends in Washington.

When Ken Holland, D-S.C., calls roll in the House of Representatives textile caucus he chairs, more than 240 representatives from 30 states answer. Sen. Ernest Hollings, D-S.C., leads an equally potent, though less formal, Senate coalition.

Congressional supporters rallied when American textile and apparel manufacturers felt they weren't being protected in 1978 international trade talks in Geneva. Congress exempted textiles from tariff cuts, which could hurt domestic manufacturers by allowing cheaper imports into the country. The move brought the Geneva talks to a standstill.

President Carter later vetoed the exemption bill but the industry had made its point. Carter instructed trade negotiators to make better deals for American textiles.

Such an obvious display of power is rare, said one senior U.S. Commerce Department official.

"In a sense, " he said, textiles "are powerful enough that they don't have to prove it. Everybody knows the power is there."

The industry's clout has also helped it fight federal regulations.

In early 1972 the U.S. Labor Department's Occupational Safety and Health Administration (OSHA) announced it would regulate five toxic substances, including cotton dust. OSHA adopted a temporary cotton dust standard until researchers developed tougher, permanent regulations.

Industry leaders oppose the standards and asked OSHA for a delay.

On June 14, 1972, George Guenther, a former Pennsylvania textile executive who headed OSHA, wrote a confidential memorandum to

Labor Under Secretary Lawrence Silberman, listing ways to raise money for Richard Nixon's 1972 reelection campaign. Guenther recommended using "the great potential of OSHA as a sales point for fund raising and general support by employers."

Cotton dust was the memo's first topic.

"While promulgation and modification activity must continue, no highly controversial standards (i.e., cotton dust, etc.) will be proposed by OSHA or NIOSH" (National Institute of Occupational Safety and Health), Guenther wrote. NIOSH didn't recommend a standard until 1974 and OSHA didn't issue one until 1976.

Former U.S. Commerce Secretary Maurice Stans also urged textile executives to support Nixon in 1972. They responded with nearly $1 million, including $430,000 before a federal law took effect April 7 requiring public disclosure of campaign contributions.

Roger Milliken, who heads Spartanburg's Milliken and Co., gave Stans $363,122.50 in checks and cash only hours before the April 7 deadline.

Frederick Dent, president of Mayfair Mills in Arcadia, S. C., and former president of the American Textile Manufacturers Institute, gave $10,500 before the April 7 deadline, and marshaled industry support for Nixon in the Carolinas, Kentucky, and Georgia.

A month after the election, Nixon named Dent U.S. Secretary of Commerce, a post crucial to textile interests concerned with trade tariffs and agreements. In March 1975, President Ford named Dent special representative for trade negotiations.

Although the focus is in Washington, most state officials know before they get to Raleigh and Columbia that the textile industry is important to them, their counties—and their election campaigns.

"There's no question if the textile industry is strongly and adamantly opposed to a bill, we'll have a real hard time passing it," said S.C. Sen. Isadore Lourie, D-Richland, head of the legislature's workers' compensation study and review committee. "Their prestige is immense."

The S. C. Textile Manufacturers Association (SCTMA) has 75 member firms. The group spent $28,252 during the 1979 General Assembly session—more than twice as much as any of the 220 other registered lobby groups—entertaining state legislators and otherwise lobbying for favorable legislation.

The manufacturers' group has led the fight against proposed changes in laws to make it easier for brown lung victims to win compensation.

Mill executives last year wrote letters, made phone calls, and buttonholed state senators to oppose a bill which would ease compensation. Senators voted 27-11, with eight not voting, to return the bill to committee, killing it for at least a year.

"Our position over there has been to do what we think is good for South Carolina," said John Beasley, SCTMA executive vice president. Beasley is a former assistant to the president of the University of South Carolina and former assistant to U.S. Rep. William Jennings Bryan Dorn.

The SCTMA Good Government Fund spent $30,584 before the November 1978 elections, contributing to more than 100 candidates for local and state offices, state ethics commission reports show. Political action committees at individual companies such as Riegel Textile Corp., Dan River, and Springs Mills, reported handing out a total of $8,430 in the past two years.

Dunn, the spokesman for the N.C. Textile Manufacturers Association (NCTMA), reported spending only $1,500 lobbying last year. But the industry doesn't have to spend money to have influence in Raleigh.

The chairman of the N.C. Senate's Committee on Manufacturing and Wages, the committee which deals with most bills affecting textiles, is Sen. Jack Childers, D-Lexington, a retired textile executive and former president of the NCTMA.

Last year Dunn and Cone Mills attorney Jack Elam had little trouble convincing legislators to weaken a workers' compensation bill that prohibited employers from firing workers who filed claims.

Keeping Unions Out

Textile companies also have used their power, sometimes illegally, to keep unions out of the Carolinas, the nation's least unionized states.

The National Labor Relations Board (NLRB) has cited J.P. Stevens for unfair labor practices 22 times since the Amalgamated Clothing and Textile Workers Union began an organizing drive in 1963.

A federal appeals court last month upheld an NLRB order saying Stevens had a "long history of violations of employee rights and flagrant disregard of board decisions and court orders."

The company still hasn't signed a contract in Roanoke Rapids, six years after the union won a controversial election recently publicized in the film "Norma Rae."

In South Carolina, Deering Milliken's Darlington Manufacturing Co. closed six days after 556 millworkers voted to join the Textile Workers Union of America in 1956.

The union sued the company, now called Milliken and Co., for lost wages. The case went to the U.S. Supreme Court twice, and courts repeatedly ruled the millworkers were fired illegally and ordered Milliken to pay their lost wages.

The company disputes the number of workers affected and how

much they should be paid. The Darlington workers still have not been paid 24 years after they lost their jobs. At least 75 have died.

The Carolinas textile companies pay among the lowest wages of any manufacturing industry in the nation, an average of $4.73 an hour to N. C. textile workers in 1979, and about $4.82 to S.C. workers.

Partially as a result, the Carolinas have among the lowest manufacturing wages in the nation, according to the U.S. Labor Department. South Carolina ranks 48th and North Carolina ranks 50th.

Carolinas' governors have courted companies with higher-paying jobs to the two states, saying they don't want more low-wage industry. But top state officials still come to the industry's aid.

In September 1978, S.C. Gov. Jim Edwards and N.C. Gov. Jim Hunt supported a resolution at the Southern Governors' Conference at Hilton Head, S. C., urging federal officials to delay new, tougher federal standards to lower cotton dust in the mills.

Hunt said in November that he supported the delay at the request of his own commerce department.

Said Hunt: "Anybody who provides the large investment and employs a lot of people" is going to be listened to.

DOES GROUP HELP OR HURT THE CAUSE?

By Bob Drogin

Paul Cline, 58, a sixth-grade dropout who heads the Greenville, S.C., chapter of the Brown Lung Association, does not mince words.

"The good Lord give man the breath to breathe and I don't think the textile mills have the right to take it away," Cline said recently. "They sacrifice our lives for profits."

Harsh words, but they sum up much of what the loosely organized and financially strapped Brown Lung Association is about: a bitter fight between mostly uneducated, poor, and disabled cotton-mill workers, their paid organizers, and the most powerful industry in the Carolinas.

The issues are compensation for the estimated 18,000 active and retired workers disabled by byssinosis—the lung disease cotton dust causes—and reducing cotton dust for the 115,000 Carolinians who work in cotton mills. The Carolinas have 391,500 textile workers.

In five years, the 5,000-member, non-profit Brown Lung Association has helped reform state and federal laws, helped disabled workers win compensation, and fought to focus public concern on the dangers of cotton dust.

The group's opponents don't mince words either. State officials and textile spokesmen say the association has run bogus medical clinics, violated state fund-raising laws, juggled facts and statistics, staged sensational media events, disrupted meetings and offices, and manipulated workers for political ends.

"I don't have any relations with them today," said William Stephenson, chairman of the N. C. Industrial Commission, which has approved 286 of the 913 byssinosis [brown lung] compensation claims filed. "They haven't accused me of bastardy but they have of everything else."

"It's very difficult to work with them," said Dr. Don Robinson, head of occupational safety and health in the S. C. Department of Health and Environment Control. "They antagonize everybody instead of accepting help. . . . I feel like they kicked me in the teeth."

The criticism doesn't bother Brown Lung members.

"We're not running a popularity contest," said Charlotte Brody, 31, who lives in Charlotte and is the association's chief organizer. "We're an organization of people fighting back. ... When they stop killing people, we'll stop fighting." Ms. Brody, a registered nurse from Detroit, also has worked in groups supporting striking Kentucky coal miners, counseling soldiers against the Vietnam War at Fort Campbell, Ky., and for the Student Nonviolent Coordinating Committee in Detroit.

The Brown Lung Association's fighting sometimes is rough. But it has led to some impressive achievements.

On the federal level, the association has lobbied and testified in favor of stricter regulations to reduce cotton dust in the mills. U.S. Labor Secretary Ray Marshall cited the group's support in a May 1978 memorandum to President Carter recommending the White House give its blessings to the standards.

The standards, first proposed in 1974, are to go into effect March 25. Textile industry spokesmen said they will appeal the standards to the U.S. Supreme Court.

In the Carolinas, the group has helped dozens of the 320 disabled workers who have won more than $4 million in brown lung awards and settlements. Organizers have sought out disabled workers, filed their claims, gotten them lawyers and doctors, and sometimes even carried workers into compensation hearings.

The group also has pressured both states to reform compensation laws and procedures. In North Carolina, Gov. Jim Hunt last December ordered an investigaton of delays in brown lung compensation. He appointed a Brown Lung member, Florence Sandlin of Greensboro, to the seven-member panel.

In South Carolina, Brown Lung pressure since 1977 led the General Assembly to amend laws to make byssinosis compensable, ease the statute of limitations, increase potential benefits, and eliminate a conservative medical panel that had rejected most brown lung cases.

"The Brown Lung Association really deserves credit," says S.C. Sen. Isadore Lourie, D-Richland, chairman of the General Assembly's workers' compensation study and review committee. "If it weren't for them, I don't think we would have gotten the legislation through."

The association—which has 13 chapters and about 40 paid staffers—got its start late in 1974 following a 13-month strike against Duke Power Co.'s Brookside coal mines in Harlan County, Ky. Five Brookside organizers, veterans of anti-war, labor, and political movements, attended an occupational health conference organized by students near Knoxville, Tenn. They left with a new cause—brown lung.

Consumer Advocate Ralph Nader had written about brown lung five years earlier, but few Carolinas doctors, lawyers, or workers knew about the dangers of cotton dust. Some textile industry executives still denied byssinosis existed, or said it didn't affect American workers.

Armed with $5,000 from the United Church of Christ, Frank Blechman and two other former Brookside organizers started knocking on mill-workers' doors in Greensboro, Columbia, Roanoke Rapids, and Spartanburg.

"Folks were real scared," recalled Blechman, 32, a former newspaper photographer from Virginia who now organizes a charity called The Other Way of South Carolina. "It was too risky for most people."

In Greensboro, Lacy Wright, now 75, a disabled Cone Mills worker, "got up out of my rocking chair" to call friends and hold living-room meetings after organizer Thad Moore visited his home. More than 100 people turned out at the first Brown Lung meeting at a Columbia textile union hall in April 1975.

Support grew slowly. Many retired workers were too old or sick to come to meetings. Others, crippled by breathing problems, died.

"When I first got here there was someone dying every eight weeks," said Mike Russell, a former Greenville, S. C., staff member whose wife, Kathy, now works for the group. "That's what made this job so hard."

In November 1975, the group organized its first mass filing of brown lung compensation claims. About 70 disabled millworkers filed claims simultaneously in Spartanburg, Columbia, Greensboro, and Roanoke Rapids. Staffers acknowledge now the event was staged mostly for publicity; only a few workers ever won compensation.

"Many were marginal cases," said Ben Bowen, a Greenville lawyer who works closely with the association. "It was just a way to draw attention for the public and the politicians."

The group also began brown lung screening clinics to identify workers with breathing problems who might be eligible for compensation.

The first clinic was June 12, 1975, at Hope View Presbyterian Church in north Greensboro. Medical students and doctors took medical histories and gave breathing tests and physical examinations. More than a third of the 92 active and retired workers were diagnosed disabled due to cotton dust.

In a September 1975 clinic in Columbia, association doctors found 68 of the 97 millworkers to be totally or partially disabled from the cotton dust. About 25 announced they would file for compensation.

Brown Lung spokesmen announced to the media that the clinics showed byssinosis was a serious problem. But others attacked the clinic results as inaccurate and misleading.

An S.C. Department of Health and Environment Control report called the Columbia findings "an insult to one's intellect" because they didn't account for smoking, genetic background, and other possible lung problems.

"You cannot diagnose brown lung with just a screening clinic," said Haven Newton, vice president of Fieldcrest Mills Co. of Eden, a mill community where several clinics have been held.

The Brown Lung Association ran into another problem when the few doctors sympathetic to its cause began facing troubles of their own.

Two Columbia doctors who diagnosed dozens of byssinosis cases at clinics in 1975 and 1976 went to federal prisons on separate, unrelated charges. Several other doctors, including two who were shot to death at an anti-Ku Klux Klan rally in Greensboro Nov. 3, began using the clinics as a political forum. Dr. Paul Bermanzohn, partially paralyzed from the Greensboro shootout, was particularly active.

"He'd get up in front of a group of doctors and castigate them for not being Communist," one former organizer recalled. "And he did that saying he was representing the Brown Lung Association. We pulled him aside quietly and told him if he ever did that again we'd . . . break his knees."

Some doctors who work with the association say clinics often raise unrealistic hopes of compensation. Worse, they say, workers apparently coach clinic patients on what to tell other doctors to strengthen their cases.

Dr. Leo Heaphy, a Winston-Salem pulmonary specialist whose office is decorated with Brown Lung Association posters, said these workers leave the clinics convinced they can file for workers compensation for byssinosis, when they really have other breathing problems.

37 Clinics Last Year

"These [patients] take nastily to the suggestion, 'You really do not have brown lung disease,' " Heaphy said.

Brown Lung members say the clinics educate victims, doctors, and the public. The association sponsored 37 clinics last year, screening about 1,500 people.

The Carolina Brown Lung Association formally was chartered in August 1976. "Carolina" was dropped last year when the group decided to expand into Virginia and Georgia. A $60,000 budget came mostly from the Campaign for Human Development, an arm of the U.S. Catholic Conference.

The budget has grown steadily.

The group took in $156,347 between Jan. 1 and Sept. 1, 1979, including $25,000 from the federal Community Services Administration, $37,880 from the United Presbyterian Church USA, $40,000 from the U.S. Labor Department's Occupational Safety and Health Administration (OSHA), and $19,500 from the Youth Project, a Washington foundation for community groups. The rest came from private foundations and donations.

This year's $250,000 budget begins with a $95,000 OSHA grant to buy audio-visual equipment, hold 12 workshops, six screening clinics, and other programs to educate active workers about brown lung. The budget does not include government-paid salaries of $250 a month for up to 20 VISTA, and about 12 part-time CETA workers.

The association has chapters in Eden, Erwin, Greensboro, Laurinburg, Lincoln/Gaston, Roanoke Rapids, Rockingham, and Stanly County in North Carolina, and Aiken, Anderson, Columbia, Greenville, and Spartanburg in South Carolina. New chapters are planned this year in Danville, Va., and Augusta, Ga.

The chapters raise money through fish fries, auctions, cookbook sales, and gospel sings. Copy machines, office space, and supplies often are borrowed or donated. Paychecks are low and frequently late.

Twelve full-time staff members, including an attorney in Durham, were supposed to make $8,500 last year. They each made $6,600 instead.

High staff turnover has led to confusion. A Greenville, S.C., staffer recently found files of about 35 workers diagnosed in 1977 clinics with breathing problems which no one had followed up. Columbia chapter members rumored a staffer was an FBI agent; she says she isn't.

"I quit because I wasn't getting paid and it was so disorganized," said another former staffer. "Nobody was in a position to make a decision."

Members and organizers often face hostility, fear, and distrust.

"I been harassed by company people, I've had trouble in my own church over it, and the company personnel office called the mayor to try to keep us from having meetings," said John Cobb, a disabled worker in West Pelzer who is president of the S.C. Brown Lung Association. "I've lost a good many friends about this thing."

Bruce Dew, a Columbia lawyer who works with the group, said, "The Brown Lung people are regarded as anarchists, radicals, Communists, hippies, and labor agitators. One top lawyer in the state told me, 'Hell, they're nothing but a bunch of damn Catholics and labor unions agitating.' "

The organization has worked closely in some communities with the Amalgamated Clothing and Textile Workers Union (ACTWU). But the two groups have feuded recently. Brown Lung members such as Lacy Wright, a former Greensboro textile union local president, say the union ignores disabled workers; ACTWU organizers say Brown Lung doesn't do enough for workers still in the mills.

"Hell, anybody can organize retired textile workers," complained one ACTWU organizer, who asked not to be identified. "They got nothing to lose. It's active workers who are at risk and Brown Lung don't do nothing for them."

From the start, organizers said Brown Lung should be a self-help, democratic organization of byssinosis victims. Members were to speak publicly, lobby, testify, and organize. Staffers were to stay in the background, talking to reporters only if they wouldn't be quoted or identified.

Actually, staffers do most of the routine work—writing and mailing newsletters and press statements, organizing protests, coordinating compensation claims, calling lawyers and doctors. Only a handful of members are active in each chapter.

"They're Sick, They're Old"

"It's really a task even to get them [members] to the office," said Rosa Hankerson, 32, a registered nurse who is the Columbia staff member. "They're sick, they're old."

But members do turn out for protests. Each year, dozens of elderly, sick retired millworkers troop into plush government and industry offices, ready to tell their stories in wheezes and whispers.

They are not always welcome. Wearing buttons saying "Cotton Dust Kills," and carrying signs reading "We swallowed your dust, we won't swallow your lies," they sometimes block doors and refuse to leave. Some cry. Others sing.

"They come in here and some old person tells me his story," said Harold Trask, chairman of the S.C. Industrial Commission, which has approved about 40 brown lung compensation claims of about 200 filed. "I feel compassion, sure, but it really doesn't accomplish anything. . . . They are all laymen. They don't understand the intricacies of the law."

Stephenson, head of the N.C. commission, met Brown Lung members several times but stopped in 1978 after "they showed up one morning with 75 people and used it as a platform to espouse their views to the press."

The association demanded Stephenson's resignation last fall, claiming he hadn't made changes in commission procedures he'd promised in early, less contentious, meetings.

Last August, about 20 Brown Lung members dumped 300 empty prescription bottles on the desk of state S.C. Sen. David Taylor, D-Laurens, saying he had helped kill a proposed byssinosis compensation bill. Picketers carried signs reading "Taylor is Industry's Boy" and "Taylor Lied to Us."

Attracting Attention

In November, eight members marched into the economics classroom of Clemson University Professor Hugh Macaulay, saying he had written a column on compensation that was "irrational, immoral and a contradiction of the facts" in the *Greenville News and Piedmont*. Macaulay threatened to call the police and his students told the group to leave.

The Brown Lung Association achieved its greatest publicity in April 1977 when about 50 members, some in wheelchairs or breathing from oxygen tanks, went to Washington to talk to Congressional delegations and to testify at OSHA hearings for new cotton dust standards.

The Brown Lung Association attracted national attention again last September after five N.C. United Way chapters and the United Way of South Carolina, the state umbrella group, turned down all association requests for financial aid. Association members picketed mills in both states, urging millworkers to give money to Brown Lung instead of the United Way, the Carolinas largest charity.

The association's anti-United Way drive was "technically in violation of the law" in South Carolina because the group wasn't registered to solicit contributions, said Eric Pantsari, head of the charities division of the S.C. secretary of state. He said the association later filed the proper papers.

Brown Lung members and staffers say the organization's future is unclear. They'll continue to push for federal standards to reduce cotton

crowd because all we do is sit on our butts and do nothing." I advised him I was making a change in residence from Birmingham to Cullman. Did his organization have anybody in Cullman I could contact?

Black had told me that Wilkinson had a tough Klan Klavern in Cullman.

Torbert gave me the name of the Cullman den commander, Terry Tucker. "He is our E.C. up in Cullman," Torbert said, "our Exalted Cyclops." He promised to call Tucker for me. I was elated. I notified John Seigenthaler, my publisher in Nashville. We agreed the time had come to move on to the next Empire.

Within no time I had rented an apartment in Cullman, an hour's drive north of where I had lived for months in Birmingham.

I arranged for a telephone call service to take messages while I was away from the apartment. I told my "boss," David Skelton—who had employed me for months as a cabinetmaker's helper in Homewood, a Birmingham suburb—that I was having to move away.

He was my friend. He wished me well, suspicious but not sure of what my relationship with the Klan was all about.

When I called Terry Tucker, the "E.C." for Wilkinson's den in Cullman, he was delighted to hear from me—a real, live defector from the KKK Knights of Don Black. He said he would put the question of my membership to his Klansmen at their next meeting.

Three days later he called me back to say everything had been approved and that I could be sworn in at the next meeting, which was two weeks away. It was another great example of KKK "security" techniques.

I decided to push him to try to bring about a personal meeting of myself with Wilkinson. Torbert urged me to call the Wizard and gave me his phone number in Denham Springs, La. I made the call.

"You don't know me," I told the Imperial Wizard over the phone, "but I'm J. W. Thompson and I've been a member of David Duke's and Don Black's Klan. Now, I'm getting ready to come over to your group.

"I'm doing this because I'm so upset that Duke tried to sell my membership. I've got to ask you, Mr. Wilkinson: If and when you decide to sell my membership to someone, will you notify me first?"

Wilkinson's response was immediate. "I don't sell anyone out," he said. "And I don't buy anyone either. My record will show that."

I expressed satisfaction with his reply. I asked if he would be in Alabama soon so that we could talk personally. He would not be there for almost two months, he said. In fact, I never got to meet him face to face. Now I was ready to become a member of Wilkinson's group— while secretly retaining my membership in Black's organization.

So, on a Saturday night—this past Oct. 4—I arrived at the same isolated farmhouse where a few weeks earlier Bill Wilkinson and David Duke had their confrontation. As I drove up, Gerald Briscoe, the den's Nighthawk, fumbled with the lock on the front door. But the key he had been given didn't work.

"How are we going to get in?" Briscoe finally asked. I had no idea. Other Klan members arrived.

Finally one of them, Red Willingham, said he would go look for a key somewhere else. And while we were waiting for his return, we watched the children of Klan members ride a white horse from a nearby shed.

Klansman Jim Logan—who later told me he had owned the farmhouse before selling it to a relative—drove up. He had a key.

Inside, it appeared that only the living room was in use. The front window was boarded up and old theater seats and church pews were lined up in front of a table. Behind the table a Klan flag and a Confederate battle flag hung on the wall.

Beside the table was a handmade cross that held 13 candles in little glass cups. The room was lighted by a single bulb hanging at the end of a cord from the ceiling.

I was introduced to another KKK "recruit," James Johnson, who was identified as a city fireman. He was also there to be inducted into Wilkinson's Invisible Empire.

Briscoe and Willingham, I noticed, had briefcases. Opening them, they took out their Klan robes and hoods. Briscoe had a revolver, which he laid on the table.

The weapons should not have surprised me. I never went to a meeting of Wilkinson's Klan group where rifles and pistols, and sometimes bayonets, were not displayed.

It is necessary, Wilkinson tells his members, that they arm themselves for what he predicts will be "a race war."

In the way it is armed, Wilkinson's Klan is different from Black's. Black preaches that acts of violence result in Klan members' going to jail, and usually only his security guards are armed.

On this night at the farmhouse, Nighthawk Briscoe was serving as Exalted Cyclops during the ceremony, in the absence of Terry Tucker, who was out of town.

Willingham was appointed the Klaliff—second in command—for the night. The regular Klaliff, Dudley Ham, was out of town with Tucker. Jim Logan served as Chaplain. All three were dressed in their Klan garb, the white robes.

Meanwhile, an older man whose name I never learned served as

Nighthawk, or guard at the front door. Wearing a 38-caliber revolver in a shoulder holster, he stood in the doorway to make sure no unauthorized persons came in.

I had expected all the other Klan members—18 were there that evening—to attend the ceremony. But most of them declined, remaining outside on the front porch and in the front yard. They obviously had seen such ceremonies dozens of times. It was routine for them, and something of a bore.

The Klan calls such a ceremony a "naturalization," meaning that the recruit is accepted from an "alien world"—a racially integrated world, of course—into "citizenship in an empire that believes in the purity of the white race for America."

In most respects the ceremony for Wilkinson's group is exactly like that for Black's—a ceremony in which I had participated nearly a year before.

. . . .

Now I had been baptized twice into the Klan. The second time was just as silly as the first.

Actually the fiery cross—with the 13 candles—wasn't lit. When I had been initiated into Black's group, a single candle had been lit, but the only lighting in the Invisible Empire ceremony came from the bare light bulb.

The Chaplain—Jim Logan—then prayed for "our white race in your sublime image, Amen."

We all said "Amen."

. . . .

Johnson and I then attended our first business meeting with the Cullman den. It was less than impressive.

For one thing the secretary of the den was out of town—in Ohio—and so there could be no reading of the minutes of the last meeting. The treasurer was not present, so no one could pay dues. Tucker, the Exalted Cyclops, was away, so other business matters could not be attended to.

Briscoe talked for a while about the "Special Forces"—a paramilitary group of Klansmen in training at a camp nearby—which, according to Wilkinson, will be used as a "defensive force" when the race war starts.

"Those of you who know anything about the Special Forces, just forget what you know," said Briscoe. "And those of you who don't know anything—well, that's OK. Just don't even ask. The Special Forces are the hottest thing in the country right now."

He was referring to the publicity the group received after the *Ten-*

nessean's correspondent, Bob Dunnavant, had disclosed that Klan members were in training at the secret hideaway, using live ammunition and dressing in camouflage clothing, just like in the Army.

Briscoe then asked if anyone had anything else to talk about. Nobody did, and so we broke up for the night.

The next meeting, we were told, would be two weeks later.

Now I could say "AKIA"—"A Klansman I Am"—and it would be twice as true as before.

CHILDREN IN ROBES OF HATE . . . IT MADE ME WANT TO CRY

By Jerry Thompson

As I reflect on more than a year as a reporter working as an undercover Klansman there are vivid flashbacks of moments that saddened me, frightened me, worried me.

Here are some of those recollections that caused me sadness, fear, and concern:

• I was saddened every time I saw Klan children at a KKK function. In the flickering light of huge crosses in vacant fields there were always the beautiful, shining faces of small children—boys and girls—not yet in their teens: Klan children. They are being indoctrinated with the Klan's racist doctrine of white supremacy. Each time I saw them I felt sorry for them. And then, there was a Sunday afternoon, just two weeks ago, during a march of the Knights of the KKK through the streets of Birmingham when, suddenly, in the midst of two dozen Klan people wearing robes and hoods, there appeared this petite girl, striding along fully robed and hooded, her lovely face reminding me of my own 9-year-old daughter. Her left arm was in a cast. Her eyes looked straight ahead. She was expressionless. I have no idea what she was thinking. Our Klan people kept referring to her as "cute." Seeing her made me want to cry.

• Inevitably when I marched in my Klan garb, I would be moved by a sense of sadness and guilt when my eyes would lock into the gaze of black people standing along the sidewalks of our parade route.

I remember well the Labor Day march at Tuscumbia, Ala., in which I carried a sign which attacked public welfare. We were strolling along bellowing silly chants like, "White Power!" and "Wake Up White People, Wake Up!"—and I glanced suddenly to my right and met the gaze of a wrinkled old black woman, seated on a bench. I knew that she hated me. Worse, her look of contempt made it clear that she pitied me. I wanted, for just a moment, to rush over, smile at her, and tell her, "I'm not really part of this."

• Fear? I lived with fear for more than a year every time I attended a Klan function of either the Knights of the KKK or its rival group, the Invisible Empire of the KKK.

• There was the fear of being discovered—by Klan members, or by reporters covering Klan functions who had previously known me.

. . . .

• I became fearful on another occasion when I telephoned Bill Wilkinson long distance at his national headquarters of the Invisible Empire of the KKK in Denham Springs, La.

Later, after I ended the conversation, I played back the legal tape recording I had made of our conversation. Suddenly, I was scared out of my wits. It happened as I listened to the recorded voice of Wilkinson's secretary answering the phone. When I told her my name was "J. W. Thompson" calling Imperial Wizard Wilkinson, I could have sworn that she said, "Jerry?" I hadn't caught it when I was actually talking to her on the phone. But now the recording sounded as if she called me by my given name.

Could somebody have revealed to Wilkinson's Klan that I was not J. W. Thompson, retired Army sergeant, but Jerry Thompson, reporter? I rushed home to Nashville, and Seigenthaler and I listened as we played and re-played the tape. We became convinced that it was the recording re-play, not reality. Once again, my paranoia was working overtime.

• The time I became most frightened during my life with the Klan was a night when Terry Tucker, the Exalted Cyclops of my Cullman Klavern, told us we were to stage an armed march in Birmingham to confront the Communist Workers Party—"just like Greensboro." Five people had been shot to death when the Klan confronted the Communist Workers Party in Greensboro, N.C.

Now Tucker was telling us all to take weapons to confront the CWP in Birmingham.

Lawyers for the newspaper had instructed me before I took on the Klan assignment that I was not to participate in any unlawful activity, and that if I heard that violence was threatened by a Klan group I was to notify my publisher or the lawyers so that steps could be taken to halt the danger.

I called Seigenthaler. He notified the Justice Department in Washington that such a threat existed in Birmingham. As a result, Birmingham SWAT team police surrounded us that day on the Birmingham march. They ordered us to disarm, and they meant business. We loaded up tool boxes in two pickup trucks with an arsenal of weapons. We marched, with police helicopters hovering overhead and motorcycles escorting us.

There was no confrontation, and the only thing that got hurt was our feet from the three-mile walk.

• I remember worrying the night I sat in on my first den meeting with members of the Cullman Klavern of the Invisible Empire. Many of them routinely flashed and fondled their pistols and automatic rifles with something close to affection.

It dawned on me for the first time then: these people are ready for the "race war" their Imperial Wizard, Bill Wilkinson, keeps predicting.

The den to which I belonged in Cullman is an angry armed band whose members include people who are active in a paramilitary guerrilla warfare training unit near Hanceville, Ala. I am concerned that they are, in fact, promoting that race war.

• It worried me that day last April when I sat in the Birmingham City Council Chamber and saw Klan members sneer and heard them jeer and applaud as a black Army veteran, Willie James Williams, told about KKK members shooting into his home at night, endangering his wife and children.

Not one of those Klansmen would have wanted his own family to go through such an ordeal; still they clapped their hands with joy as Williams, a leader of the NAACP in Sylacauga, Ala., told the anti-Klan group conducting a hearing on Klan violence that police had ignored his pleas for help because they were busy investigating a television theft.

That display of pleasure in the knowledge that a black man was in danger and could not get police aid was an attitude that I regret was shared by too many members throughout the KKK factions to which I belonged. At that time I was a journalist posing as a KKK member, and I was worried about being discovered. But I couldn't bring myself to applaud.

• It concerned me to see how members of the Klan seemed to "turn on" when one of their leaders, such as Imperial Wizards Don Black or David Duke, launched into a discussion about about the "problems" that they claim are being caused by the "niggers and the Jews."

. . . .

I had been prepared in advance during prepping sessions with a psychiatrist to expect the Klan to be filled with angry, insecure people. Without that advance warning I could never have been ready for the unreasoned dogma of dislike for blacks and Jews that rules the KKK.

• And I always worried when I saw so-called "respectable" people expressing sympathy for Klan actions and Klan literature.

It disturbed me when I attended a meeting at the home of a Birmingham area physician, Dr. Frank Abernathy, where Imperial Wizard Black was introduced by the host. Dr. Abernathy clearly seemed to me to be sympathetic to the Klan.

I was gravely concerned because Don Black actually recruited new Klan members at that meeting and urged the guests to sign Klan application blanks and read Klan materials that were spread out on a table nearby.

I wrote about this meeting earlier in this series. Since then Dr. Abernathy told a United Press International reporter that I was wrong in saying this was a "Klan recruiting meeting" in his home. He said it was not a Klan meeting "per se"—and that he has all sorts of meetings in his fashionable residence at Alabaster, Ala. He insisted he was not a Klan member, and I never suggested that he was. I can only report what I saw at his home. And I stand by what I wrote.

I come away with these strong impressions about the Klan:

1. The KKK today is a growing threat to peace and order in cities all across the country. Whenever Klan members gather with guns concealed beneath their robes or on the hips of their so-called "security officers"—or in their automobiles nearby—it will only take a confrontational spark to set off a raging war.

The gunfire that has rocked a dozen cities and the blood that has stained the streets of Chattanooga, Decatur, Ala., and Greensboro is due to be repeated elsewhere unless authorities find some way to legally disarm the Ku Klux Klan.

2. Communities must find ways to deal openly, candidly, and forcefully with the sense of false security Klan leaders somehow are able to impart.

Actually, the Klan has no answers for its members. It only has empty promises to offer. It cannot do anything to curb crime, help the police, improve the economy, or assist society. In fact, were its rhetoric not so hateful and its potential for terror not so great, it would appear ludicrous. It is a silly organization whose members and especially their children must come to understand how irrational they appear.

Every city in America needs to have its leaders well informed about Klan activities. Educational programs need to be initiated by human relations organizations to alert the public to the very real physical and social dangers posed by a growing KKK.

3. The news media should make every effort to make investigative studies of all aspects of the Klan so that reporters, interviewers, and commentators are prepared to deal with glib, crafty, intelligent Klan leaders.

Too often journalists throw general questions at KKK Wizards like Don Black, Bill Wilkinson, and former Wizard David Duke, giving them the opportunity to make generalized statements that should be challenged with facts.

There has been criticism that the media have given the KKK "too much publicity." My own view is that too often the media have given the Klan too much superficial coverage. Rarely is Imperial Wizard Don Black asked about his background as an anti-Semitic racist, dating back to his teens when he was investigated for making threats against a Jewish schoolmate—threats he told *Tennessean* correspondent Robert Dunnavant were misinterpreted. He claims he was trying to make friends with the Jewish girl. She says she still fears him.

Nor is he ever usually questioned about how he got shot several years ago by Jerry Ray, brother of James Earl Ray, or about why military officials found him unacceptable as an Army officer because of his racist attitudes.

Nor is Imperial Wizard Bill Wilkinson, of the rival KKK group, asked about the Klan front business he operated in New Orleans under the name "E.C. Productions" which sold advertising for a festival in that city—a promotion that fell through after it was exposed by colleagues of mine on the *Tennessean.*

Bill Wilkinson was born "Elbert Claude" but changed his name to Bill—thus the name, "E.C. Productions."

Nor is he asked about his "mail order ministry" in the Universal Life Church of Modesto, Calif. He had himself declared a mail order preacher in this church, then transferred personally owned real estate of his to the name of the church. Again, all that has been published in this newspaper.

4. Despite suspicions to the contrary by many people, my own impression is that the Klan today is poorly financed. Black's operation seems to live hand-to-mouth and Wilkinson's organization seems only slightly better off.

They deal in sales of gadgets, tee shirts, trinkets (I purchased from a Klan member a wristwatch that plays *Dixie* for $25), and racist books, in addition to the initiation fees and dues. They also conduct roadblocks and turkey shoots to try to raise cash. True enough, Wilkinson flies his own private plane. But my observations convince me neither faction of the Klan to which I belonged has much money.

5. There is a concern that the KKK has infiltrated the police establishment.

My own experience suggests, at least at this point, that the Klan is so nervous about taking in new members who might be police spies that the concern is unfounded. When I was being "recruited" into the Knights of the KKK, a fellow recruit, Jim Huslander, who has said he was not a spy, was rejected as suspect because his father was a Birmingham policeman. While he was rejected, I was accepted.

And the strong response of the Metropolitan Nashville police to the efforts of the KKK to create disorder during the Nashville Christmas parade made me proud of my city and its Police Department.

There may be places where the Klan has risked letting in police officers as members. It won't happen where the police departments believe in upholding the law.

My year and more in the Ku Klux Klan now has ended. It was never a pleasant experience. I went into the assignment with my eyes wide open. I discussed it with my wife, Linda, in advance. The strain on her during much of this time has been nearly unbearable. I can never thank her enough for being both father and mother to our four children during this time. She is a brave lady, and I love her for many things— not the least of which is her support of me in this most dangerous news story of my 20-year career.

I also must express my appreciation to all of the members of the *Tennessean*'s news staff—those few who knew of the role I was playing and the many who did not and who telephoned my wife and other relatives with words of encouragement during a time when they thought I was trying to lick a liquor "problem."

Many other friends who were worried that I lost my job also telephoned or came by my house to offer words of encouragement to Linda. I thank them all.

To *Tennessean* Publisher John Seigenthaler, whose idea it was to infiltrate the Klan and who selected me for the job, I am appreciative for the confidence and his day-to-day advice and simple availability to talk over progress—or lack of it—and problems.

And I cannot forget my debt to other reporters who during my life with the Klan discovered me and kept the secret: Joe Holloway, a photographer for the AP Bureau in Atlanta; Jon Smith, cameraman for CBS-TV; Larry Brinton and Chris Clark with WTVF in Nashville. They could have blown my cover and made my life more problematical.

This has been a trying and troublesome time. It does not end with this series of stories. I know that the manuals of both factions of the Klan to which I belonged threatened "direful things" and "disgrace, dishonor, and death" for those who violate the Klan oath.

This means that my life will be different for a long time to come. I will have to have police protection in our house and when we travel.

That will be unpleasant. But while the story of the Klan will not end for me with this series, neither will it end for my community, the South, or for the nation.

The Klan is a menace. It is racist and anti-Semitic, and it threatens violence to any city where it has a Klavern or where it holds a rally.

I suspected as much before I joined the KKK. I know it positively now. I only hope my life with the Klan and these articles have helped others understand it.

CONCLUSION

All good reporting is investigative reporting, Carl Bernstein said, commenting on the lessons of Watergate.[1] We heard reporters repeat the sentence again and again, citing the need to probe beyond the obvious and the routine.

Yet, in-depth, investigative journalism is a different breed from even the best day-to-day coverage. It takes a step back to look at the larger picture, to search for patterns. Some journalists object to the word "investigative" because it does not necessarily involve detective work or result in catching a crook. In the sense we use the word, investigative refers to a method of research that is more scientific than even the most thorough reporting of a mayor's press conference or a sewer board meeting. The reporter begins with a tentative hypothesis, then sets up a method of investigation to determine the truth.

Breaking news usually involves an event—an accident, fire, announcement, or meeting. Events only trigger these investigative pieces. The questions asked by reporters and editors in this book go beyond the who, what, where, and when of today's news event. What investigative reporters look for is a pattern over time, a pattern that usually indicates something is wrong in some part of society. Their news does not get stale with the next day's edition. They may work on a story for months or even years. And their perspective often enables them to paint a broader picture than can be seen by any of the experts who may be their sources.

The story idea is usually germinated in that most basic of reportorial instincts—curiosity. Why, wondered Jonathan Neumann of the *Philadelphia Inquirer* as he sat through trial after trial in the city courts, were so many defendants testifying that police officers had beaten them during interrogation? And why was no one else in the court horrified?

Gordon Eliot White of Salt Lake City's *Deseret News* wondered, if

[1]Bill Kirtz, "Investigative Reporters Relate How They Operate," *Editor & Publisher*, May 3, 1975, p. 24.

Nevada bomb tests had caused cancer in the Army men who witnessed them, could they also have caused health problems in Utah citizens who were showered by the same fallout?

Howard Covington at the *Charlotte Observer* questioned what the effect of brown lung was on the cotton mill industry and its workers. A source convinced John Fried at the *Long Beach Independent, Press-Telegram* that he should inquire why private hospitals were dumping indigent patients out of their emergency rooms without proper care.

In two of the six cases in this book, the story idea sprang from the head of an editor. John Seigenthaler in Nashville wanted to get behind the new public relations front of the old Ku Klux Klan. Managing editor Frank Johnson at the *Arizona Daily Star* in Tucson saw a pattern of scandal in the football and basketball programs of the nation's major universities and sent two reporters to check out the local scene.

Unlike other areas of reporting, investigative journalism may not tell the public something new, something it did not already know or strongly suspect. "I imagine that 90 percent of all major investigative stories that are done are stories that are already known," Jonathan Neumann said.

For years homicide defendants in Philadelphia had been testifying that police were beating them to obtain a confession. Judges routinely had thrown out such confessions on the grounds that they had been illegally coerced. Police brutality was no secret in Philadelphia before the *Inquirer* documented it.

Brown lung in Carolina cotton mills was well known. The abuses in bigtime college football were a scandal most fans and sportswriters chose to wink at. Not many Tennesseans were really fooled by the Klan's new image, but Seigenthaler was determined to expose it.

Getting at the truth is where the reporter's work begins. As reporters frequently told us, the purported glamor of investigative reporting quickly frays. The initial excitement of the story idea will not sustain them through the long, tedious months of research. Only a dogged determination to get at truth enables them to do so.

Jerry Thompson endured months under the strain of a false identity and the virtual abandonment of his family. Gordon Eliot White pursued a paper chase through Washington's bureaucracy for years. Howard Covington had to carry his paper work around in a newspaper delivery sack. Bill Marimow and Jonathan Neumann spent long hours holed up with dusty files in an attic room of Philadelphia's City Hall.

Then sometime in the midst of this tedium, the pieces fell into place or the smoking-pistol piece of evidence was found, and suddenly the reporters saw the enormous scope of their discoveries. They knew, for the first time, that they had the goods, the documentation they needed, and they were onto a really big story.

We might have predicted that the reporters' reaction would be elation, pride, even exhilaration as they faced the prospect of the biggest stories of their careers, stories that brought each of them national renown. Instead, almost all told us what they felt was humility, even self-doubt. Were they up to the job? Did they want to be the ones to document this story?

Obviously, in each of these six cases, the reporters resolved their doubts and got on with the job. In fact, in many cases they came back from the pause with renewed commitment to get the whole story and to get it in such a way that it was beyond question, beyond reproach.

"I wanted to make sure that this story was documented in an ironclad way," Neumann recalled. "I wanted to make 100 percent sure that we were totally thorough, fair, and accurate."

None of the investigations in this book, except for the one from Nashville, would have been possible without state and federal open-record laws that gave reporters access to documents. In Tucson, the story pivoted on records—the airline and hotel bills charged to the university and the athletic department's phone records. Tony Mason's antics might have gone unnoticed if he had worked in a state with less liberal open-record laws.

For John Fried and Gerald Merrell in Long Beach, Los Angeles County's records of each patient's diagnosis, treatment, transfer, and final result were "pay dirt" in their attempt to uncover abuses in the Emergency Aid Program.

Howard Covington began his research with a list from the North Carolina Labor Department of all the cotton mill plants that had been inspected for cotton dust. "The Homicide Files" began with a search of court records. And although Gordon Eliot White seldom actually invoked the federal Freedom of Information Act, its existence and ever-present threat made his paper chase possible.

Throughout any major investigation, reporters face serious journalistic and ethical questions, questions that can be hampered by their own emotional involvement and their quest to get a good story. Reporters in North Carolina felt deeply that the victims of brown lung whom they interviewed "were getting screwed" by the cotton mill industry. Reading the court records of police brutality in Philadelphia, Marimow and Neumann began to see a picture of torture and suffering that aroused their sympathies. Neumann admits he was moved. "I don't think there's any such thing as objectivity," he explained. But his emotions were tempered by a deeper commitment to get all sides of the story.

Ironically, reporters often feel sympathy also for people they originally think of as "the other side." Some of the worst perpetrators of violence on the Philadelphia homicide squad tugged at Marimow's and Neumann's feelings when they finally interviewed them. Howard Covington came to feel sorry for the overworked labor inspectors who had neglected to inspect the state's mills for cotton dust levels. Jerry Thompson found that the Klan member he sought to expose strongly resembled the rural Tennesseans he had grown up beside.

The Tucson reporters were in a sticky mess when they found coach Tony Mason was apparently flying in girl friends at the university's expense. Where was the line between what was public and what was private when public monies were being privately exploited? Did reporters have to worry who might get hurt by such revelations?

Reporters consider the readers' sympathies as well. Gordon White refused to do stories about cancer victims. Cancer is always a personal tragedy, he noted. But was it fair to play on the readers' emotions when there was no sure evidence that any given cancer was related to bomb-testing fallout?

The reporters' job must be to get at the truth, and that inevitably turns out to be larger and more complex than simply pointing a finger at a bad guy. No story unsupported by a thorough, accurate, and fair investigation could achieve the stature of the six included in this book. If someone can poke holes in the findings, the public will simply write off the reporter's work as a cheap shot. Remarkably, in none of the six examples here were any of the newspapers seriously accused of inaccuracy or bias. In each case reporters built into their investigations special precautions against their own biases and those of their sources.

Using anonymous sources for information vital to a story has long been controversial in journalism. While reporters can readily justify why a source's identity must be kept secret, the technique raises questions about the reliability of a source unwilling to take public responsibility for his word.

Neumann and Marimow used anonymous sources to report on the politically sensitive meeting in which the district attorney decided not to prosecute any police officers in a brutality case. Neumann since has hardened his views. "I don't think unnamed sources should be used in a newspaper," he now says, because the practice diminishes the story's credibility, he contends. "I just don't think it's worth it."

Yet both he and Marimow argued that, in this instance, anonymity was justified. The outcome of the meeting was a public record, they noted. Only political nuance was attained from unnamed sources.

Fried and Merrell could not get Los Angeles doctors to cooperate unless they agreed not to name names in the patient-dumping scandal. In the end, the sources argued, it was abuses in the whole Emergency Aid Program and not individual doctors and hospitals that were their target.

Even with sources who are named, reporters must often be cautious about what ax they may have to grind. Gordon Eliot White weighed carefully the merits of a document handed to him by Stewart Udall, a former politician and then legal representative for the fallout victims. Fried and Merrell were acutely aware that many of their sources were intimately involved with the problem they were researching.

Jerry Thompson's work illustrates one of the most thorny investigative techniques in journalism—deception. *Tennessean* publisher Seigenthaler wondered if the newspaper could regain credibility with its readers after its reporters had misrepresented themselves to get the story. He concluded that it could. But the use of deception raises yet again the question of whether the ends justify the means.

We have devoted considerable attention in these chapters to the writing and editing of the final products. The process was often agonizingly tedious, stretched out over several weeks as reporters and editors debated and sometimes argued about how to express and organize the material.

There are several recurring reasons for the problems. Having amassed so much material, the reporters experience difficulty in organizing it. They want to tell everything they have learned right away. Having been immersed in the story for so long, they have trouble standing back and looking at the whole picture in a coherent fashion. And having spent several months on the research, they are eager to get the story into print. As one editor after another picks over the copy, asks endless questions, and proposes changes, the reporters grow edgy, fearful that the story they worked so hard to gather will be cut to pieces by editors who do not understand its significance.

For their part, the editors know that they must take extraordinary pains to be sure that the stories are fair to all sides, pose no legal problems, and above all are accurate in all details. They realize that their reporters care about these matters as well, but they also know that fresh eyes may spot errors or gaps that the reporters missed. And the editors want to be sure that the sheer volume of the copy does not overwhelm the reader, so they try to reduce the length without eroding the substance, and they strive for means of presentation that will help the reader grasp and follow the material.

"If you're going to inflict 10,000 to 50,000 words on the reader," editor Gene Roberts of the *Philadelphia Inquirer* told us, "you owe it to the reader, to the paper, and to yourself to make sure it is well organized, that it reads well, that it flows properly, and that it's accurate, accurate, accurate. That takes some time."

Meanwhile, he added, the reporters are eager to get the story they've labored so long over into the paper. "At that point," Roberts said, "I always try to go into a stall and see that the institutional forces slow the process down—we check and double-check and we write and rewrite."

Given all of this, it is not surprising that patience grows short and tempers flare. We are inclined to agree with Rich Oppel, editor of the *Charlotte Observer*, that "there is almost no way to avoid that kind of agony." It may even be beneficial because reporters and editors are likely to develop increased understanding and respect for each other as a result of the shared ordeal.

But so vigorous a bloodletting could lead to enduring hard feelings, too. If little evidence of that emerges from these pages, it may stem partly from the special relationship between the reporters and their immediate supervising editor that was forged during the information-gathering phase of the project.

Listen to reporter Bob Lowe talking about his city editor, Jon Kamman, in Tucson: "You need to know there's someone ready to go to the wall for you." Or to reporter Bill Marimow talking about how he and Jonathan Neumann worked with city editor John Carroll in Philadelphia: "When we found something that made us gasp, he would gasp with us. And when we needed time or freedom, he was always supportive." For investigative reporters working on highly sensitive and controversial stories, having an editor such as Kamman or Carroll to turn to and to rely on may well be crucial. The reporters come to know that the newspaper supports them and will stand behind them in a crisis, that they do not stand alone. And the final editing process may seem less dangerous to them because at least one editor, they know, has a stake in the outcome nearly as large as their own.

For its part, the newspaper's management is probably more willing to undertake major investigations and see them through because it has confidence in the judgment of a seasoned editor.

A good line editor is not the only factor that contributes to the success of an in-depth reporting project. Four of our six cases involved more than one reporter, and in each one the chemistry between or among the collaborators played an important role. The three two-member teams all agreed that having a partner to talk to helped them generate and test ideas and hypotheses. They also found each other's support helpful. Interestingly, they often preferred to work together even though dividing assignments between them might have improved efficiency.

Only in Long Beach were the two men already friends when the collaboration began, and in no case had the pair worked together on previous stories, so the harmonious blending was entirely fortuitous. For what it's worth, we might note that the teams saw each other as opposite personality types: in Philadelphia, the deliberate, detached Marimow and the emotional Neumann; in Tucson, the seasoned veteran Hallas and his excitable younger colleague Lowe; in Long Beach, the patient, persistent Fried and the volatile Merrell.

A newspaper planning to launch an investigative project must be prepared to help the participants in a variety of ways. The reporters must be relieved of their beat responsibilities or at least given some help; a reporter doing the research that a project requires cannot keep up with developments on his beat as well. Large dailies have no trouble freeing up reporters for months at a time, but our chapters demonstrate that smaller ones can bring off major projects if they are willing to stretch their resources. That sometimes makes other reporters resentful, but the problem is manageable if the importance of the project is made clear to the staff and if every reporter has the opportunity to suggest project ideas and participate in investigations of his own. The *Charlotte Observer* found that involving many hands in approving and planning the project paid off in widespread staff support, although we found that approach to be the exception.

Top management must be prepared to respond to criticism and pressure generated by controversial stories. This included resisting advertising boycotts and even personal threats in Tucson and making an indefinite commitment to ensuring the safety of the reporter's family in Nashville. Less dramatically, *Charlotte Observer* editors visited a textile plant and invited industry officials to come to the newspaper in an effort to deflect criticism of the brown lung series. Even those executives not involved in the project (or who work in departments other than editorial) may be called on to defend it; they have to be sufficiently conversant with the material and the decisions surrounding its publication to speak for the paper if necessary.

All of this requires a deep institutional commitment to in-depth reporting. It is surely no accident that most of the newspapers represented in this book had distinguished records of achievement in investigative reporting long before launching their latest projects.

But the most important factor in determining whether an investigative effort will succeed is the most obvious one: the reporters. The stories in this book were the result of their skill and dedication, from the quiet courage of Nashville's Jerry Thompson to the insight and persistence of Salt Lake City's Gordon Eliot White. They are all experienced professionals who had earned the confidence of their editors; investigative work is not for the tyro.

You have to wonder why anyone would want to be an investigative reporter. "I go to dinner with my sources, christenings, weddings, you name it," said Nicholas Gage of the New York Times some years ago.[2] "I live with them. Seventy percent of my social life is with my sources. My job is round-the-clock. Sources won't trust you unless you're close to them. If these people were discovered, they would lose their jobs."

"I'm away from home a lot, doing a lot of travel, and there's a definite breakdown in communications in the family," said Frank Lalli of Forbes.[3] "After I've been away, my wife asks, 'What did you learn?' and I don't want to repeat it." Lalli says that "brains have a lot less to do with investigative reporting than strong legs."

For the news organization, investigative reporting can be equally frustrating. Although a project may turn a reporter loose for months, the result may be no story; Nick Gage estimated that two-thirds of his projects come up dry. And the results of these stories that make it into print, as the examples in this book illustrate, may seem anticlimatic in terms of miscreants jailed and major reforms implemented.

In fact, the news media's devotion to investigative reporting may be exaggerated. "The volume of hard investigative journalism has dropped off considerably," according to Bob Porterfield, who helped win a Pulitzer prize for the Anchorage Daily News and the Boston Globe. "There was a real increase in investigative reporting after the Watergate stories, but now a lot of newspapers are not really making the commitment."[4]

Why? Porterfield cited several factors, including reporters being preoccupied with routine beat coverage and editors unwilling to give them the time for lengthy probes. Too much Washington coverage

[2]Carla Marie Rupp, "Investigative Reporters Reveal How They Do It," Editor & Publisher, January 11, 1975, p. 12.
[3]Ibid.
[4]Bill Bellows, "Why Investigative Reporting Is Dying," Editor & Publisher, March 14, 1981, p. 60.

concentrates on superficial political jockeying and overlooks important stories about regulatory agencies and other governmental activities that require tough digging, he argued. He also cited the increasing group ownership of newspapers, contending that chains care more about earning profits than publishing high-quality newspapers, so they produce cautious products that eschew investigative reporting so as not to offend advertisers and readers.

But the case is not entirely persuasive. Three of the newspapers represented in this book belong to the Knight-Ridder group (Philadelphia, Long Beach, Charlotte); a fourth is part of Gannett (Nashville). Few newspapers have a better record of investigative achievement than Long Island's *Newsday*, which belongs to the Times-Mirror group. Clearly, whether a paper is independently owned or part of a chain does not automatically determine its willingness to do in-depth reporting.

And the frustrating nature of investigative reporting may be more apparent than real. Few of Woodward and Bernstein's counterparts around the nation can match their impact, but there appears to be a growing realization that a new yardstick is needed. "Don't measure success in indictments or convictions," Bob Greene of *Newsday* told an IRE convention not long ago. "The people understand right and wrong whether there's a penal law violation or not."[5] In Tucson, the *Arizona Daily Star* staff seemed undismayed that more people exposed by its investigation were not convicted. City Editor Kamman talked about "serv[ing] notice" that public officials will be held to the same standards of accountability as private citizens, and reporter Hallas spoke of a "national debate" on collegiate athletics generated in part by the *Star*'s work.

A prominent editor complained a few years ago that many journalists were motivated primarily by an urge to "get somebody," to rack up forced resignations and indictments as a sure path to a Pulitzer prize or other major award.[6] But what could be further from that stereotype than the *Long Beach Independent, Press-Telegram*'s decision not to publish the names of the hospitals charged with mistreatment of indigent patients? Reporter John Fried said the paper wanted to "expose a situation that is inimical to the public good," not point fingers.

The *Philadelphia Inquirer*'s commitment to in-depth reporting, editor Gene Roberts told us, stemmed from "a deep-seated conviction in

---

[5]"280 Reporters Jam IRE's 2-Day Workshop," *Editor & Publisher*, March 11, 1978, p. 14.
[6]Roscoe C. Born, "Journalistic Instinct: To 'Get' People," *National Observer*, August 3, 1974, p. 10.

our newsroom that [because] society has grown ever more complex, if all a paper is [doing] is conventional what-happened-yesterday reporting, the chances are it's not really adequately reporting on its community to its community."

Cynicism may be fashionable, but Hallas, Kamman, and Fried seemed motivated more by an old-fashioned desire to do good than to "get somebody." *Newsweek* suggested once that "the main interest of investigative journalism should perhaps not be to ferret out wrongdoers but to explain why government works the way it does—to enlighten and not just to indict."[7] There is encouraging evidence that this approach is taking hold, if not because of a resurgence of altruism, then because journalists may be recognizing the limits of their trade. Woodward and Bernstein did not bring down Richard Nixon, after all; Congress and the courts did. "The press cannot save society; it can only be a catalyst," said Nick Gage. "There's too much emphasis on the effectiveness of the press and not enough on the agencies which have the power. Reporters don't have subpoena power. They provoke."[8]

[7] David Gelman, "Jugular Journalism?" *Newsweek*, May 10, 1976, p. 79.
[8] Carla Marie Rupp, "Investigative Reporters Reveal How They Do It," *Editor & Publisher*, January 11, 1975, p. 12.

DISCUSSION QUESTIONS

NOTE: Instructors and students who use this book may find the following questions useful for class discussion.

THE *PHILADELPHIA INQUIRER*

Jonathan Neumann said he imagines "90 percent of all major investigative stories that are done are stories that are already known." The job of the reporter is to document and publish the evidence. Is Neumann right? Why do not more reporters go beyond the day-to-day reporting and ferret out the investigative story?

What are some of the emotions Neumann and Bill Marimow felt while working on "The Homicide Files"? Did these emotions help or hinder them?

According to the reporters' own descriptions, Marimow is even-tempered and relatively slow to react, while Neumann is emotionally volatile. How did the reporters' personalities complement one another?

Why did the reporters choose always to research together rather than split the work?

Should editors follow city editor John Carroll's practice and keep in close contact with reporters on an investigation to give them support and keep them on the right track? At other papers, reporters might not see an editor more than once or twice during an investigation. What difference does an editor make to reporters when they are doing their research?

The *Inquirer* requires painstaking editing and rewriting before an in-depth series goes to print. Why? Does the hard work show in the final product?

Is editor Gene Roberts right that today's complex society requires more than "a conventional what-happened-yesterday type of reporting"?

THE *ARIZONA DAILY STAR*

Was it ethical for the *Star* to examine the university's telephone records?

Should the *Star* have published its initial story with its vaguely worded allegations about the coaching staff and the women visitors to Tucson?

The *Star*'s revelations generated intense opposition and hostility, not only from the university but also from the community. On what grounds, then, could the paper justify pressing its investigation of this cherished local institution? If the community wanted to protect its football team, shouldn't the paper have bowed to its wishes?

How would you explain the behavior of the *Star*'s rival media, the *Tucson Citizen* and the local TV stations? How should they have responded to the university's efforts to discredit the *Star?*

Hallas and Lowe tape recorded many telephone conversations without their sources' knowledge. How can such a practice be ethically justified?

Was the *Star* justified in withholding its first story until after the football team had played in the Fiesta Bowl?

Many of the stories relied heavily on unattributed sources. How did the *Star* justify that? Do you find its explanation persuasive?

THE *LONG BEACH INDEPENDENT PRESS-TELEGRAM*

Fried and Merrell were turned loose on a three-month investigation after only a brief discussion with an editor, and they were left largely on their own throughout the project. Contrast this with the elaborate procedures used by the *Philadelphia Inquirer* before a major investigation can be undertaken and with the close supervision exercised by the editors at Philadelphia and the other papers examined in this book. What are the advantages and drawbacks of each approach? Which do you prefer and why?

Why did Fried and Merrell grant anonymity to their physician sources? Should they have forced the doctors to go on the record with their names and accusations? Specifically, Merrell wanted to threaten a recalcitrant physician with public exposure if he did not show the reporters his private study of patient transfers. Would Merrell have been justified in doing that?

Fried and Merrell disagreed over whether to identify the hospitals accused of inadequately treating indigent patients. What arguments did each man use to support his position? What is your view?

Fried and Merrell wondered what they would have said if they had been able to interview any of the indigent patients. Would you have told such a patient that you believed he had been treated negligently, knowing that this might trigger a lawsuit against the hospital? How did the *Charlotte Observer* reporters deal with this problem in talking to brown lung victims?

THE *SALT LAKE CITY DESERET NEWS*

In his earlier days as a reporter Gordon Eliot White had dismissed scares about the hazards of low level radiation. Yet when the case of Sgt. Paul Cooper pointed toward a story that countered his beliefs, White pursued it wholeheartedly. Is it the mark of a good reporter to pursue the truth despite his own preconceived notions? How should a reporter handle his biases when he is on a story?

How did White use the methods of scientific research to put together his first story on cancer statistics in southern Utah? Was he right to doubt his own judgment and seek verification?

Was White correct to resist reporting human interest stories about leukemia victims in southern Utah when he had no way clearly to link any specific victim's cancer to fallout?

White did not identify himself when he went to the briefing by Dr. Joseph L. Lyon about his research findings that linked fallout and cancer. Should a reporter always identify him/herself?

Was the *News* right to decide to hold the story about Lyon's findings until they could be published in the *New England Journal of Medicine?* Should newspapers consider the effect of what they publish or should they publish the news when they know it?

How did the Freedom of Information Act help White with his research? Could he have done these stories without it?

How did White's experience in Washington help him to research this story?

THE *CHARLOTTE OBSERVER*

The reporters said they were deeply moved by the plight of the brown lung victims and felt they had been "screwed." How should reporters deal with such feelings in reporting and writing their stories?

Howard Covington said he tried to remain detached when interviewing the brown lung victims. Why did he feel he had to do that? Do you agree? Did the reporters have any responsibilities to help the ailing workers other than by writing their stories?

Writing the massive series involved six weeks of "agony" involving many reporters and editors. Why did the paper adopt so tortuous a process? Why did so many clashes develop? Do you agree with editor Rich Oppel that "there is almost no way to avoid that kind of agony?"

The *Observer* expected to be criticized for publishing the series. Why? What steps did it take to deflect the criticism? Should newspapers regularly take these or similar steps to explain their activities and decisions to the public and to give their readers greater opportunities to voice their views?

Readers around the country praised the *Observer* for daring to undertake the brown lung and tobacco series, but the reporters and editors denied that they had acted courageously. Explain. Is editorial-writer Williams correct in his indictment of American newspapers for cowardice?

What factors help explain the scanty coverage of brown lung prior to the series?

In the absence of dramatic, highly visible change or reform in the wake of the series, what results did it achieve? Do these results justify the enormous commitment of time and resources made by the newspaper? Try to answer this question for all of the investigations studied in this book.

THE *NASHVILLE TENNESSEAN*

Nashville Tennessean publisher John Seigenthaler believed reporter Jerry Thompson had to work undercover to get a picture of the Ku Klux Klan that the *Tennessean* investigative team working out in the open would never be able to see. Does a news organization, which bases its reputation on telling the truth, risk its credibility with readers when its reporters use deception? Could the story be reported without the use of deception? Does the end—the story—justify the means? Do people have an ethical right to know when they are talking to a reporter and when what they say may be quoted in a newspaper?

Thompson uses an unusual journalistic style in writing this series. He writes in the first person and includes his opinions. Is it appropriate for him to deviate from the usual objective voice of reporting?

Should Thompson have put his opinions into separate editorials?

Was publisher Seigenthaler on a crusade against the Klan? Is there a difference between crusading and watch-dogging by a journalist? Is it right for a newspaper to crusade against an organization like the Klan or is it a misuse of the newspaper's power to target a group?